P9-CEZ-343

MIKE AND ELAINE CARTER
SUNRIDER DISTRIBUTORS
1984 NORTH 275 WEST
OREM, UTAH 84057
(801) 224-2748

Sacred Truths
of the
Doctrine and Covenants

Volume One

L.G. Otten
C.M. Caldwell

Copyright © 1982

Library of Congress Catalog Number: 82-71971

Published by
LEMB, Inc.
Springville, Utah
Third Edition

To Rae and Bonnie

Acknowledgments

We express our sincere appreciation to all who have, in any way, encouraged and assisted the authors in the preparation and publication of this book.

Specifically, we express our heartfelt thanks to former Dean Ellis T. Rasmussen, and Dean Robert J. Matthews, of the Department of Religious Instruction, and also Larry C. Porter, Chairman of the Church History and Doctrine Department of the Department of Religious Instruction, Brigham Young University. These men have provided encouragement and helpful suggestions which have been very beneficial in the preparation of this material.

Key to Abbreviations

AGQ	Answers to Gospel Questions
BofM	Book of Mormon
CHMR	Church History and Modern day Revelation
CR	Conference Report
D&C	Doctrine and Covenants
DCC	Doctrine and Covenants Commentary
DS	Doctrines of Salvation
DWW	Discourses of Wilford Woodruff
HC	History of the Church
GD	Gospel Doctrine
IE	Improvement Era
JD	Journal of Discourses
LDSBE	L.D.S. Biographical Encyclopedia
LHCK	Life of Heber C. Kimball
MD	Mormon Doctrine
MDC	The Message of the Doctrine and Covenants
MS	Millennial Star
PofGP	Pearl of Great Price
TPJS	Teachings of the Prophet Joseph Smith

Suggested Titles

Table of Contents

Preface

Ideas and techniques for effectively teaching the Doctrine and Covenants began to germinate in the minds of the authors while studying in graduate classes at the Brigham Young University early in the 1960's. Shortly thereafter, Brother Otten was assigned to teach the Doctrine and Covenants at the Logan Institute of Religion, adjacent to the Utah State University campus. While serving in that capacity, he compiled materials that would assist the students and supplement their study of the Doctrine and Covenants. These materials were published in a booklet in April 1970 under the title "Historical Background and Setting For Each Section of the Doctrine and Covenants." We would insert here an extract from the preface of that publication:

> For the past several years it has been my privilege to teach the Doctrine and Covenants to the L.D.S. college student as well as townspeople of the university community. I have endeavored to accomplish two major goals while teaching from this great volume of scripture.
>
> First, to unfold to the student, to the best of my ability, the messages of salvation, exaltation, and the perfection of a Zion people that the Lord has revealed to us through his Prophet Joseph Smith Jun.
>
> Second, to help the student know the Doctrine and Covenants, that is, to know where to find the various concepts and the circumstances surrounding each revelation . . . .
>
> Many requests have been made by students for a compilation of the historical background and setting of each section, together

with suggested titles. For this reason I have compiled this work. This is not to say that the material presented is exhaustive, or that the suggested section titles are the most appropriate. My desire has been to make the study of the Doctrine and Covenants more rewarding.

In the fall of 1970, Brother Caldwell was assigned to teach at the Logan Institute of Religion and together the authors developed a teaching course outline for their classes in the Doctrine and Covenants.

In June 1972, some minor revisions were made and a revised edition of the original supplementary text was published.

At about this time, Brother Otten gave permission to William O. Nelson to use his compilation in the preparation of the LDS Church Education Home Study Course on the Doctrine and Covenants. Consequently, the Church published a booklet entitled "Historical Vignettes." Subsequently, the format ideas as well as some of the materials, have been used in additional publications by the Church as well as some other independent authors.

By 1978, both authors were teaching at the Brigham Young University. They decided, at that time, to expand upon the original compilation and place additional materials in the hands of students to further aid them in their study of the Doctrine and Covenants. This two-volume work is the result of that endeavor.

The purpose of this book is that it should serve as a supplement to the individual's study of the Doctrine and Covenants. It is not to be construed as a substitute for either studying or teaching the scriptures. This book should strengthen the individuals conviction that the scriptures are the source of truth and the depository of the gospel of Jesus Christ. This book is intended to direct the readers attention to the scriptures and encourage an increased study thereof.

The authors accept full responsibility for the contents of this book. Any errors or mistaken conclusions that may be found herein are the responsibility of the authors. Earnest effort has been made to present the truth as it has been revealed by the Lord and taught by the General Authorities of the Church.

Chapter 1

Introduction

Gospel Scholarship

A study of the Doctrine and Covenants is a study of the Lord's doctrine. By this study one also learns of man's opportunity to enter into covenants with the Lord that makes possible man's eventual exaltation. Such a study is not limited to historical events and sayings. The gospel scholar who studies the Doctrine and Covenants will seek not only to learn and understand the truths revealed by the Lord, but he will also endeavor to discover and make application of these truths in his own life. Ultimately, the purpose of all gospel scholarship is to enhance the opportunity for the individual to attain unto personal salvation. This concept of gospel scholarship is the basis upon which this book has been written.

There is another dimension of gospel scholarship. The way the gospel is taught, whether verbally or in written form, should be consistent with principles of simplicity. Two great gospel scholars have emphasized this dimension of gospel presentation:

> The Lord has a great many principles in store for us; and the greatest principles which he has for us are the most simple and plain. The first principles of the Gospel which lead us unto eternal life are the simplest, and yet none are more glorious or important unto us. Men may labour to make a great display of talent, learning, and knowledge, either in printing or preaching. They may try to preach the mysteries and to present something strange, great, and wonderful, and they may labour for this with all their might, in the

spirit and strength of man without the aid of the Holy Spirit of God, and yet the people are not edified, and their preaching will not give much satisfaction. It is the plainest and the most simple things that edify us the most, if taught by the Spirit of God; and there is nothing more important or beneficial unto us. (Wilford Woodruff, J.D., Vol. 5, p. 50)

Make quality performance a goal. Seek the Spirit of the Lord. Study the scriptures. Work in unity. Stay close to the fundamentals so that what you teach will be true. Strengthen your lessons by making them simple. (Spencer W. Kimball, "Men of Example," p. 11)

Based upon these two fundamental principles of gospel scholarship (application of salvation principles and simplicity), this book presents information pertinent to each section of the Doctrine and Covenants. Each presentation provides the following:

1. *Suggested Title*

Each section of the Doctrine and Covenants has been given a suggested title which will serve as a capsulized summary of the content of the section. It will also serve as a guide to the gospel scholar and assist him to find and remember the content of the various sections. Several of the sections have been given titles by the Lord or by His prophet Joseph Smith, Jun. The Savior called Section 1, His "Preface" and Section 42, His "Law." The Prophet Joseph Smith referred to Section 76 as "The Vision" and Section 88 as "The Olive Leaf."

By formulating a title for each section of the Doctrine and Covenants, the gospel scholar will be able to more effectively use this volume of scripture. To assist in the effective use of these titles, a complete list of all section titles is provided in the front of the book and a cross-reference index of all titles is provided as Appendix 1 at the end.

2. *Overview of Section Content*

For each section of the Doctrine and Covenants, an overview is provided of the content of the section. This overview gives emphasis to the various doctrinal teachings and concepts as contained within the section. It is not strictly a listing of sequential verses except in those cases where it lends itself to a separation of concepts. This overview should aid the gospel scholar to become familiar with the content of each revelation.

3. *Historical Setting*

Each section of the Doctrine and Covenants must be studied in light of its historical setting. President Joseph Fielding Smith has stressed the importance of this approach:

> You may take it up if you want to by topics, or doctrines, that is good; but you are not going to understand the Doctrine and Covenants, you are not going to get out of it all there is in it unless you take it up section by section; and then when you do that, you will have to study it with its setting as you get it in the history of the Church. (D. of S., Vol. 3, p. 199)

In this book, a historical setting for each section of the Doctrine and Covenants has been provided. This historical information is not exhaustive, but has been selected to assist the gospel scholar to better understand the content of each revelation.

4. *Sacred Truths*

As previously mentioned, an important dimension of gospel scholarship is the transfer of gospel principles into the behavioral patterns of the individual.

In this book, various gospel principles will be discussed from each section of the Doctrine and Covenants. An attempt has been made to point out the importance of applying these principles in a meaningful way to one's life and circumstances today.

All truth is sacred to the Lord. Truth becomes sacred to the individual when it is understood and applied. The Doctrine and Covenants is a depository of sacred truths as revealed by the Lord.

The Doctrine and Covenants—The Lord's Book

To help us more fully appreciate the inestimable values of the Doctrine and Covenants, the words of Rudger Clawson, a latter-day apostle, are quoted as follows:

> I have here in my hand a most wonderful book, its value cannot be estimated in dollars and cents. It is one of the sacred books of the world; there are none greater perhaps. It is the Doctrine and Covenants, one of the standard works of the Church. This book, my brethren and sisters, is a book containing the revelations of God given unto this people through Joseph Smith, the Prophet . . . They

constitute the pure word of God to us. We can depend upon the teachings of this book, and you should know that a deep and thorough study of the book before me is more than equivalent to a university education. You may wonder why I say this, but as a matter of fact the university education does not and could not give us the actual saving principles of eternal life. That information comes direct from our Heavenly Father.

The book of Doctrine and Covenants covers every phase of the Gospel of salvation. (*CR*, October 1939, pp. 28-29)

As a preview of the sacred teachings which are in store for us in this study, we note that the Lord has declared the following:

> For I will raise up unto myself a pure people, that will serve me in righteousness. (D&C 100:16)

The Doctrine and Covenants is the Lord's book and serves as a means to help us become a pure people before the Lord. In the Lord's preface to His book, He gave directions as to how His revelations in this dispensation should be used to bring about His purposes for the salvation of mankind.

1. *Publish the Commandments*

> Behold, this is mine authority, and the authority of my servants, and my preface unto the book of my commandments, which I have given them *to publish* unto you, O inhabitants of the earth. (D&C 1:6, italics added)

The Lord wanted His book published. This was an essential step in the raising up of a pure people. Of course, Lucifer has always opposed purity in people and consequently took steps to prevent the publishing of the book. A mob gathered in Jackson County and destroyed the printing press of W. W. Phelps and most of the papers and publication work. Bishop Partridge and Charles Allen were tarred and feathered, and members of the Phelps family were thrown outside with their furniture. (See HC, Vol. 1, pp. 390-393)

Notwithstanding this opposition, the revelations were preserved and subsequently published. How grateful the world should be to have access to the Lord's book containing His revelations.

2. *Search the Commandments*

> Search these commandments, for they are true and faithful, and the prophecies and promises which are in them shall all be fulfilled. (D&C 1:37)

The Lord wants us to know the contents of His book. Once the book was published, the directive was given to "search" the contents.

President Kimball has emphasized the need to evaluate our scripture "searching" habits. He has said:

> . . . I ask us all to honestly evaluate our performance in scripture study. It is a common thing to have a few passages of scripture at our disposal, floating in our minds, as it were, and thus to have the illusion that we know a great deal about the gospel. In this sense, having a little knowledge can be a problem indeed. I am convinced that each of us, at some time in our lives, must discover the scriptures for ourselves—and not just discover them once, but rediscover them again and again. (*Ensign*, September 1976, p. 4)

3.   *Teach the Commandments*

And also gave commandments to others, that they should proclaim these things unto the world; . . . (D&C 1:18)

The Lord commanded that the revelations contained in His book should be taught, not only to the Latter-day Saints, but to all the world by the mouth of His servants. (See D&C 1:1-6) Clearly, this commission to teach the contents of the Lord's book can only be fulfilled by those who come to know the contents of His book by searching and obtaining personal understanding. (See D&C 11:21)

Summary and Conclusion

The Doctrine and Covenants is the Lord's book. He has commanded that it be published, that we search its contents and teach the principles contained therein.

To more effectively search and teach the principles of salvation contained in the Lord's book, we must study the Doctrine and Covenants section by section with its setting as found in the history of the Church and then make application of the principles in our lives today.

Chapter 2

Doctrine and Covenants Section 1

Suggested Title

The Lord's Preface

Overview of Section Content

1. To whom is the message written? (vs. 1-7, 34-36)
2. Need for the message. (vs. 8-23, 29-33)
3. Purpose of the Doctrine and Covenants. (vs. 24-28)
4. Challenge and promises. (vs. 37-39)

Historical Setting

Joseph Fielding Smith

Section one in the Doctrine and Covenants is not the first revelation received, but it is so placed in the book because the Lord gave it as the preface to the book of his commandments. The Doctrine and Covenants is distinctively peculiar and interesting to all who believe in it that it is the only book in existence which bears the honor of a preface given by the Lord himself. This, however, is consistent and should be the case, for it is as he declares his book. It was not written by Joseph Smith, but was dictated by Jesus Christ, and contains his and his Father's word to the Church and to all the world that faith in God, repentance from sin and membership in his

Church might be given to all who will believe, and that once again the New and everlasting covenant might be established.

This revelation known as section one, was given at the wonderful conference held in Hiram, Ohio, November 1 and 2, 1831 when the publication of the commandments was under consideration. The Lord here gives approval to the publication of his word for he is desirous that his will might be made known. The Gospel had been restored and the elders of the church had been sent forth to proclaim salvation to an unbelieving world that once again men might find their way into the kingdom of God. This preface stamped the revelations with divine endorsement and therefore the revelations went forth with greater power than otherwise would have been the case, and should impress all who read them, especially members of the Church, with their responsibility to keep the commandments which the revelations contain. (CHMR, Vol. 2., p. 24)

Sacred Truths

Introduction

It would be well to consider the purpose of the preface before we discuss the contents thereof. Elder John A. Widtsoe, a member of the Quorum of Twelve Apostles has written:

> A good preface should prepare the reader for the contents of the book. It should display in a concentrated manner the full content of the book. (MDC, pp. 11-12)

In His preface, the Lord provided capsulized glimpses of the content of His book of commandments. A reader should keep in mind that he is seeing a synopsis of the book. He is going to be introduced to many subject areas and will look forward to having those subjects expanded upon in greater depth throughout the book. It is suggested that after being alerted to each idea, the reader should anticipate and watch for it as it is enlarged upon in future sections.

For the purpose of this discussion, we will not endeavor to provide a comprehensive analysis of the Lord's preface. Rather, we will select some topical examples that will illustrate the nature of this section as a preface. We will group these selections into four major areas.

To Whom Is The Message Written?

From verses 1-6, and 34-36, we note the Lord's book is for all men. However, the Lord has charged the Church with the custodial responsibility for His book. The Church is to both publish and proclaim His messages and revelations to the world. The Lord is speaking to every member of the Church and has let it be known that we must take these sacred truths to all of His children. So, when our priesthood leaders give us an opportunity to perform such a task or participate in that endeavor, we must remember the request comes from the Lord. We are not responding to mortal leadership only, but to the declared directive of the Lord. Throughout the book, we will see how the Lord speaks to members and non-members alike and reminds us of the need to proclaim the message to both. He will consistently teach the Church membership how to more effectively prepare and how to carry out this divine directive.

The Need For The Message

How is the message to be conveyed, and why is it being delivered? In verses 8-23, we note the following:

Because the fulness of gospel truth was not to be found at that time in the earth, the Lord called and authorized servants to bear the message of truth to the world. They have been given the power to seal that message as they testify of the restored truth. Among the Lord's children are those who will receive and those who will reject these messengers. Those rejecting the message are referred to by the Lord as "...unbelieving and rebellious;" (D&C 1:8) Through the testimony of the Lord's servants, the hearer is left without excuse.

It is interesting that the Lord calls His servants "...the weak and the simple..." (D&C 1:23) It is not to be understood to be derogatory but rather that the receiver of the truth might look past the servant and not place his:

...trust in the arm of flesh.
But that every man might speak in the name of God the Lord, even the Savior of the world;
That faith also might increase in the earth;
That mine everlasting covenant might be established;
That the fulness of my gospel might be proclaimed by the weak and simple unto the ends of the world, and before kings and rulers. (D&C 1:19-23)

As we see in verses 29 and 30, the fulness of the gospel referred to above was placed in the hands of the Lord's servant, Joseph Smith, Jun. The Lord gave him power to translate the Book of Mormon and also gave him revelations (commandments) as published in the Doctrine and Covenants.

Through these revelations, the Lord authorized Joseph to organize His Church as the means by which His message could be taken to all mankind. He declared His Church to be "the only true and living church upon the face of the whole earth...." (D&C 1:30) Why is it referred to as a "living"

Church? Whenever there is life, there is spirit. The Lord has breathed into His Church the breath of life, even the Holy Ghost. Such life cannot be found existing in any man-made organization upon the earth.

Purposes Of The Doctrine and Covenants

Some of the Lord's purposes in bringing forth the Doctrine and Covenants are described in verses 24 through 28. We call attention to five specific ways by which lives will be changed as people adhere to the contents of the Lord's book.

1. We will come to an understanding
2. Errors will be made known
3. Wisdom will be obtained
4. We will be chastened that we might repent
5. We will be made strong, blessed from on high, and gain knowledge from time to time

May we point out the personal nature of these objectives. The Lord's book is for each of us today. The teachings can and must be applied in our lives. Thus, every revelation in the Lord's book has meaning, application, and purpose for each of us.

Might we suggest an illustration of items 4 and 5 above. Anyone who searches the contents of the Lord's book will hear the Lord frequently calling attention to the need for repentance. Every one of us has sinned and made mistakes from time to time. The Lord will chasten us as a means of helping us to change our lives. Such chastening may come from the printed pages of the Lord's book, or perhaps through His authorized servants, or indeed through personal revelation by the Holy Spirit. The issue at stake is: What will be our attitude at the time, and how will we receive such chastisement? Ought we not to remember that the love of the Lord prompted the correcting process in the first place? If we will always keep in mind the Lord's desires for us, we will gratefully receive His correcting counsel. By doing so, we will be made strong and blessed with knowledge from on high.

A continued emphasis on this subject is declared by the Lord in verses 31 through 33. The Lord makes it clear that sin, however inconsequential we may see it to be, is still sin. Even a small amount of it is still a blot on the human soul and must be dealt with. It cannot be "allowed" (excused).

> Nevertheless, he that repents and does the commandments of the Lord shall be forgiven;

And he that repents not, from him shall be taken even the light which he has received; for my Spirit shall not always strive with man, saith the Lord of Hosts. (D&C 1:32-33)

Challenge and Promises

Now as we conclude our brief analysis of the Lord's preface, we would emphasize that the Lord gave the following challenge and promises in verses 37-39:

Search these commandments, for they are true and faithful, and the prophecies and promises which are in them shall all be fulfilled.

What I the Lord have spoken, I have spoken, and I excuse not myself; and though the heavens and the earth pass away, my word shall not pass away, but shall all be fulfilled, whether by mine own voice or by the voice of my servants, it is the same.

For behold, and lo, the Lord is God, and the Spirit beareth record, and the record is true, and the truth abideth forever and ever, Amen. (D&C 1:37-39)

The Challenge

The challenge to us as we read the Lord's book is to search its contents. The Lord has taught us in His preface the rewards to be had from such an effort. He has also warned us of the consequences for failure to respond to this challenge.

The Promises

As to the promises they can be grouped into three categories:

1. Every prophecy and every promise contained in the Doctrine and Covenants will be fulfilled. (See D&C 1:37) We must realize that part of that which was prophetic in Joseph Smith's day is now historical. Many of these promises and prophecies have already been realized. What a great testimony we have before us that all remaining ones will likewise be fulfilled. Joseph Smith was and is the Lord's prophet.

2. The Lord's work will be directed by Him. However, the world will see that direction as it is carried out by and through His servants. His promise assures the world that He endows His servants with His power to accomplish His purposes upon the earth. His servants are the reflection of His mind and will. (See D&C 1:38)

3. To the honest-in-heart who search these commandments comes the promise of a spiritual witness. Each is entitled to receive the testimony of the Spirit that this book is of the Lord and is therefore true. (See D&C 1:39) The Lord bore His own testimony and added His personal witness:

> ...these commandments,...are true and faithful....
> (D&C 1:37)
> ...the record is true, and the truth abideth forever and ever. Amen. (D&C 1:39)

Summary and Conclusion

This is the Lord's book. Its message is for all mankind. In the preface to His book, the Lord has endorsed its contents and assured all men that adherence to these revealed truths is an essential preparation for His second coming in this dispensation. He has commanded that all should search His book for the saving truths contained therein.

Chapter 3

Doctrine and Covenants Section 2

Suggested Title

The Coming of Elijah

Overview of Section Content

1. Revealing of Priesthood (vs. 1)
2. Promises made to the fathers (vs. 2)
3. Clarification of penalty (vs. 3)

Historical Setting

The night of September 21, 1823, the angel Moroni appeared to the Prophet Joseph Smith. In addition to instructing Joseph relative to the gold plates from which the Book of Mormon was translated, Moroni quoted certain Old Testament prophecies. Among others, he quoted the last two verses of Malachi, though he did so with a little variation from the biblical text. Section two is the quotation as delivered by Moroni. (See P. of G.P., Joseph Smith History 1:27-39)

Sacred Truths

Introduction

We ought not to assume Moroni was correcting the text of Malachi. The Savior quoted the same passages verbatim as they appear in the Old Testament. (See B. of M., III Nephi 25:5-6) Rather, Moroni was likely giving new or additional insights to the meaning of those verses.

There are four significant contributions summarized as follows:

1. Priesthood
2. Promises
3. Penalty
4. Priorities

Priesthood

Elijah was not to restore the Priesthood. (This was to be done by John the Baptist, Peter, James, and John.) His mission was to *reveal*. To reveal is to bring from the heavens something which is not at that time, to be found on the earth.

The nature of the mission, as pertaining to the Priesthood and its powers, is described by Elder Joseph Fielding Smith as follows:

> Elijah restored to this Church and, if they would receive it, to the world, the keys of the sealing power; and that sealing power puts the stamp of approval upon every ordinance that is done in this Church...(D.S., Vol. 3, p. 129, underlining added)

Were it not for these keys, there could be no eternal purposes to our Priesthood work. A person could be baptized by the Priesthood and would be a member of the Church in this life, but not beyond it. A man could be ordained to the Priesthood and could be actively involved in using it during mortality. But after death, he would be without Priesthood power. Marriages performed would be for this life but could not endure throughout eternity. There could not be eternal family relationships. We would all be single and alone and without ties to the Savior in any covenant relationship.

All such relationships are now possible but only because those keys were revealed by Elijah to the Prophet Joseph Smith, April 3, 1836, and are available to the Church through the authority of each succeeding Prophet of the Church. This concept has been stressed by President Joseph F. Smith:

> ...it is necessary that every act performed under this authority shall be done at the proper time and place, in the proper way, and after the proper order. The power of directing these labors con-

stitutes the keys of the Priesthood. In their fullness, the keys are
held by only one person at a time, the prophet and president of the
Church. He may delegate any portion of this power to another, in
which case that person holds the keys of that particular labor. (G.D.,
p. 136)

Promises

What were the promises made to the "Fathers"? Who made them?
When? Elder Joseph Fielding Smith answers as follows:

> The question is asked: "What is meant by the 'promises made
> to the fathers' in the instruction of Moroni to the Prophet Joseph
> Smith, as recorded in the second section of the Doctrine and
> Covenants?"
> This expression has reference to certain promises made to
> those who died without a knowledge of the Gospel, and without
> the opportunity of receiving the sealing ordinances of the Priest-
> hood in matters pertaining to their exaltation. According to these
> promises, the children in the latter days are to perform all such
> ordinances in behalf of the dead. (I.E., Vol. 25, p. 829, July 1922)

The Lord made these promises to His children before they ever entered
mortality. He assured them that their ordinance work would be done for
them in the latter days when temples would be available for such work.
Many of these people would be coming to earth during periods when the
gospel was not available and they would not have opportunity to receive it.
Many came to earth with pre-arranged assignments to perform in fulfillment of the Lord's plans but oftentimes without access to the Priesthood
and the ordinances thereof. To illustrate the fullfillment of the Lord's
promises in connection with the powers revealed by Elijah, certain of those
fathers from ages past appeared and requested their work to be done.
President Wilford Woodruff described the experience:

#6

> I will here say that two weeks before I left St. George, the spirits
> of the dead gathered around me, wanting to know why we did not
> redeem them. Said they, 'You have had the use of the Endowment
> House for a number of years, and yet nothing has ever been done
> for us. We laid the foundation of the government you now enjoy,
> and we never apostatized from it, but we remained true to it and
> were faithful to God.'
> These were the signers of the Declaration of Independence,
> and they had waited on me for two days and two nights. I thought it

very singular, that notwithstanding so much work had been done, and yet nothing had been done for them. The thought never entered my heart, from the fact, I suppose, that heretofore our minds were reaching after our more immediate friends and relatives.

I straitway went into the baptismal font and called upon Brother McAllister to baptize me for the signers of the Declaration of Independence, and fifty other eminent men, making one hundred in all, including John Wesley, Columbus, and others. I then baptized him for every President of the United States, except three; and when their cause is just, somebody will do the work for them. (D.W.W., pp. 166-161)

Moroni used the phrase "...plant in the hearts..." (D&C 2:2) The heart is often referred to as the depository of feelings. In other words, Elijah's coming would result in the development of feelings for these promises in relation to the salvation of Father's children. Thus, this feeling is manifest among the Savior's people as they develop and establish eternal relationships with ancestral fathers. These family ties are made possible beyond the grave through the sealing powers of the Priesthood revealed by Elijah.

Furthermore, these feelings are not limited to fathers of ancient time. President Harold B. Lee has said:

Now keep in mind this: that when the full measure of Elijah's mission is understood, that the hearts of the children will be turned to the fathers, and the fathers to the children. It applies just as much on this side of the veil as it does on the other side of the veil. If we neglect our families here in having family home night and we fail in our responsibilities here, how could we feel that we are doing our full duty in turning the hearts of our children to their fathers.

How would heaven be if we lost some of those we love through our own neglect? The blessings in heaven won't be ours until we have done everything we can to save those whom the Lord has sent through our lineage. So, the hearts of you fathers and mothers must be turned to your children right now, if you have the true spirit of Elijah, and not think that it applies merely to those who are beyond the veil. Let your hearts be turned to your children, and teach your children; but you must do it when they are young enough to be properly schooled. If you are neglecting your family home evening, you are neglecting the beginning of the mission of Elijah just as certainly as if you were neglecting your genealogy research work. (Priesthood Genealogy Seminar, 1973)

Penalty

The curse mentioned describes the earth as being wasted. This suggests that the earth has purpose and would be denied the fulfillment of such were the powers of Elijah not returned in this day. This purpose of the earth was described by the Lord:

> And again, verily I say unto you, that whoso forbiddeth to marry is not ordained of God, for marriage is ordained of God unto man.
> Wherefore, it is lawful that he should have one wife, and they twain shall be one flesh, and all this that the earth might answer the end of its creation;
> And that it might be filled with the measure of man, according to his creation before the world was made. (D&C 49:15-17)

The earth is to be a celestial habitation and/or a dwelling place forever for faithful covenant children of the Lord. The Priesthood sealing powers revealed by Elijah are now available to bring about this plan. As Moroni explained, the absence of such powers would result in an earth being barren of eternal family units and thus void of purpose. Hence, man's mortal experience and the earth's purpose would be wasted.

Priorities

It is interesting to note that as the Doctrine and Covenants is presently compiled, Section 2 is the first revelation chronologically recorded in the Lord's book. Perhaps such position is not by chance. Following Joseph Smith's first vision, his first recorded encounter with divine revelation included a message on the importance of the eternal nature of the family. The Lord stressed the overall objective of His work—Family Exaltation.

President Lee emphasized:

> . . .the most important of the Lord's work that you will ever do will be within the walls of your own home. (Area Conference Report, Mexico City, Mexico, August 26, 1972, p. 77)

Summary and Conclusion

The primary purpose of mortality is to organize and function in family units. The coming of Elijah restored the power by which the family units are able to remain intact throughout eternity. The Lord's church is the custodian of that power. Thus, through the church, all of Father's children who come to this earth may have access to the promises of eternal family relationships.

Chapter 4

Doctrine and Covenants Sections 3 and 10

Suggested Titles

Section 3—The Lost Manuscript

Section 10—Do Not Re-Translate—The Reality of Satan

Overview of Section Content

Section 3

1. Works of God cannot be frustrated (vs. 1-3)
2. Lesson to Joseph-Trust God, not man (vs. 4-8, 12-15)
3. Mercy of God-Joseph is reassured (vs. 9-11)
4. Purposes of the Book of Mormon (vs. 16-20)

Section 10

1. Gift of translation restored (vs. 1-4)
2. Satan's opposition to the Lord's work (vs. 5-29)
3. Alternate plan of translating—The wisdom of God (vs. 30-45)
4. Faith and desires of Book of Mormon prophets-The Lord to fulfill (vs. 46-70)

Historical Setting

These two sections are studied together since the subject matter discussed flows through both revelations. The subject is addressed in section 3; whereas, the Lord's counsel in the matter is recorded in section 10.

Section 3

Joseph Fielding Smith

Section three is a revelation given in consequence of the loss of the 116 pages of manuscript of the Book of Mormon which had been translated by Joseph Smith when Martin Harris was his scribe . . . (CHMR, Vol. 1, p. 23)

Joseph Smith, Jun.

Mr. Harris, having returned from his tour, left me and went home to Palmyra, arranged his affairs, and returned again to my house about the 12th of April, 1828, and commenced writing for me while I translated from the plates, which we continued until the 14th of June following, by which time he had written one hundred and sixteen pages of manuscript on foolscap paper. Some time after Mr. Harris had begun to write for me, he began to importune me to give him liberty to carry the writings home and show them; and desired of me that I would inquire of the Lord, through the Urim and Thummim, if he might not do so. I did inquire, and the answer was that he must not. However, he was not satisfied with this answer, and desired that I should inquire again. I did so, and the answer was as before. Still he could not be contented, but insisted that I should inquire once more. After much solicitation I again inquired of the Lord, and permission was granted him to have the writings on certain conditions; which were, that he show them only to his brother Preserved Harris, his own wife, his father and his mother, and a Mrs. Cobb, a sister to his wife. In accordance with this last answer, I required of him that he should bind himself in a covenant to me in a most solemn manner that he would not do otherwise than had been directed. He did so. He bound himself as I required of him, took the writings, and went his way. Notwithstanding, however, the great restrictions which he had been laid under, and the solemnity of the covenants which he had made with me, he did show them to others, and by stratagem they got them away from him, and they never have been recovered unto this day. (HC, Vol. I, pp. 20-22)

For additional information see History of Joseph Smith by his mother Lucy Mack Smith, pp. 124-132.

Section 10
Joseph Smith, Jun.

After I had obtained the above revelation [Section 3], both the plates and the Urim and Thummim were taken from me again; but in a few days they were returned to me, when I inquired of the Lord, and the Lord said thus unto me: [Section 10] (HC, Vol. 1, p. 23)

B.H. Roberts

. . .this revelation was given at Harmony, Pennsylvania, in the summer of 1828, a short time after the revelation known as section 3, in the Doctrine and Covenants. (HC, Vol. 1, p. 23 Footnote)

Sacred Truths

Introduction

What is the problem discussed by the Lord in section 3? It would be easy to conclude that the loss of the Book of Mormon manuscript was the disturbing issue. Before doing so, let us remember that the lost manuscript was not a problem to the Lord; he had made provision for that eventuality in his directions to Nephi over two thousand years earlier. (see B of M., I Nephi 9:5-6) Rather, the problem dealt with in this section is threefold:
1. Trusting in man instead of God (vs. 7, 13)
2. Delivering sacred things unto wickedness (vs. 12)
3. Breaking covenants with the Lord (vs. 13)

Trusting In Man Instead of God

When Martin requested the privilege of showing the manuscript, he was certain he could protect it and was willing to make promises before the Lord. As he persisted in that desire, Joseph was apparently convinced that Martin was capable of handling such a sacred document. Joseph pleaded with the Lord asking that the plans of mortals be given divine approval. Knowing the weakness of men, the Lord allowed them to learn a difficult lesson by simply granting them the object of their desire.

When failure resulted, as the Lord knew it surely would, He proceeded to teach His youthful prophet a significant principle. Listen to the Lord:

For although a man may have many revelations, and have power to do many mighty works, yet if he boasts in his own strength, and sets at naught the counsels of God, and follows after the dictates of his own will and carnal desires, he must fall and incur the vengeance of a just God upon him. (D&C 3:4)

This is a very common weakness in all of us. We may fear man more than God and often depend upon our own judgment instead of the Lord's counsel. Take, for instance, the many items of instruction given by the Lord through his prophet to us. We are taught on such matters as:

1. Abortion
2. Sabbath Day Shopping
3. Grooming Standards
4. Birth Control
5. Missionary service
6. Dating Standards
7. Home and Property Appearance
8. Fidelity in Marriage
9. Cleanliness of Speech
10. Honesty in Business and School Activities

Do we always follow the direction of the Lord? Or do we sometimes consider we are an exception and therefore justify our disobedient behavior?

How many people have fallen and incurred the vengeance of a just God because they set at naught the counsel of God and followed after the dictates of their own will and desires?

Might we not well expect the result of such decisions to be remorse and suffering? Joseph and Martin couldn't avoid it. And neither can we.

What is the counsel of the Lord to avoid such regret and unhappiness? Joseph was told:

> For, behold, you should not have feared man more than God. Although men set at naught the counsel of God, and despise his words—
>
> Yet you should have been faithful; and he would have extended his arm and supported you against all the fiery darts of the adversary; and he would have been with you in every time of trouble. (D&C 3:7-8)

Delivering Sacred Things Unto Wickedness

The gravity of their errors was emphasized when the Lord pointed out another aspect of their transgression:

> And when thou deliveredst up that which God had given thee sight and power to translate, thou deliveredst up that which was sacred into the hands of a wicked man. (D&C 3:12)
>
> Therefore, you have delivered them up, yea, that which was sacred, unto wickedness. (D&C 10:9)

Joseph seemingly was not fully aware of the sacred nature of the plates and the translation thereof. He apparently hadn't considered all that had been done to bring that ancient record into his hands. Perhaps he hadn't thought about all the spiritual strugglings, hours of labor and toil, days of fasting, praying, pondering and worrying to properly prepare those records. He may have overlooked how involved the Lord had been in the unnumbered spiritual and sacred experiences in the lives of ancient prophets. Possibly Joseph had not sensed how very sacred this book really is.

Now the issue in our lives today is not plates and manuscripts, but the principle is the same. We need to avoid a repetition of that same mistake. We have all been entrusted with sacred things. The reminder given to Joseph is just as appropriately applied to us as well.

> Behold, you have been entrusted with these things, but how strict were your commandments; and remember also the promises which were made to you, if you did not transgress them. (D&C 3:5)

So it seems imperative that each of us ascertain for ourselves the answer to the question: What things are sacred? Might each of us take time to ponder that question? Might we consider the following:

1. Children—Do we treat them properly; teach them adequately; correct them appropriately?
2. Marriage—Do we prepare for it as we should? Are we loyal to our companions and our covenants at all costs?
3. Presiding Authorities—Do we realize those titles and callings are sacred and revealed from above?
4. Our Mind—Do we nourish it with a proper balance of nutritional thoughts?
5. Our Body—Is it seen as a temple and a home for our spirit to dwell? Is it protected from the forces that might be destructive of its intended purpose?

Each of us would do well to make our individual lists and then exert all efforts towards protecting the items thereon. We must be sure that we are never guilty of delivering sacred things unto wickedness.

Breaking Covenants With The Lord

The breaking of covenants is a grave offense before God. The Lord indicated the seriousness of this action. Referring to Martin, the Lord said:

> ...[he] has broken the most sacred promises which were made before God, and has depended upon his own judgment, and boasted in his own wisdom. (D&C 3:13)

Martin had made a solemn promise that he would show the manuscript to five people only. He did not keep that covenant but instead chose to show the manuscript to others. This action brought upon him the charge of wickedness from the Lord. Anyone who violates covenants with God puts himself in the same position. Such violation suggests that an understanding of the sacred nature of covenants is lacking. Pres. Marion G. Romney has explained:

A covenant is a binding and solemn agreement between two or more parties. From the beginning God's people have been a covenant people . . .

No man who comprehends, believes and lives according to the gospel covenants will be inactive in the Church. When one understands the gospel of Jesus Christ—which is the Lord's new and everlasting covenant—and realizes that he himself accepted it in the spirit world, fought for it in the war in heaven, and entered mortality pursuant to the Lord's promise that if he here proves faithful he shall inherit eternal life—anyone who understands that has the needed background to understand the covenants entered into here in mortality. (CR, October 1975, p. 109)

Whenever one abuses his relationship with the Lord, he will find certain distasteful or unpleasant results. In the case at hand, the Lord told Joseph:

And you also lost your gift at the same time, and your mind became darkened. (D&C 10:2)

What was true for Joseph is true today. The principle is the same. To illustrate the point, we might refer to an incident when a young man was struggling to learn the gospel and prepare himself to teach it to others. For several weeks he could make no progress. He couldn't understand meanings or remember passages. Finally, in desperation, he approached his priesthood leader and sought counsel from him. In the course of their discussion, the young man felt a need to confess a sin that had never been cleared from his life before. He had delivered up things that were sacred unto wickedness. The leader referred him to the counsel the Lord gave Joseph at the time Joseph's mind was darkened.

. . .remember, God is merciful; therefore, repent of that which thou has done which is contrary to the commandment which I gave you, and thou art still chosen, and art again called to the work. (D&C 3:10)

. . .it is now restored unto you again; therefore, see that you are faithful and continue on unto the finishing of the remainder of the work of translation as you have begun. (D&C 10:3)

The young man was told not to rely on his own judgment and strength; not to break any of his covenants again. Again the leader referred him to the counsel the Lord had given Joseph:

Do not run faster or labor more than you have strength and means provided to enable you to translate; but be diligent unto the end.

Pray always, that you may come off conqueror; yea, that you may conquer Satan, and that you may escape the hands of the servants of Satan that do uphold his work. (D&C 10:4-5)

In section 10, the Lord provided a solution to the problems caused by the loss of the 116 pages of manuscript. The Lord gave Joseph instructions how to proceed to conquer Satan and his plan. He told him not to retranslate the same material. But instead, he was to translate from the plates of Nephi; " . . .which doth throw greater views upon my gospel . . ." (D&C 10:45)

Summary and Conclusion

We should never lose sight of the fact that,

. . .[the Lord's] wisdom is greater than the cunning of the devil. (D&C 10:43)

His counsel then and now is:

But as you cannot always judge the righteous, or as you cannot always tell the wicked from the righteous, therefore I say unto you, hold your peace until I shall see fit to make all things known unto the world concerning the matter. (D&C 10:37)

We see why the Lord said at the beginning of these sections:

The works, and designs, and the purposes of God cannot be frustrated, neither can they come to naught. (D&C 3:1)

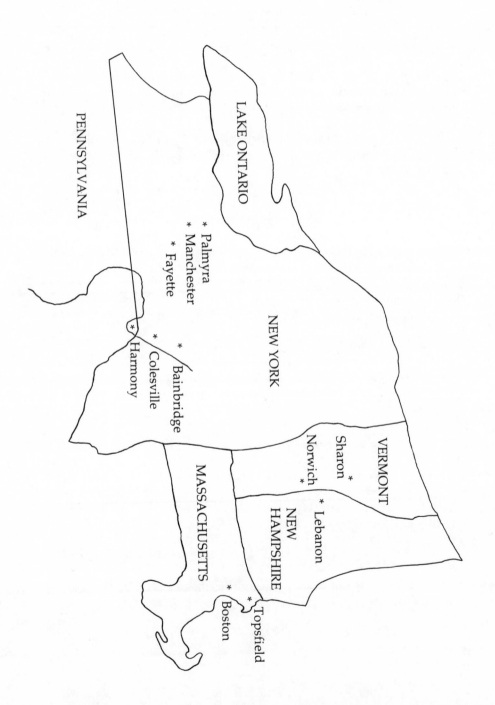

Chapter 5

Doctrine and Covenants Sections 4, 11, 12, 14, 15, 16

Suggested Titles

Section 4—The Call to Labor—Joseph Smith, Sr.
Section 11—The Call to Labor—Hyrum Smith
Section 12—The Call to Labor—Joseph Knight, Sr.
Sections 14, 15, 16—The Call to Labor—David, John and
Peter Whitmer, Jun.

Overview of Section Content

Section 4

1. A marvelous work to come forth (vs. 1)
2 Attitude of those who serve God (vs. 2-4)
3. Qualifications of those who serve God (vs. 5-7)

Section 11

1. The marvelous work and the laborers (vs. 1-5)
2. The Lord's counsel to Hyrum Smith
   a. Seek to bring forth Zion (vs. 6)

   b. Seek for true riches (vs. 7-8)
   c. Seek to teach repentance (vs. 9)
   d. Gift of Hyrum Smith (vs. 10)
   e. Trust in the power of the Lord's spirit (vs. 11-14)
   3. Preparation to labor in the Lord's kingdom (vs. 15-30)

Section 12

   1. The marvelous work and the laborers (vs. 1-5)
   2. Seek to bring forth Zion (vs. 6)
   3. Qualifications of those who serve God (vs. 7-9)

Section 14

   1. The marvelous work and the laborers (vs. 1-5)
   2. Seek to bring forth Zion (vs. 6)
   3. Counsel and promises to David Whitmer (vs. 7-11)

Section 15

   1. Desires of John Whitmer (vs. 1-5)
   2. The Lord's response to his desires (vs. 6)

Section 16

   1. Desires of Peter Whitmer, Jun. (vs. 1-5)
   2. The Lord's response to his desires (vs. 6)

Historical Setting

The nature of the contents of each of these sections suggests that they could all be profitably studied together. At the inception of the gospel restoration process, people were called by the Lord to assist in the preparatory phases of the restoration. Even prior to the organization of the Church men were called to labor with the Prophet Joseph under the direction of the Lord. These sections constitute opportunities given by the Lord for men to labor in this dispensation. We will group them together and study their contents jointly.

Section 4

In February 1829, Joseph Smith, Jun. was living with his wife Emma in Harmony, Pennsylvania. During that month, his father traveled from his own home in Manchester, New York, to Harmony to visit his son. (See map in Chapter 4) While there, he " . . .asked to know by revelation the will of the Lord. This section of the Doctrine and Covenants is the result of that humble inquiry." (CHMR, Vol. 1, pp. 32-33)

Section 11

In May 1829, Hyrum Smith, Joseph's older brother, traveled from his home in Manchester, New York, to Harmony, Pennsylvania to visit his brother Joseph. (See map in Chapter 4) "When he arrived he asked the Prophet to inquire of the Lord by Urim and Thummim what the Lord would have him do. The answer is the interesting and profitable revelation known as Section Eleven." (CHMR, Vol. 1, p. 51)

Section 12

Joseph Smith, Jun.

About the same time [see Historical Setting for Section 11] an old gentlemen came to visit us of whose name I wish to make honorable mention—Mr. Joseph Knight, Sen., of Colesville, Broome County, New York who, having heard of the manner in which we were occupying our time, very kindly and considerately brought us a quantity of provisions, in order that we might not be interrupted in the work of translation by the want of such necessities of life; and I would just mention here, as in duty bound, that he several times brought us supplies, a distance of at least thirty miles, which enabled us to continue the work when otherwise we must have relinquished it for a season. Being very anxious to know his duty as to this work, I inquired of the Lord for him, and obtained the following . . . (HC, Vol. 1, pp. 47-48)

Sections 14, 15, 16

Joseph Smith, Jun.

Shortly after commencing to translate, I became acquainted with Mr. Peter Whitmer, of Fayette, Seneca County, New York (see map in Chapter 4), and also with some of his family. In the beginning of the month of June, his son, David Whitmer, came to the place where we were residing, and brought with him a two-horse wagon, for the purpose of having us accompany him to his father's place, and there remain until we should finish the work . . . Upon our arrival, we found Mr. Whitmer's family very anxious concerning the work, and very friendly towards ourselves.

They continued so, boarded and lodged us according to arrang-
ments; and John Whitmer, in particular, assisted us very much in
writing during the remainder of the work.

In the meantime, David, John, and Peter Whitmer, Jun.,
became our zealous friends and assistants in the work; and being
anxious to know their respective duties, and having desired with
much earnestness that I should inquire of the Lord concerning
them, I did so, through the means of the Urim and Thummim, and
obtained for them in succession the following revelations. (HC,
Vol. 1, pp. 48-49)

Sacred Truths

Introduction

The emphasis of this chapter will be to focus our attention on the
teachings contained in these six revelations. They all pertain to a call to
labor in the Lord's kingdom. Each contributes to this lesson. However, the
content and breadth of section 4 is unique and must be understood by all
who serve in the Church. This section will provide a substantial portion of
the teachings presented herein. Commenting on this revelation, Elder
Joseph Fielding Smith has said:

> This revelation is very short, only seven verses, but it contains
> sufficient counsel and instruction for a life-time study. No one has
> yet mastered it. It was not intended as a personal revelation to
> Joseph Smith, [Sr.] but to be of benefit to all who desire to embark
> in the service of God. It is a revelation to each member of the
> Church, especially to all who hold the Priesthood. Perhaps there is
> no other revelation in all our scriptures that embodies greater
> instruction pertaining to the manner of qualification of members of
> the Church for the service of God, and in such condensed form than
> this revelation. It is as broad, as high, and as deep as eternity. No
> elder of the Church is qualified to teach in the Church, or carry the
> message of Salvation to the world, until he has absorbed, in part at
> least, this heaven-sent instruction. (CHMR, Vol. 1, pp. 32-33)

We will present three essentials that are necessary to characterize
proper or correct service unto the Lord.

Proper Attitude

Why does the Lord call His children to serve in His kingdom? And
what are our reasons for accepting such calls? What are our purposes as we

serve in various positions? A list of our motives could include the following:

1. Fear
2. Self-improvement
3. Prestige
4. Desire to help others
5. Social advancement
6. Business advantages
7. Service to the Lord

As appropriate as some of the above might be, do we have in mind the same purpose as does the Lord when He extends the call? What is the purpose? We suggest the answer is two-fold.

1. *An Invitation to Work with Father*

Listen to the words of the Savior:

Now behold, a marvelous <u>work</u> is about to come forth . . .
Therefore O ye that embark in the <u>service of God</u>, see that ye <u>serve him</u> . . .
Therefore, if ye have desires to <u>serve God</u>, ye are called to the <u>work</u> . . . (D&C 4:1-3, underlining added; See also D&C 15:6; 16:6)

What is the work of our Father in Heaven? And how do we <u>serve</u> Him? "For behold, this is my <u>work</u> . . . to bring to pass the immortality and eternal life of man." (P of GP, Moses 1:39, underlining added)

Simply and respectfully said, Father's employment is to save the souls of His children. His efforts are to assist and help them become like Him. Are we aware and do we realize that when we are called to His work we are actually being invited to labor with Him for the souls of men? With such an understanding, how could any of us refuse to work with Him and say "No" to His authorized servants who extend His calls? With this proper attitude, we welcome the opportunities to hold family home evening, be a home teacher, give missionary service, pay our tithes, teach quorums and auxiliary classes, perform vicarious work for the dead, etc.

King Benjamin saw this relationship with our Father and taught his people:

. . .I have spent my days in your service, . . .for I have only been in the <u>service of God</u>.
. . .I tell you these things that ye may learn wisdom; . . .when ye are in the service of your fellow beings, ye are only in the <u>service of your God</u>. (B of M, Mosiah 2:16-17, underlining added)

As we serve in our several capacities in the kingdom, it would be well for us to remind ourselves of our objectives. Can we pray and say, "Father, I enjoy working with thee. Help me retain this proper attitude. Thanks for this opportunity to labor for the souls of my brothers and sisters. Help me never to lose sight of why we labor together."

2.   Salvation For My Soul

We must not forget that our first responsibility is the salvation of our own soul. How is it accomplished? There is a relationship between working for others and obtaining our own salvation. Speaking of those who labor in the kingdom, the Savior said, " . . .he that thrusteth in his sickle with his might, the same layeth up in store that he perisheth not, but bringeth salvation to his soul . . ." (D&C 4:4, underlining added; See also D&C 11:3, 12:3; 14:3)

Again, may we be reminded that our salvation depends upon our positive responses to the Lord's authorized servants as they extend to us opportunities to labor. May we not shun such opportunities and put our salvation in jeopardy. Elder Joseph Fielding Smith has warned:

> Wo be to the man who sets his hand to the sickle and is not diligent, or who leaves the unharvested field. The Lord says of him that he stands in danger and may perish and lose salvation to his own soul. (CHMR, Vol. 1, p. 34)

In summary, it should be remembered that the Lord's purpose in extending calls to labor is to save souls; both those who labor and those for whom the labor is performed.

Tools for the Laborer

A laborer in any field of endeavor must have certain tools to accomplish his work. From these sections, we will identify some significant "tools" for saving souls.

1.   Authority

The Lord instructed Hyrum Smith as follows: "Behold, I command you that you need not suppose that you are called to preach until you are called." (D&C 11:15)

No one assumes the right to function in any official capacity in the Lord's Church. Each must be called by proper authority. (See P of GP, Articles of Faith, No. 5; also, D&C 42:11)

2.   Knowledge

Additional instructions to Hyrum Smith included:

Seek not to declare my word, but first seek to obtain my word, and then shall your tongue be loosed; then, if you desire, you shall have my Spirit and my word, yea, the power of God unto the convincing of men. (D&C 11:21)

A knowledge of gospel truths is absolutely essential for the laborer in the kingdom. A person cannot give or follow a principle he does not know for himself.

The Holy Ghost is a testator of truth. When the laborer presents divine truth, there is, for the hearer, an accompanying witness of the Lord's spirit. Such a process is the way men are convinced of truth when they hear it. Might we reflect again on the Lord's promise to the knowledgeable laborer: " . . .you shall have my spirit and my word, yea, the power of God unto the convincing of men." (D&C 11:21, underlining added)

3. Attributes

In order that a laborer might more effectively work with Father in saving souls, he must seek to develop and acquire the attributes of Father. We could refer to these tools as attributes of Godliness. A partial list of these attributes was given by the Savior in the revelation to Joseph Smith, Sr. as follows: (See D&C 4:2-6; 12:8)

1. Desire to serve with all of one's heart, might, mind, and strength
2. Faith
3. Hope
4. Charity
5. Virtue
6. Knowledge
7. Temperance
8. Patience
9. Brotherly kindness
10. Godliness
11. Humility
12. Diligence

To illustrate some of the above attributes: As we labor with Father to save the soul of a child, it is vital that we develop patience and draw close to that child.

In our hope to influence family members for good, we must exhibit brotherly kindness towards them. We must remember they are indeed children of God.

In courting relationships, a couple can only labor to save souls as they practice the principles of virtue and chastity.

Control of one's passions is only achieved as we develop temperance which is self-control.

It is interesting that the Savior listed faith and charity twice. Probably no other qualities are more essential than these two attributes. They are prerequisites to service in behalf of others. We may not have certain skills or talents, but if we have faith in God and charity (love) towards men, the Lord will make us equal to our tasks.

It would be well to remind ourselves again that the above list and illustrations are tools which are essential and must be developed by the laborer to effectively work with Father for the salvation of His children.

Correct Teachings

The Savior has given the laborer the following injunctions:

> Say nothing but repentance unto this generation. (D&C 11:9)
> . . .the thing which will be of the most worth unto you will be to declare repentance unto this people, that you may bring souls unto me, . . .(D&C 15:6, 16:6)

In commenting on the meaning of these verses, Elder Joseph Fielding Smith has explained:

> When the Lord calls upon his servants to cry nothing but repentance, he does not mean that they may not cry baptism, and call upon the people to obey the commandments of the Lord, but he wishes that all that they say and do be in the spirit of bringing the people to repentance. (CHMR, Vol. 1, p. 52)

Everything that we teach in the Lord's Church needs to be presented with the intent of helping people improve their lives and place themselves more in conformity with the teachings of Jesus Christ. Regardless of the subject being treated, the laborer needs to remember the purpose of it all and keep an eye single to the glory of God. We must not teach facts without purpose. We must not teach principle or concept without application. If we are to teach within the spirit of these inspired injunctions, we must assist in making the transfer of the teaching principle into the lives of the hearers.

Summary and Conclusion

We have been taught by the Lord the nature of a call to labor in His kingdom. Every laborer is extended an invitation to work with our Father for the salvation of His children. By doing so, the servant brings salvation to his own soul.

We have seen there are certain tools for the work. Effective labor is dependent upon having and properly using them.

We have been directed to teach Father's children in such a way as to bring them closer to Him.

Chapter 6

Doctrine and Covenants Sections 5 and 17

Suggested Titles

Section 5—Witnesses of The Book of Mormon—Martin Harris
Section 17—The Three Witnesses of The Book of Mormon

Overview of Section Content

Section 5

1. Martin Harris desires a witness-View of the plates (vs. 1, 24)
2. The Lord provides witnesses of the Book of Mormon
   a. Joseph Smith (vs. 2-10)
   b. Three servants as witnesses (vs. 11-15)
   c. Power of the Lord's spirit (vs. 16)
   d. The Lord's covenant people (vs. 16-20)
3. Requirements for Martin Harris to become a witness (vs. 23-32)
4. The Lord cautions and counsels Joseph Smith (vs. 21-22, 33-35)

Section 17

1. The Lord's requirements of the Three Witnesses to the Book of Mormon
   a. Have faith and rely on the Lord (vs. 1-2)
   b. Testify by the power of God (vs. 3, 5)

2. The witnesses to view the plates and other sacred things (vs. 1)
3. Purposes and power of the testimony of the Three Witnesses (vs. 3-4, 7-9)
4. The Savior's testimony of the Book of Mormon (vs. 6)

Historical Setting

We will discuss these two sections together since they both pertain to witnesses of the Book of Mormon.

Section 5

From this revelation and from the prophet Joseph Smith we learn that Martin Harris was desirous of viewing the plates. (See HC, Vol. 1, p. 28)

Section 17

Joseph Smith, Jun.

In the course of the work of translation, we ascertained that three special witnesses were to be provided by the Lord, to whom He would grant that they should see the plates from which this work (the Book of Mormon) should be translated; and that these witnesses should bear record of the same, as will be found recorded, Book of Mormon, page 581 [Book of Ether, chapter 5, verses 2, 3, and 4, p. 487, edition 1920], also page 86 [II Nephi, chapter 11, verse 3, p. 73, edition 1920]. Almost immediately after we had made this discovery, it occurred to Oliver Cowdery, David Whitmer and the aforementioned Martin Harris (who had come to inquire after our progress in the work) that they would have me inquire of the Lord to know if they might not obtain of him the privilege to be these three special witnesses; and finally they became so very solicitous, and urged me so much to inquire that at length I complied; and through the Urim and Thummim, I obtained of the Lord for them the following: (HC, vol. 1, pp. 52-53)

Sacred Truths

Introduction

As we explore the nature of the witness given by the Lord to these men, we will discuss both the physical and spiritual aspects of that witness. We will see the hand of the Lord in both as He unfolds the witness process.

Physical

Martin Harris was desirous of having a personal witness as to the reality of the plates from which Joseph Smith translated the Book of Mormon. (See D&C 5:1) Apparently, he considered that viewing the plates could constitute such a witness. It would appear that Martin's approach to this phase of the Lord's work was primarily a physical orientation. Such an approach is consistent with the world's view of acceptable evidence. It seems there is a place for such an experience in the Lord's program, as He promised Martin a view of the plates. (See D&C 5:23-24)

However, there are limitations to this type of witness. Though it would be supportive, it would not be adequate. The Lord counseled Joseph Smith that faith and testimony could not be built on tangible evidence alone. Addressing the children of men, He said, "Behold, if they [the world] will not believe my words, they would not believe you, my servant Joseph, if it were possible that you should show them all these things [the plates, etc.] which I have committed to you." (D&C 5:7)

Spiritual

Speaking of the witnesses of the Book of Mormon, the Lord said "...they shall know of a surety that these things are true." (D&C 5:12) This suggests an irrefutable witness and such a witness must include a "...manifestation of my Spirit." (D&C 5:16)

The Lord was willing that Martin should become a witness to the Book of Mormon, but He made it clear that Martin was not yet prepared to be such.

> And now, except he humble himself and acknowledge unto me the things that he has done which are wrong, and covenant with me that he will keep my commandments, and exercise faith in me, behold, I say unto him, he shall have no such views, for I will grant unto him no views of the things of which I have spoken. (D&C 5:28)

Joseph Smith reinforced the need for Martin to repent properly when he said:

> Martin Harris, you have got to humble yourself before God this day, that you may obtain a forgiveness of your sins. If you do, it is the will of God that you should look upon the plates in company with Oliver Cowdery and David Whitmer. (HC, Vol. 1, p. 55)

Apparently Martin was unprepared for either kind of witness because of his unworthiness. The question is, why was he unworthy? We do not suggest he was not willing to repent. But rather his orientation was in physical things. He had not yet realized that his breaking of a covenant with the Lord was the principal thing—not the loss of 116 pages of manuscript (see chapter 4). He apparently was not aware of the additional difficulties of being in transgression spiritually.

Oft times members of the Church have similar difficulties in recognizing the spiritual dimensions of transgression.

To illustrate:

A Sunday afternoon of sports and athletics instead of Sacrament Meeting attendance may be much more appealing to physical appetites. However, to one who is aware of covenant relationships with the Master, the spiritual opportunities take precedence over physical satisfactions.

We all ought to be aware that spiritual harm is being done when we violate any commandment of the Lord. This principle is one of the important concepts for us to glean from this revelation.

The Lord Gives the Witness

> Behold, I say unto you, that you must rely upon my word, which if you do with full purpose of heart, you shall have a view of the plates, and also of the breastplate, the sword of Laban, the Urim and Thummim, which were given to the brother of Jared upon the mount, when he talked with the Lord face to face, and the miraculous directors which were given to Lehi while in the wilderness, on the borders of the Red Sea. (D&C 17:1)

The Lord said he would give the witnesses a view of several things related to the translation of the Book of Mormon. The fullfillment of the promise was beautifully described by David Whitmer, one of the Three Witnesses as he was interviewed September 7, 1878, by Orson Pratt and Joseph F. Smith:

> It was in June, 1829, the latter part of the month, and the eight witnesses saw them, I think, the next day or the day after (i.e., one or two days after). Joseph showed them the plates himself, but the angel showed us (the Three Witnesses) the plates, as I suppose to fulfill the words of the book itself. Martin Harris was not with us at this time; he obtained a view of them afterwards (the same day). Joseph, Oliver, and myself were together when I saw them. We not only saw the plates of the Book of Mormon, but also the brass plates, the plates of the Book of Ether, the plates containing the records of the wickedness and secret combinations of the people of the world down to the time of their being engraved, and many other plates.

The fact is, it was just as though Joseph, Oliver and I were sitting just here on a log, when we were overshadowed by a light. It was not the light of the sun, nor like that of a fire, but more glorious and beautiful. It extended away around us, I cannot tell how far, but in the midst of this light about as far off as he sits (pointing to John C. Whitmer, sitting a few feet from him) there appeared as it were a table with many records or plates upon it, besides the plates of the Book of Mormon, also the sword of Laban, the directors (i.e., the ball which Lehi had) and the interpreters. I saw them just as plain as I see this bed (striking the bed beside him with his hand), and I heard the voice of the Lord, as distinctly as I ever heard anything in my life, declaring that the records of the plates of the Book of Mormon were translated by the gift and power of God. (Life of Joseph F. Smith, pp. 242-243)

The witness given by the Lord was more than just seeing. As He said,

. . .after that you have obtained faith, and have seen them with your eyes, you shall testify of them, by the power of God; (D&C 17:3)

Yea, they [Three Witnesses] shall know of a surety that these things are true, for from heaven will I declare it unto them. I will give them power that they may behold and view these things as they are; And to none else will I grant this power, to receive this same testimony . . . (D&C 5:12-14)

The true Church of Jesus Christ is not man-made. Thus, God provides and gives his own witness by His power. The strength of the testimony of these three men did not come from any mortal man, including Joseph Smith. Therefore, the knowledge of the truthfulness of the Lord's work is not an issue between the world and Joseph Smith. (See D&C 17:4) Rather it is a matter between each individual and the Savior Himself. Each person must accept the responsibility to accept or reject the Lord's witness as declared by these three men:

. . .we know of a surety that the work is true. And we also testify that we have seen the engravings which are upon the plates; and they have been shown unto us by the power of God, and not of man. (Book of Mormon, Testimony of Three Witnesses, underlining added)

These men testified of the divine source of this work. Acceptance or rejection of that testimony will have an influence upon our salvation. (See D&C 5:15-18)

Frequently the question is asked, "Why did the Three Witnesses leave the Church after such a powerful experience with the Lord?" Though they left the Church, it should be pointed out they never did deny their experience as a witness of the plates. The problem was not the denial of their testimony (which never occurred). Rather it was their failure to remain in harmony with the Lord and His church.

What of our spiritual standing? Do we know this work is true? To obtain our own witness from the Lord, we must qualify the same ways these men did. And once it is obtained, we must continue to live in such a way as to retain our spiritual standing with the Lord.

Summary and Conclusion

Along with the strength of the testimony borne by the Three Witnesses, and in addition to the personal witness granted by the Lord to each individual who properly seeks, the Savior gives us His personal witness as follows:

> And he [Joseph Smith] has translated the book, even that part which I have commanded him, and as your Lord and your God liveth it is true. (D&C 17:6)

Chapter 7

Doctrine and Covenants Sections 6, 8, 9

Suggested Titles

Section 6—What Greater Witness Can You Have Than
From God?—Oliver Cowdery
Section 8—The Spirit of Revelation—Oliver Cowdery
Section 9—Oliver Cowdery's Calling in the Translation
of the Book of Mormon

Overview of Section Content

Section 6

1. The marvelous work and the laborers (vs. 1-5)
2. The Lord's counsel to Oliver Cowdery
   a. Seek to bring forth Zion (vs. 6)
   b. Seek for true riches (vs. 7)
   c. Seek to teach repentance to this generation (vs. 8-9)
   d. Further counsel (vs. 18-21, 26-37)
3. Gifts of Oliver Cowdery (vs. 10-13, 25)
4. The Lord's witness to Oliver Cowdery (vs. 14-17, 22-24)

Section 8

1. How to seek revelation from the Lord (vs. 1, 9-12)

  2. The spirit of revelation (vs. 2-3)
  3. Gifts of Oliver Cowdery (vs. 4-8)

Section 9

  1. Oliver's calling (vs. 1-4, 13-14)
  2. Why the gift of translation was taken from Oliver Cowdery (vs. 5-12)

Historical Setting

At this point of time in the restoration process, Oliver Cowdery met Joseph Smith. During the first month of their association, the Lord gave Oliver three revelations through the Prophet Joseph. The content of these revelations is such that it lends itself to a combined study. We will discuss all three of them in this chapter.

Section 6

Joseph Smith, Jun.

On the 5th day of April, 1829, Oliver Cowdery came to my house [in Harmony, Penn.] until which time I had never seen him. He stated to me that having been teaching school in the neighborhood where my father resided, and my father being one of those who sent to the school, he went to board for a season at his house, and while there the family related to him the circumstances of my having received the plates, and accordingly he had come to make inquiries of me. Two days after the arrival of Mr. Cowdery (being the 7th of April) I commenced to translate the Book of Mormon, and he began to write for me, which having continued for some time, I inquired of the Lord through the Urim and Thummim, and obtained the following: ... (HC, Vol. 1, pp. 32-33)

Section 8

In the first revelation given to Oliver Cowdery (section 6) the Lord said,

...I grant unto you a gift, if you desire of me, to translate, even as my servant Joseph. (D&C 6:25)

Undoubtedly, this promise remained in Oliver's mind and he desired to have the promise fulfilled as indicated by the Prophet Joseph:

Joseph Smith, Jun.

Whilst continuing the work of translation, during the month of April, Oliver Cowdery became exceedingly anxious to have the power to translate bestowed upon him, and in relation to this desire the following revelations were obtained [Sections 8 and 9]. (HC, Vol. 1, p. 36)

Section 9

Joseph Fielding Smith

It seems probable that Oliver Cowdery desired to translate out of curiosity, and the Lord taught him his place by showing him that translating was not the easy thing he had thought it to be. In a subsequent revelation (Sec. 9), the explanation was made that Oliver's failure came because he did not continue as he commenced, and the task being a difficult one his faith deserted him. The lesson he learned was very necessary for he was shown that his place was to act as scribe for Joseph Smith and that it was the latter who was called and appointed by command of the Lord to do the translating. There must have been some desire on the part of Oliver Cowdery to be equal with the Prophet and some impatience in having to sit and act as scribe, but when he failed to master the gift of translating, he was then willing to accept the will of the Lord who said to him: "Be patient, my son, for it is wisdom in me, and it is not expedient that you should translate at this present time..." (CHMR, Vol. 1, p. 47)

Sacred Truths

Section 6

A Witness From the Lord

To more fully understand the importance of the message contained in section 6, it is vital to understand the circumstances under which these two men met.

At this time, (1828-29) Joseph and Emma were living in Harmony, Pennsylvania and Oliver Cowdery was teaching school in Manchester, (Palmyra area) New York. (See map chapter 4) While thus engaged in teaching in the Palmyra area, Oliver became aware of the story of Joseph Smith and the gold plates. Because of his desire to investigate futher, he traveled (in April 1829) approximately 100 miles from New York to Pennsylvania to see Joseph. (See Historical Setting for section 6)

It is of interest to note, that of all the people residing in the Palmyra area who most cetainly were aware of the story concerning Joseph Smith and the angel, few men put forth special effort to inquire personally of Joseph himself. Why would Oliver do so? Listen to the Lord's explanation:

Verily, verily, I say unto thee, blessed art thou for what thou hast done; for thou hast inquired of me, and behold, as often as thou hast inquired thou hast received instruction of my Spirit. If it had not been so, thou wouldst not have come to the place where thou art at this time.

Behold, thou knowest that thou hast inquired of me and I did enlighten thy mind; and now I tell thee these things that thou mayest know that thou hast been enlightened by the Spirit of truth;

Yea, I tell thee, that thou mayest know that there is none else save God that knowest thy thoughts and the intents of thy heart. (D&C 6:14-16)

It is significant that after the Lord revealed the thought and intent of Oliver's heart with reference to his coming to Harmony, Pennsylvania Oliver confided in Joseph Smith. Commenting on what Oliver said, Joseph recorded:

After we had received this revelation [section 6], Oliver Cowdery stated to me that after he had gone to my father's to board, and after the family had communicated to him concerning my having obtained the plates, that one night after he had retired to bed he called upon the Lord to know if these things were so, and the Lord manifested to him that they were true, but he had kept the circumstance entirely secret, and had mentioned it to no one; so that after this revelation was given, he knew that the work was true, because no being living knew of the thing alluded to in the revelation, but God and himself. (HC, Vol. 1, p. 35)

The Lord had given a witness to a man who had never seen the Prophet. Yet, when he met Joseph, he knew he stood in the presence of a prophet of God, a man who received revelation from Jesus Christ. Joseph told him things known only by the Lord. Thus, Oliver Cowdery received divine confirmation of the prophetic calling of Joseph Smith.

Oliver shared this special confirmation experience with David Whitmer, a friend of his residing in Fayette, New York. Commenting on this experience, David said:

When Oliver Cowdery went to Pennsylvania, he promised to write me [David Whitmer] what he should learn about these matters, which he did. He wrote me that Joseph had told him his (Oliver's) secret thoughts, and all he had meditated about going to see him, which no man on earth knew, as he supposed, but himself, and so he stopped to write for Joseph. (Historical record, May 1887, Vol. 6, p. 208)

Let us recall that while residing in the Joseph Smith, Sr. family home in Manchester, Oliver had sought for and received a personal witness from the Lord concerning the story of Joseph and the gold plates. He had told no one of this sacred, personal experience.

To remind Oliver that his witness had truly come from a divine source, and to verify Joseph's divine appointment, the Lord gave a further witness through His prophet:

> Verily, verily, I say unto you, if you desire a further witness, cast your mind upon the night that you cried unto me in your heart, that you might know concerning the truth of these things.
>
> Did I not speak peace to your mind concerning the matter? What greater witness can you have than from God?
>
> And now, behold, you have received a witness; for if I have told you things which no man knoweth have you not received a witness? (D&C 6:22-24)

The strength of the Lord's Church lies in the personal revelations received by the individual members. After receiving the Lord's witness, Oliver's life was never the same. His trip to Harmony, his subsequent service as a scribe, his relationship and association with Joseph Smith in the ministry, his sharing of many spiritual manifestations and experiences with Joseph in the kingdom—all of this resulted from this pivotal point in his life. What greater witness can you have than from God?

Our lives must likewise be influenced and changed. We also must know and have the assurance and direction from the Savior on a personal basis. However, such a realization and result will only come as we seek for it with the same desire and effort as did Oliver.

Sections 8 and 9

The Spirit of Revelation

We would recall that Oliver was promised by the Lord that he could have the opportunity to translate, even as Joseph Smith. (See D&C 6:25) Because of Oliver's desire to have this promise fulfilled, Joseph sought for and received section 8. (See Historical Setting for section 8)

After permission to proceed was granted and the Lord had given instructions as to how divine help could be obtained, Oliver made the attempt to translate. As a result of his failure in that endeavor, the Lord kindly explained the cause of his failure and revoked Oliver's privilege to translate as recorded in section 9 of the Doctrine and Covenants. (See Historical Setting for section 9)

These two revelations combined, describe a process for seeking and receiving divine revelation. The process was revealed to Oliver but the principles are applicable to all mankind. In fact, the entire work of the restoration of the Lord's kingdom is a process of the Lord communicating with man. It is not man's initiative to organize—but only to inquire. In order that man might properly seek revelation and know how to obtain divine direction, the Lord gave these two revelations as instructions to Oliver and to all His children who would seek His mind and will.

The process referred to above might be called the Lord's formula for revelation. This formula will be presented in two categories—asking and answer.

Asking Formula	Answer Formula
1. Ask in faith (See D&C 8:1)	1. Impression on the mind-ideas (See D&C 8:2)
2. Honest heart (See D&C 8:1)	
3. Believe answer will come (See D&C 8:1)	2. Impression in the heart-feelings (See D&C 8:2; 9:8-9)
4. Study problem in own mind (See D&C 9:7-8)	(Both of the above are given by the power of the Holy Ghost) (See D&C 8:2)

Asking Formula

In the Savior's sermon on the mount, He taught the people to pray for divine guidance in their lives. He said:

> Ask, and it shall be given you; seek, and ye shall find; knock and it shall be opened unto you:
>
> For every one that asketh receiveth; and he that seeketh findeth; and to him that knocketh it shall be opened.
>
> Or what man is there of you, whom if his son ask bread, will he give him a stone?
>
> Or if he ask a fish, will he give him a serpent?
>
> If ye then, being evil, know how to give good gifts unto your children, how much more shall your Father which is in heaven give good things to them that ask him? (Bible, Matthew 7:7-11)

To more fully appreciate the scope of these teachings and to realize the seriousness with which the Lord has given this instruction, we must come to know that these promises of the Lord are extended to all of His children.

To one of those children, Oliver Cowdery, the Lord reaffirmed that personal revelation is available to each of us today. He said,

> Oliver Cowdery, verily, verily, I say unto you, that assuredly as the Lord liveth, [and there is nothing more certain that that] who is your God and your redeemer, even so surely shall you receive a knowledge of whatsoever things you shall ask . . . (D&C 8:1)

With such an assurance, might we proceed now to learn the process by which such revelation is obtained.

1. *Ask in Faith*

The first principle of the gospel is faith in the Lord Jesus Christ. Anyone seeking revelation from God must have faith that the Lord lives and answers prayers. To illustrate the principle we will refer to the following incident that occurred during the march of the Mormon Battalion:

> We resumed our march, camping in the evening near some springs. One yoke of our oxen got mired in the mud. We took off the yoke when one got out. The other we undertook to pull out with a rope and unfortunately broke his neck. Our team was now too weak for our load . . .
>
> What to do for a team we did not know. This was a dark time, and many were the earnest petitions that went up to our God and Father for Divine aid.
>
> The next morning we found with our oxen a pair of splendid young steers, which was really cheering to us. We looked upon it as one of the providences of our Father in Heaven. Thus provided for, we pursued our march. (Mormon Battalion History, p. 191)

Why would anyone out in the middle of nowhere think that offering a prayer to some unseen being would produce any assistance to pull a wagon? The only real answer to such a query is that they had faith that Jesus Christ could and would help them. Such a simple faith is a vital ingredient in this asking formula.

2. *Honest Heart*

What does it mean to be honest? Moroni said we need to " . . .ask with a sincere heart, with real intent . . ." (B. of M. Moroni 10:4, underlining added) Is he not suggesting that we must be seriously and sincerely seeking and doing whatever is necessary to prepare ourselves for answers? As an illustration, we will refer to the descriptive words of Huckleberry Finn, as written by Mark Twain:

It made me shiver, and I about made up my mind to pray and see if I couldn't try to quit bein' the kind of a boy I was and be better.

So I kneeled down. But the words wouldn't come. Why wouldn't they? It weren't no use to try and hide it from Him . . .

I knowed very well why they wouldn't come. It was because my heart wasn't right; it was because I was playin' double.

I was tryin' to make my mouth say I would do the right thing and the clean thing, but deep down in me I knowed it was a lie and He knowed it. You can't pray a lie. I found that out. (Adventures of Huckleberry Finn, p. 283)

3. Believe Answer Will Come

There is a relationship between belief and receiving revelation. We remember that an angel asked Nephi if he believed. Such a condition was apparently a requirement for him to receive the marvelous revelation that followed. (See B. of M., I Nephi 11:4-6) The Savior was not able to do many mighty works among His people because of their unbelief. (See Bible, Matthew 13:58) And again in our dispensation, Joseph Smith said on one occasion:

. . .on account of the unbelief of the people, I cannot reveal the fullness of these things at present. (HC, Vol. 5, p. 510)

What will a person do who truly believes he will receive revelation? Will he take time to inquire but fail to provide time to listen for an answer? Or will he instead prepare himself and provide a time and a place to hear the expected response from the Lord? The latter approach is a demonstration of one who believes he will receive revelation from the Lord.

4. Study Problem in Own Mind

The Lord said " . . .study it out in your mind, . . ." (D&C 9:8) This might suggest two avenues of thought:

a. The Prophet Joseph taught " . . .we never inquire at the hand of God for special revelation only in case of there being no previous revelation to suit the case . . ." (HC, Vol. 1, p. 339)

It would be inappropriate to ask the Lord to reveal information which had already previously been given through his authorized servants and made available to mankind. It would be especially so if we are unaware of such information only because of our failure to study. Hence, we see the necessity and value of regular scripture study and a constant awareness of the counsel that is given by the Brethren who guide and direct the Lord's Church.

b. Whenever a decision is to be made, the Lord expects us to evaluate the alternatives and form our own conclusions. In such cases, we must not ask the Lord to make decisions for us. It is our responsibility to initiate the study process along with our inquiring of the Lord.

Answer Formula

Not only has the Savior taught His people to ask and seek for guidance, but He has also promised:

> ...every one that asketh, receiveth; and he that seeketh, findeth . . . (Bible, Matthew 7:8)

Such answers come as the Lord has said:

> ...I will tell you in your mind and in your heart, by the Holy Ghost, . . . Now, behold, this is the spirit of revelation . . . (D&C 8:2-3 underlining added)

1. *Impression on the Mind*

As to one of the ways this process takes place, the Prophet Joseph taught:

> The Spirit of Revelation is in connection with these blessings. A person may profit by noticing the first intimation of the spirit of revelation; for instance, when you feel pure intelligence flowing into you, it may give you sudden strokes of ideas, so that by noticing it, you may find it fulfilled the same day or soon; (i.e.) those things that were presented unto your minds by the Spirit of God, will come to pass and thus by learning the Spirit of God and understanding it, you may grow into the principle of revelation . . . (HC, Vol. 3, p. 381)

To illustrate: Consider the dilemma Moses faced at the shores of the Red Sea when Pharoah's armies were determined to destroy the Israelites. It was not the natural thing for Moses, to think of separating the sea. But as he sought for divine help, the Lord presented an idea to his mind, and by the power of the Lord the people were led through the sea on dry ground.

> ...this is the spirit of revelation; behold, this is the spirit by which Moses brought the children of Israel through the Red Sea on dry ground. (D&C 8:3)

The scriptures are rich with examples of the above process taking place. Today, Latter-day Saints continue to enjoy the spirit of revelation. Every faithful bishop, parent, home teacher, missionary, etc. is entitled to experience personal revelation. All are in need of ideas from a divine source to function effectively in their various responsibilities. We need to seek for and be receptive to those ideas presented to our minds by the Holy Ghost.

2. *Impression in the Heart*

In addition to the impression on the mind, the Lord said He would also touch the heart by the Holy Ghost. (See D&C 8:2) As we follow instructions and make personal efforts to obtain revelation we are taught by the Lord as follows:

> . . .you must ask me if it be right, and if it is right I will cause that your bosom shall burn within you; therefore, you shall feel that it is right.
>
> But if it be not right you shall have no such feelings, but you shall have a stupor of thought that shall cause you to forget the thing which is wrong . . . (D&C 9:8-9)

One of the more difficult things to do is to describe a feeling. For insight and description of the experience we will refer to statements made by two of the General Authorities:

H. Burke Peterson

As you feel the need to confide in the Lord or to improve the quality of your visits with him—to pray, if you please—may I suggest a process to follow: go where you can be alone, go where you can think, go where you can kneel, go where you can speak out loud to him. The bedroom, the bathroom, or the closet will do. Now picture him in your mind's eye. Think to whom you are speaking, control your thoughts—don't let them wander, address him as your Father and your friend. Now tell him things you really feel to tell him—not trite phrases that have little meaning, but have a sincere, heartfelt conversation with him. Confide in him, ask him for forgiveness, plead with him, enjoy him, thank him, express your love to him, and then listen for his answers. Listening is an essential part of praying. Answers from the Lord come quietly— ever so quietly. In fact, few hear his answers audibly with their ears. We must be listening so carefully or we will never recognize them. Most answers from the Lord are felt in our heart as a warm comfortable expression, for they may come as thoughts to our mind. They come to those who are prepared and who are patient. (CR, October 1973, p. 13)

Spencer W. Kimball

In our day, as in times past, many people expect that if there be revelation it will come with awe-inspiring, earthshaking display. For many it is hard to accept as revelation those numerous ones in Moses' time, in Joseph's time, and in our own year—those revelations which come to prophets as deep, unassailable impressions settling down on the prophet's mind and heart as dew from heaven or as the dawn dissipates the darkness of night.

Expecting the spectacular, one may not be fully alerted to the constant flow of revealed communication. (CR, April 1977, p. 115)

Summary and Conclusion

What have we learned from these revelations given to Oliver Cowdery? Would it be well to ask ourselves these questions:

1. Do we seek revelation and ask for it in faith?
2. Do we seek out of honest hearts?
3. Do our actions and attitudes reflect a belief that answers will come?
4. Do we study the Lord's teachings before seeking additional revelation?
5. Whenever decisions need to be made, do we evaluate alternatives and reach tentative conclusions and then ask for the Lord's confirmation?
6. Are we seriously listening and looking for revealed ideas from the Lord?
7. Are we sensitive to feelings created in the heart by the Holy Ghost?
8. As the Prophet Joseph has suggested, we "...may grow into the principle of revelation..." (HC, Vol. 3, p. 381) Are we?

Finally, for our help and guidance in these matters, we will hear from three General Authorities of the Church. Their counsel will summarize many of the points presented herein.

Melvin J. Ballard

You do not know what to do today to solve your finacial problems, what to plant, whether to buy or sell cattle, sheep, or other things. It is your privilege to study it out; counsel together with the best wisdom and judgment the Lord shall give you, reach your conclusions, and then go to the Lord with it, tell him what you have planned to do. If the thing you have planned to do is for your good and your blessing, and you are determined to serve the Lord, pay your tithes and your offerings and keep his commandments, I promise that he will fulfill that promise upon your head, and your bosom shall burn within by the whisperings of the Spirit that it is right. But if it is not right, you shall have no such feelings, but you shall have a stupor of thought, and your heart will be turned away from that thing.

I know of nothing today that the Latter-day Saints need more than the guidance of the Holy Spirit in the solution of the problems of life. (CR, April 1931, pp. 37-38)

Marion G. Romney

Now, my brothers and sisters, we need to seek that Spirit. We need to realize that it is a real guide. The Lord has given us several tests by which we may know when we have that Spirit . . .

Now, I tell you that you can make every decision in your life correctly if you can learn to follow the guidance of the Holy Spirit. This you can do if you will discipline yourself to yield your own feelings to the promptings of the Spirit. Study your problems and prayerfully make a decision. Then take that decision and say to him, in a simple, honest supplication, "Father, I want to make the right decision. I want to do the right thing. This is what I think I should do; let me know if it is the right course." Doing this, you can get the burning in your bosom, if your decision is right. If you do not get the burning, then change your decision and submit a new one. When you learn to walk by the Spirit, you never need to make a mistake. I know what it is to have this burning witness. (CR, October 1961, pp. 60-61)

Paul H. Dunn

Leaders sometimes tend to neglect using the Spirit of the Lord, when actually it should finalize every decision. If we do all within our power to solve our problems and make the proper decisions, and then ask the Lord for confirmation and verification, we soon discover we never err in our plans and decisions . . .

All leaders and members of the Church need to learn this process of receiving and interpreting correctly the spirit as it comes from the Lord. It forms the very heart of the working relationship between man and God. But the individual needs to understand that he must make the first move. As James summed it up so well, "Submit yourselves therefore to God . . . Draw nigh to God, and he will draw nigh to you." (Jas. 4:7-8)

This principle of receiving help from the Lord is always the same, but the method or process involved will change with each experience. No two experiences will be exactly alike except in principle. We must always study it out to the best of our ability and the Lord will finalize. Whenever the principle is followed effectively, we can act with confidence and be assured of being in agreement with God. (The Ten Most Wanted Men, pp. 21, 23)

Chapter 8

Doctrine and Covenants
Section 7

Suggested Title

The Parchment of John

Overview of Section Content

1. John's status in the flesh (vs. 1-4, 7)
2. The influence of desires (vs. 3, 8)
3. Peter's desire (vs. 4-5, 7)
4. John's desire (vs. 2, 4-6)

Historical Setting

Joseph Smith, Jun.

During the month of April I continued to translate, and he [Oliver Cowdery] to write, with little cessation, during which time we received several revelations. A difference of opinion arising between us about the account of John the Apostle, mentioned in the New Testament, [Jesus saith unto him, If I will that he tarry till I come, what is that to thee? follow thou me. Bible, John 21:22] as to whether he died or continued to live, we mutually agreed to settle it by the Urim and Thummim and the following is the word which we received. (HC, Vol 1, pp. 35-36)

Joseph Fielding Smith

...There arose a difference of opinion between Joseph Smith and Oliver Cowdery as to whether John remained in the flesh or had died. They inquired of the Lord by Urim and Thummim and the answer was the revealing of the record made by John on parchment and hidden up by himself. This record is section seven of the Doctrine and Covenants . . . (CHMR, Vol. 1, p. 44)

Sacred Truths

Introduction

Very often when someone seeks direction from the Lord, he is directed to a source containing previously recorded information that provides the direction being sought. In response to Joseph's inquiry, the Lord revealed to the Prophet statements written by John the Beloved which made it possible for Joseph to obtain the desired information. As a result, the Prophet gained additional insights pertaining to the desires and mission of John.

We will discuss the content of this revelation under two topics:

1. John's status in the flesh
2. The influence of desires.

John's Status in the Flesh

The contents of the parchment revealed that John would not die or go through a change equivalent to death before the Savior's second coming. He asked for power over death. (See D&C 7:2) The Lord responded by saying:

...Verily, verily, I say unto thee, because thou desirest this thou shalt tarry until I come in my glory . . . (D&C 7:3)

John became a ministering angel with a ministry that would not end until the second coming of Jesus Christ. At the present time John has a body of flesh and bones that has been changed in such a way that death is postponed for a period of time. Such a condition is described as a state of being translated. Commenting on such persons, the Prophet Joseph Smith said:

He [Joseph] explained the difference between an angel and a ministering spirit; the one a resurrected or translated body, with its spirit ministering to embodied spirits—the other a disembodied spirit, visiting and ministering to disembodied spirits. Jesus Christ became a ministering spirit (while His body was lying in the sepulchre) to the spirits in prison, to fulfill an important part of His mission, without which He could not have perfected His work, or entered into His rest. After His resurrection He appeared as an angel to His disciples.

Translated bodies cannot enter into rest until they have undergone a change equivalent to death. Translated bodies are designed for future missions. (HC, Vol. 4, p. 425)

For additional insight as to the nature of translated beings, see B. of M., III Nephi 28:9, 19-22.

The Influence of Desires

It is a fundamental principle of the gospel that the Lord grants unto men according to their own desires. God allows us to receive that which we would truly desire to have. (See B. of M., Alma 29:4-5) We are not describing wants or wishes, but rather those internal qualities that motivate men to action. Ultimately we determine our own destiny. One of the finest illustrations of the above principle can be seen in the conversation the Lord had with Peter and John. Each of their desires is identified by Him.

Peter's Desire

The Lord described Peter's desire as follows:

...thou [Peter] desiredst that thou mightest speedily come unto me in my kingdom. I say unto thee, Peter, this was a good desire... (D&C 7:4-5)

We note the Lord called this kind of desire, good. It is a righteous desire that all of us should be seeking to be in the presence of the Lord. Peter expressed such a desire to the Lord the night of the last supper. During their conversation the Savior had indicated Peter's conversion and the realization of that desire was yet future. (See Bible, Luke 22:31-32) Peter's response was as follows:

...Lord, I am ready to go with thee, both into prison, and to death. (Bible, Luke 22:33)

A history of the events of that same night reveal that he really was not ready. There isn't any question but what his desire existed in his heart. But, though he was willing, he was not able. He lacked the spiritual power to keep his commitments. He had not yet received the spiritual gifts of the

Holy Ghost. They would subsequently come from a divine source and would enable him to remain a loyal servant of the Master. Ultimately, Peter did realize the fulfillment of his desires. He became a stalwart leader in the Church and was assigned to come to the earth in the present dispensation to restore the priesthood and the keys of the kingdom of Jesus Christ.

Every member of the Church can relate to Peter's experience. We all must develop the desire to be with the Lord. The achieving of this goal is dependent upon our acquiring spiritual power from the Holy Ghost through the process of obedience to the Savior's commandments.

John's Desire

As great as it is and will be for individuals to come into the presence of Jesus Christ, there is a greater work—help others experience the same glory. This was the desire of John the Beloved. He recorded as follows:

> And the Lord said unto me: John, my beloved, what desirest thou? For if you shall ask what you will, it shall be granted unto you.
> And I said unto him: Lord, give unto me power over death, that I may live and bring souls unto thee. (D&C 7:1-2, underlining added)

In conversing with Peter concerning John's desire, the Savior referred to John and said,

> . . .my beloved has desired that he might do more, or a greater work yet among men than what he has before done. (D&C 7:5, under-lining added)

A reported incident in John's own life will serve as an example of the sincerity of his desire. This experience was recorded by an ancient historian. We note the phraseology and use of words is sometimes foreign to those who have the benefit of the restored gospel. However, the principle portrayed is John's great concern and love for the souls of his fellowmen.

> When the tyrant [Domitian ?] was dead, and John had moved from the island of Patmos to Ephesus, he used to go when asked to the neighboring districts of the Gentile peoples, sometimes to appoint bishops, sometimes to organize whole churches, some-times to ordain one person of those pointed out by the Spirit. So it happened that he arrived at a city not far off, named by some, [Smyrna] and after settling the various problems of the brethren, he finally looked at the bishop already appointed, and indicating a

youngster he had noticed, of excellent physique, attractive appearance, and ardent spirit, he said: "I leave this young man in
your keeping, with all earnestness, in the presence of the Church
and Christ as my witness." When the bishop accepted him and
promised everything, John addressed the same appeal and ad-
juration to him a second time.

He then returned to Ephesus, and the cleric took home the
youngster entrusted to his care, brought him up, kept him in his
company, looked after him, and finally gave him the grace of
baptism. After this he relaxed his constant care and watchfulness,
having put upon him the seal of the Lord as the perfect protection.
But the youngster snatched at liberty too soon, and was led sadly
astray by others of his own age who were idle, dissolute, and
evil-livers. First they led him on by expensive entertainments; then
they took him with them when they went out at night to commit
robbery; then they urged him to take part in even greater crimes.
Little by little he fell into their ways; and like a hard-mouthed
powerful horse he dashed off the straight road, and taking the bit
between his teeth rushed down the precipice the more violently
because of his immense vitality. Completely renouncing God's
salvation, he was no longer content with petty offences, but, as his
life was already in ruins, he decided to commit a major crime and
suffer the same fate as the others. He took these same young
renegades and formed them into a gang of bandits of which his was
the master mind, surpassing them all in violence, cruelty, and
bloodthirstiness.

Time went by, and some necessity having arisen, John was
asked to pay another visit. When he had dealt with the business for
which he had come, he said: "Come now bishop, pay me back the
deposit which Christ and I left in your keeeping, in the presence of
the Church over which you preside as my witness." At first the
bishop was taken aback, thinking that he was being dunned for
money he had never received. He could neither comply with a
demand for what he did not possess, nor refuse to comply with
John's request. But when John said, "It is the young man I am
asking for, and the soul of our brother", the old man sighed deeply
and shed a tear.

"He is dead."

"How did he die?"

"He is dead to God: he turned out wicked and profligate, in
short, a bandit; and now, instead of the Church, he has taken to the
mountain with an armed gang of men like himself."

The apostle rent his garment, groaned aloud, and beat his

head. "A fine guardian," he cried, "I left our brother's soul! However, let me have a horse immediately, and someone to show me the way." He galloped off from the church, then and there, just as he was. When he arrived at the place, and was seized by the bandits' sentry-group, he made no attempt to escape and asked no mercy, but shouted: "This is what I have come for: take me to your leader." For the time being the young man waited, armed as he was; but as John approached he recognized him, and filled with shame, turned to flee. But John ran after him as hard as he could, forgetting his years and calling out: "Why do you run away from me, child—from your own father, unarmed and very old? Be sorry for me, child, not afraid of me. You still have hopes of life. I will account to Christ for you. If need be, I will gladly suffer your death, as the Lord suffered death for us; to save you I will give my own life. Stop! believe! Christ sent me."

When he heard this, the young man stopped and stood with his eyes on the ground; then he threw down his weapons; then he trembled and began to weep bitterly.

. . .[John] did not leave him, we are told, till he had restored him to the Church, giving a perfect example of true repentance and a perfect proof of regeneration . . .(Eusebius, The History of the Church, pp. 128-131)

Summary and Conclusion

Is there a message for us? Has the Savior given us access to John's record that we might come to an understanding of a vital principle? The message for us to understand is that the greater work in which we can be engaged is to labor for the soul of a child of God. Parents, bishops, teachers, and all others who labor in the kingdom need to be conscious of the greater work. By so doing they will then realize the fulfillment of their desires for the souls of others. They will be more attentive to needs and sensitive to the opportunities presented them to bless the lives and help in the saving of the souls of Father's children.

Chapter 9

Doctrine and Covenants Section 13

Suggested Title

The Restoration of the Aaronic Priesthood

Overview of Section Content

1. Keys of the ministering of angels
2. Keys of the gospel of repentance
3. Keys of baptism
4. Sons of Levi, their offering, etc.
5. Duration, or longevity, of the Aaronic Priesthood

Historical Setting

Joseph Smith, Jun.

We still continued the work of translation, when in the ensuing month (May, 1829), we on a certain day went into the woods to pray and inquire of the Lord respecting baptism for the remission of sins, that we found mentioned in the translation of the plates. While we were thus employed, praying and calling upon the Lord, a messenger from heaven descended in a cloud of light, and having laid his hands upon us, he ordained us, saying: [section 13 follows] . . .

He said this Aaronic Priesthood had not the power of laying on hands for the gift of the Holy Ghost, but that this should be conferred on us hereafter; and he commanded us to go and be baptized, and gave us directions that I should baptize Oliver Cowdery, and afterwards that he should baptize me. Accordingly we went and were baptized. I baptized him first, and afterwards he baptized me, after which I laid my hands upon his head and ordained him to the Aaronic Priesthood, and afterwards he laid his hands on me and ordained me to the same Priesthood—for so we were commanded.

The messenger who visited us on this occasion, and conferred this Priesthood upon us, said that his name was John, the same that is called John the Baptist in the New Testament, and that he acted under the direction of Peter, James and John who held the keys of the Priesthood of Melchizedek, which priesthood he said would in due time be conferred on us, and that I should be called the first Elder of the Church, and he (Oliver Cowdery) the second. It was on the 15th day of May, 1829, that we were ordained under the hand of this messenger and baptized. (HC, Vol. 1, pp. 39-41)

Sacred Truths

Introduction

As we learned in the historical setting, this section is the prayer offered at the time of the bestowal of the Aaronic Priesthood. Included within this brief statement by John the Baptist are many topics that could lead to a more exhaustive discussion or presentation. For example, see overview of section content.

Our purposes seem to be served best by limiting our discussion to the first three items listed in the overview. For additional insight and information, pertinent to items not discussed herein, the reader is referred to the following:

DS, Vol. 3, pp. 93-94
TPJS, pp. 172-173
P of GP, Joseph Smith—History 1:71, Footnote
DCC, pp. 68-70
AGQ, Vol. 1, pp. 119-120

Keys of Aaronic Priesthood

As John the Baptist bestowed this priesthood, he informed Joseph and Oliver that the Aaronic Priesthood holds specific keys, all of which are preparatory to the receiving of higher or Melchizedek Priesthood powers. (See D&C 84:26-27) We will focus our attention on each of the three keys identified by John in the prayer.

1. Keys of Ministering of Angels

As a result of the bestowal of the Priesthood of Aaron are we to expect that we might see angels? Is it to be as prevalent and common today as it was in the early history of the Church? Commenting on the subject of the ministering of angels, President Wilford Woodruff said:

> . . .One of the Apostles said to me years ago, "Brother Woodruff, I have prayed for a long time for the Lord to send the administration of an angel to me. I have had a great desire for this, but I have never had my prayers answered." I said to him that if he were to pray a thousand years to the God of Israel for that gift it would not be granted, unless the Lord had a motive in sending an angel to him. I told him that the Lord never did nor never will send an angel to anybody merely to gratify the desire of the individual to see an angel. If the Lord sends an angel to anyone, He sends him to perform a work that cannot be performed only by the administration of an angel. I said to him that these were my views. The Lord had sent angels to men from the creation of the world, at different times, but always with a message or with something to perform that could not be performed without. I rehearsed to him different times when angels appeared to men. Of course, I referred to the angel visiting Joseph Smith. The Revelator John said that in the last days an angel would fly in the midst of heaven, having the everlasting Gospel to preach to them that dwelt on the earth. The reason it required an angel to do this work was the Gospel and the Priesthood had been taken from among men. Hence God had to restore it again.
>
> . . .I have never prayed for the visitation of an angel, but I have had the ministration of an angel several times in my life.
>
> . . .I traveled thousands of miles and preached the Gospel as a Priest, and, as I have said to congregations before, the Lord sustained me and made manifest His power in the defense of my life as much while I held that office as He has done while I have held the office of an Apostle. The Lord sustains any man that holds a portion of the priesthood, whether he is a Priest, an Elder, a seventy or an Apostle if he magnifies his calling and does his duty. (Deseret Weekly News, Vol. 55, No. 21, November 7, 1896)

The principle that should be emphasized here is that angels only minister to people on earth when that ministration or service cannot be accomplished any other way.

As a result of the restoration of the gospel (which was accomplished through the ministering of angels) priesthood power has been made available to mankind. Through the use of this power, the authorized servants of the Lord are now able to render service and minister to the needs of Father's children everywhere. Thus, priesthood bearers are empowered to minister and do the work of the Lord in areas which previously would have required the services of an angel. With such an understanding, then, we can better visualize the responsibility resting upon the shoulders of the priesthood. They are expected to do the work of angels.

Since priesthood holders are designated representatives of the Lord (as angels are) it would be appropriate to ask ourselves a few questions:

1. Would an angel be concerned about his personal appearance?
2. Would an angel prepare himself for assignments and callings?
3. Would an angel willingly serve when invited to do so?
4. As an agent, would an angel be loyal to his principal?
5. Would an angel be desirous of maintaining the standards and keeping the commandments of the Lord?

Commenting upon this principle of representation, President Harold B. Lee taught:

> When we officiate in the name of the Lord, as holders of the priesthood, we are doing it in the name and in behalf of our Heavenly Father. Priesthood is the power by which our Heavenly Father works through men, through deacons, through teachers, through priests, and I have a feeling that we are not impressing that upon our young men. They are not taking the understanding of their priesthood as seriously as they might . . .They would always want to appear at their best when they are exercising their priesthood. Their hair would be properly groomed; their clothing and appearance would reflect the sanctity they should feel in the performance of their priesthood duties. I have had that same feeling. I have never performed an ordinance, such as administering to the sick, without first excusing myself, if I were out in the garden or somewhere, until I was properly clothed, to make the best appearance I could, because I felt in so doing I was drawing close to the Lord himself, and I want to appear at my best in his presence.
>
> Brethren, I am afraid that some of our elders, do not understand this, that when they are officiating as elders of the Church, or as seventies or as high priests, it is as though when they perform

the ordinance, the Lord through them is acting upon the heads of those for whom they minister. I have often thought one of the reasons why we are not magnifying our priesthood is because we don't understand that as holders of the priesthood, He is working through us by the power of the holy priesthood, and I would wish that we could all have that feeling, and so teach our young people what it means to hold the priesthood and to magnify it. (CR, April 1973, p. 129)

As an illustration of the principles taught by President Lee, Bishop Victor L. Brown's experience in Samoa is most fitting:

I was in the Pago Pago Stake in American Samoa. President Peters, the stake president, invited me to accompany him to one of the ward sacrament meetings. We arrived unannounced, so there were no special arrangements made.

It was a hot, humid day. As we approached the humble, one-room chapel with no air-conditioning, I suggested it might be appropriate to leave our jackets off. President Peters was quick to tell me that they wore jackets in sacrament meeting in their stake—no matter what the temperature—as a means of showing the Lord that they not only worshiped him but they also honored and respected him by being dressed in their very best.

As I took my place on the stand, there sat priests and deacons at the sacrament table. Each had on a shirt, tie, and jacket. It was so hot and humid.

The normal dress of the islands is very casual, as you know, but in the eyes of these wonderful Samoan leaders and their Aaronic Priesthood boys, participating in the sacred sacrament service was not a casual experience. It was a sacred duty. They felt that their appearance helped show the respect and reverence they had for the Lord. I shall never forget their influence of reverence in that meeting. Surely their understanding of their relationship with Heavenly Father is an important step in magnifying their priesthood. (Ensign, July 1972, p. 90)

2. *Keys of the Gospel of Repentance*

The privilege of holding the Aaronic Priesthood carries with it the responsibility of declaring repentance to the people of the earth. We see such a calling being fullfilled through the rendering of such services as home teaching, testimony bearing, speaking opportunities, quorum presidency efforts towards reactivation, fellowshipping activities, etc. All of the above activities are entered into for the purpose of helping others improve their lives through the process of repentance. There are those occasions when people reject such opportunities. Nevertheless, the Lord will sustain His servants while they engage themselves in such activity. President Wilford Woodruff related a personal experience as he was carrying out his duties as an Aaronic Priesthood holder. He said:

> I was once moved upon to go and warn old Father Hakeman, living on Petty-John Creek, Arkansas. He had been in Jackson County during the persecution period. His wife died there. His family consisted of five sons, all over six feet tall. Most of them had been whipped with hickory gads by mobs, and he went south into Arkansas, taking his sons with him. We went a good deal out of our way for the purpose of visiting Father Hakeman. I had a vision the night previous, in which was manifested to me the trouble that lay before us, but that the Lord would deliver us. We arrived at his house on Sunday morning. He was taking breakfast. We had had breakfast at the place where we stayed overnight. I saw a Book of Mormon on the shelf. He did not seem to pay any attention to us, or to take any interest in us. I took up the Book of Mormon, and said, "You have a very good book here."
>
> "Yes," said he, "but it is a book that came from the devil."
>
> That opened my eyes. He had been an elder; he had been in Zion; had been persecuted there and driven out; but I found that he had apostatized, and he was our enemy. I saw he would do anything he could against us.
>
> We left him and went to Brother Hubbard's and stayed with him three weeks, during which we took our axes and cleared some land for him. I was strongly impressed three times to go up and warn Father Hakeman. At last I did so, according to the commandment of God to me. The third time I met with him, his house seemed to be full of evil spirits, and I was troubled in spirit at the manifestation. When I finished my warning, I left him. He followed me from his house with the intention of killing me. I have no doubt about his intention, for it was shown to me in vision. When he came to where I was, he fell dead at my feet, as if he had been struck with a thunderbolt from heaven. I was then a priest, but God defended me and preserved my life. I speak of this because it is a principle that has been manifest in the church of God in this generation as well as in others. I had the administration of angels while holding the office of a priest. I had visions and revelations. I traveled thousands of miles. I baptized men, though I could not confirm them because I had not the authority to do it.

I speak of these things to show that a man should not be ashamed of any portion of the priesthood. Our young men, if they are deacons, should labor to fulfill that office. If they do that, they may then be called to the office of a teacher, whose duty it is to teach the people, visit the Saints and see that there is no evil or iniquity carried on. God has no respect for persons in this priesthood any further than as they magnify their callings and do their duty. (MS, Vol. 53, pp. 641-642, (1891) and DWW, pp. 297-298)

3. Keys of Baptism

From John's prayer we learn that baptism is to be performed by immersion and it is one of the steps leading to a remission of sins. This ordinance of baptism is the gate by which one enters the Savior's Church and establishes a covenant relationship with Jesus Christ. (See D&C 20:37, 73-74; B. of M., II Nephi 31:1-17) The Aaronic Priesthood has the authority to act in behalf of the Savior for those who desire to make such a covenant. It is interesting to note that the first baptisms performed in this dispensation were performed by the power of the Aaronic Priesthood. (P of GP, Joseph Smith—History 1:66-71)

Summary and Conclusion

As we analyze the restoration of the Aaronic Priesthood, we observe that many important truths were revealed at that time. We suggest several as follows:

1. The Aaronic Priesthood has the power to perform baptism.
2. Baptism must be performed by immersion.
3. Baptism satisfies part of the requirements to obtain a remission of sins.
4. Ordination to the Aaronic Priesthood is accomplished by the laying on of hands.
5. Aaronic Priesthood is limited in its powers.
6. The restoration of the Aaronic Priesthood confirms the apostasy.
7. The appearance of John the Baptist witnesses the reality of the resurrection and life after death.
8. The Aaronic Priesthood functions under the direction of the Melchizedek Priesthood. (John the Baptist acted under the direction of Peter, James and John)
9. The Aaronic Priesthood is not sufficient for the exaltation of man. (The Melchizedek Priesthood was to be conferred at a later time)

Now, in conclusion, let us point out the significance of the event that transpired on May 15, 1829. For the first time in many centuries, Father's children gained access to power from on high to seek out and obtain covenant relationships with Jesus Christ. The keys have now been restored giving man the authority to act for and in behalf of the Savior. The Church of Jesus Christ of Latter-day Saints is the custodian of those keys. Under the direction of the Lord's living prophet, ordinances are performed on earth and are made valid in the heavens for the salvation of the souls of mankind.

Chapter 10

Doctrine and Covenants Section 18

Suggested Title

The Name of Jesus Christ—The Worth of Souls

Overview of Section Content

1. The Lord counsels Oliver Cowdery to rely on the scriptures (vs. 1-5, 17)
2. The Lord reaffirms to Oliver Cowdery the divine calling of Joseph Smith (vs. 6-8)
3. The apostolic calling (vs. 9-16, 18-36)
   a. Twelve Apostles
   b. Others
   c. Knowing the name of Jesus Christ
4. The choosing of the Twelve by the Three Witnesses of the Book of Mormon (vs. 37-38)
5. The Lord counsels the Three Witnesses (vs. 39-47)

Historical Setting

At the time the Aaronic Priesthood was restored to Joseph Smith and Oliver Cowdery, they were given the promise that the "...Priesthood of Melchizedek,...would in due time be conferred..." (HC, Vol. 1, p. 40) As a result of this promise, these brethren sought for this priesthood through prayer. In response to their petition, Peter, James and John were sent by the Lord to restore the Melchizedek Priesthood. (For additional information, see:

1. HC, Vol. 1, pp. 60-61, footnote.
2. GD, pp. 193-195.
3. The Ensign, June 1979, pp. 5-10)

In section 18, the Lord revealed that the restoration of the Quorum of Twelve Apostles would be forthcoming in this dispensation. Commenting on this event, Elder Joseph Fielding Smith has said:

> . . .Nearly six years before the calling of the Twelve Apostles in this dispensation, and several months before the organization of the Church, the Lord indicated by revelation that a council of twelve Apostles would be chosen, and Oliver Cowdery and David Whitmer were informed that it was to be their privilege to choose out the Twelve and instruct them in the duties of that calling . . .
>
> . . .At this early day Oliver Cowdery and David Whitmer, who had sought the privilege of acting as two of the three witnesses of the Book of Mormon were appointed by divine revelation to seek out the Twelve. Martin Harris, who had been named as the other witness, was not named in this revelation as one who should share in this great honor. It was by sore and sincere repentance that the privilege was granted him to become a witness of the Book of Mormon, and the Lord still withheld from Martin the full exercise of his spirit when the call of the other two men came to choose out the Twelve. Before the time arrived for the choosing of the twelve special witnesses for Christ six years later, Martin had placed himself in a position where he could be recognized, and therefore the Prophet, by the revelation of the Lord, included Martin Harris with the other brethren in the choosing and ordaining of the Twelve Apostles. (CHMR, Vol. 1, pp. 75, 77)

Sacred Truths

Introduction

Our discussion of this revelation will focus on three major principles:

1. The apostolic calling of the twelve apostles.
2. A universal apostolic calling.
3. Knowing the name of Jesus Christ.

The Apostolic Calling of the Twelve Apostles

What is an apostle and what does he do? The Savior has answered that question in this revelation and others. An apostle is one who has taken upon himself the name of Jesus Christ and is specifically commissioned to bear witness of His name to the world. He is responsible for teaching all people of the earth that salvation comes only through their acceptance of the name of the Savior. (See D&C 18:21-28; 107:23, 35) This special commission is given emphasis by the Lord, who said, "Wherefore, you are called to cry repentance unto this people." (D&C 18:14)

It is interesting to note that the Lord commissioned the three witnesses of the Book of Mormon to select the members of the first Quorum of Twelve Apostles. (See D&C 18:37—Also see Joseph Fielding Smith's comments in the Historical Setting of this chapter)

Since these men did not occupy sustained ecclesiastical positions at that time, one may ask, "Why might the Lord call them to perform such an assignment?"

Elder B. H. Roberts, of the First Quorum of Seventy, has said:

> A word, by the way, in relation to the appropriateness of the Three Witnesses choosing the Twelve. In the revelation defining the special calling of the Twelve Apostles it is written: 'The Twelve traveling counselors are called to be the Twelve Apostles, or special witnesses of the name of Christ in all the world; thus differing from other officers in the Church in the duties of their calling. (Doctrine and Covenants, sec. cvii:23) From this it appears that the special calling of the Twelve is to be Witnesses for the Lord Jesus Christ in all the world; hence it was preeminently proper that these Twelve Witnesses should be chosen by the Three very special Witnesses— witnesses of the Book of Mormon in particular, and of God's marvelous work in general. (HC, Vol. 2, p. 187)

To add a further thought on the appropriateness mentioned above, it should be remembered that the Book of Mormon has come forth in this dispensation as a witness of the divine mission of the Savior. In effect, then, there were three witnesses of Christ responsible to select twelve special witnesses of Christ for service in the Lord's Quorum of Twelve Apostles.

In His instructions to the Three Witnesses, the Lord indicated that they would be able to recognize the men to be called into the Quorum. He said:

> Remember the worth of souls is great in the sight of God;
> ...the Twelve are they who shall desire to take upon them my name with full purpose of heart.

And by their desires and their works you shall know them. (D&C 18:10, 27, 38)

From the above quotations, we learn that an apostle of the Lord needs to have the same perspective towards Father's children as does the Savior— the worth of a soul is great. Equipped with such vision, the apostles must also possess the internal desires to labor with the Savior for the salvation of their brothers and sisters.

Heber C. Kimball was one of the original Quorum of Twelve in this dispensation, selected and called based upon the above criteria. An incident from his life serves as an excellent illustration of the appropriateness of his call. We call attention to the depth of his commitment and his desire to be of service to his brethren.

Brother Joseph received a revelation concerning the redemption of Zion, part of which remains to be fulfilled. He sent messengers to the east and to the west and to the north and to the south, to gather up the Elders, and he gathered together as many of the brethren as he conveniently could, with what means they could spare, to go up to Zion, to render all the assistance that we could to our afflicted brethren. We gathered clothing and other necessaries to carry up to our brethren and sisters who had been plundered; and putting our horses to the wagons, and taking our firelocks and ammunition, we started on our journey; leaving only Oliver Cowdery, Sidney Rigdon and a few aged workmen who were engaged on the temple; so that there were very few men left in Kirtland. Our wagons were about full with baggage, etc., consequently we had to travel on foot.

We started on the 5th of May (1834), and truly this was a solemn morning to me. I took leave of my wife and children and friends, not knowing whether I would see them again in the flesh, as myself and brethren were threatened both in that country and in Missouri by enemies, that they would destroy us and exterminate us from the land. (LHCK, pp. 39-40)

Universal Apostolic Calling

We have learned from a previous revelation that the Lord has extended an invitation to labor for the salvation of souls of all men. (See D&C section 4)

In preparation for this service the Lord has emphasized the covenant relationship that men must have with Him:

Take upon you the name of Christ, and speak the truth in soberness.

And as many as repent and are baptized in my name, which is Jesus Christ, and endure to the end, the same shall be saved.

Behold, Jesus Christ is the name which is given of the Father, and there is none other name given whereby man can be saved.

Wherefore, all men must take upon them the name which is given of the Father, for in that name shall they be called at the last day;

Wherefore, if they know not the name by which they are called, they cannot have place in the kingdom of my Father.

And now, behold, there are others who are called to declare my gospel, both unto Gentile and unto Jew;

Yea, even twelve; and the Twelve shall be my disciples, and they shall take upon them my name; and the Twelve are they who shall desire to take upon them my name with full purpose of heart. (D&C 18:21-27)

Once we have a covenant relationship with Jesus Christ by taking upon us His name, we also have a responsibility. And what is that responsibility? To see as the Savior has declared—the value of each soul. Once we obtain the vision, then we must be engaged in laboring for the salvation of every soul. Only then have we learned the meaning of the phrase, "...take upon them my name with full purpose of heart." (D&C 18:27, underlining added) This is a universal apostolic calling.

For those who have followed this pattern the Lord has given this promise:

And if it so be that you should labor all your days in crying repentance unto this people, and bring, save it be one soul unto me, how great shall be your joy with him in the kingdom of my Father!

And now, if your joy will be great with one soul that you have brought unto me into the kingdom of my Father, how great will be your joy if you should bring many souls unto me! (D&C 18:15-16)

Rudger Clawson, an apostle of the Lord in this dispensation, has given a beautiful insight to the principles discussed above:

And how are we to determine the value of souls? This matter has been determined for us also by revelation. The souls of men are so precious in the sight of God that He gave to the world His Only Begotten Son, that by the shedding of His blood He might draw all men unto Him. That is why the great Prophet of this dispensation, Joseph Smith, and these others, John Whitmer, Oliver Cowdery, David Whitmer, and the rest, were called to bring souls unto Christ. And if one of these men should labor all his days, and bring save it be but one soul unto Christ, and that one should be his wife, what great joy he would have with his wife in heaven. Then if he should labor all his days and bring unto Christ the souls of his wife and his children, and none else perchance, how great would be his joy in heaven with his wife and children. (CR, April 1901, pp. 7-8)

Knowing the Name of Jesus Christ

In this revelation the Savior speaks of the need to know His name. How does one know His name? Are we to simply know the words by which He is identified? Is it accomplished through the mechanics of an ordinance?

We must be aware that the Lord expects us to labor all the days of our lives in crying repentance. The objective is to make it possible for all people to know Him by receiving His name in a covenant relationship. It is through this labor that we come to know the name of Jesus Christ.

The Church of Jesus Christ of Latter-day Saints is the instrument by which the labor for souls is most effectively performed. By participating in all of the programs and organizations as revealed by the Savior to His Church, we come to experience the Christ-like joy of service in behalf of a soul. To illustrate, might we consider the following:

A father conducts a family home evening. For what purpose? For the salvation of his family; to discharge his responbility for their souls; to come to know the name of Jesus Christ. Whether one labors as a scoutmaster with his boys, or works on the welfare farm, or pays an honest tithing, or leads the primary children in song, or performs full or part-time missionary service, or participates in any other program of the Savior, the purpose of it all is to:

1. Save souls.
2. Fulfill our apostolic calling in behalf of others.
3. More fully know the name of the Savior.

Summary and Conclusion

As we participate with the Savior in these various labor opportunities it would be well that we plan and serve with the following admonitions in mind:

Remember the worth of souls is great in the sight of God; (D&C 18:10)

...Take upon them [you] my name with full purpose of heart. (D&C 18:27)

...how great will be your joy if you shall bring many souls unto me! (D&C 18:16)

Chapter 11

Doctrine and Covenants Section 19

Suggested Title

Eternal and Endless Punishment—Atonement of Jesus Christ

Overview of Section Content

1. The Savior has all power (vs. 1-3)
2. All men must choose to repent or suffer (vs. 4-5, 15-17, 20)
3. Eternal punishment is God's punishment (vs. 5-12)
4. The Savior's atonement for sin (vs. 15-20)
5. The Savior's commandments and counsel to Martin Harris
   a. Commanded to repent (vs. 13, 15, 20)
   b. Further commandments and counsel (vs. 21-41)

Historical Setting

B.H. Roberts

...No words of the Prophet introduce this revelation in his History. Nothing is known of the circumstances which called it forth. And yet there are few revelations that have been given in the present dispensation of the Gospel more important than this one. The doctrine of the atonement of the Lord Jesus, as directly applying to the individual, and God's exposition of 'Eternal

Punishment,' as here set forth, give it a place of first importance in the doctrinal development of the Church. (HC, Vol. 1, p. 72 Footnote)

Joseph Fielding Smith

...This revelation was given some time in March 1830. It would seem that Martin Harris had come to Joseph Smith seeking further assurance in relation to his standing before the Lord, being sorely troubled in his spirit because of his transgression. He had already been granted the privilege on his earnest solicitation of being one of the Three Witnesses, and that wonderful vision had been given. Perhaps out of this came much serious reflection and he sought further light. However, there is no indication in the History of the Church as to the reason why the revelation was given and the exact day is unknown when it was given. It was without question a revelation of great comfort to Martin, and it is one of the great revelations given in this dispensation; there are few of greater import than this. The doctrine of the atonement of the Lord, as directly applying to the individual, and His exposition of "Eternal Punishment," as here set forth, give to the members of the Church light which was not previously known. (CHMR, Vol. 1, pp. 80-81)

Joseph Knight, Sr.

He [Martin Harris] came to us [Joseph Smith, Jr. and Joseph Knight, Sr] and ...says, "The Books [Book of Mormon] will not sell for no Body wants them. Joseph says, "I think they will sell well." Says he, "I want a Commandment." "Why," says Joseph, "fulfill what you have got." "But," says he, "I must have a Commandment." Joseph put him off. But he insisted three or four times he must have a Commandment...

In the morning [the next day] he got up and said he must have a Commandment to Joseph and went home. And along in the after part of the Day Joseph and Oliver Received a Commandment which is in the Book of Covenants...[Section 19].
("Joseph Knight's Recollection of Early Mormon History," *BYU Studies*, Autumn 1976, p. 37)

Sacred Truths

Introduction

This revelation was directed to Martin Harris in which he was given much personal counsel from the Lord. There were a number of areas in which the Lord gave him counsel and also revealed great and glorious truths pertaining to the atonement of Jesus Christ and the benefits thereof for all mankind.

This chapter will include a discussion of two major concepts associated with the atonement:

1. Sin and its consequences
2. Mankind's opportunites to be cleansed from sin

Sin and Its Consequences

Why do men sin? What motivates people to do wrong? Sin carries its own attraction. It is desirable to many. Commenting on this, Elder Spencer W. Kimball has said:

> Whoever said that sin was not fun? Whoever claimed Lucifer was not handsome, persuasive, easy, friendly? Whoever said that sin was unattractive, undesirable, or nauseating in its acceptance?
>
> Transgression wears elegant gowns and sparkling apparel. It is highly perfumed, has attractive features, a soft voice. It is found in educated circles and sophisticated groups. It provides sweet and comfortable luxuries. Sin is easy and has a big company of bed fellows. It promises immunity from restrictions, temporary freedoms. It can momentarily satisfy hunger, thirst, desire, urges, passions, wants, without immediately paying the price. But, it begins tiny and grows to monumental proportions. It grows drop by drop, inch by inch. (CR, April 1967, p. 66)

Though sin may be called fun and desirable, there is a need to understand its consequences. There is a vast difference between so-called fun and true happiness. Alma emphasized the difference when he said, " . . .Behold, I say unto you, wickedness never was happiness." (B. of M., Alma 41:10)

What actually happens to a person when he sins? His spirit is wounded. His sensitivity to the Lord's spirit is lessened. His ability and desire to do right is weakened. In contrast to this condition, Peter described the sinless Savior as " . . .a lamb without blemish and without spot . . ." (Bible, 1 Pet. 1:19) Thus, an unrepentant or uncleansed sinner remains spiritually wounded and blemished and is in need of the healing of his soul.

Mankind's Opportunities to Be Cleansed From Sin

All mankind are afflicted with the consequences of sin and come short of the glory of God. (See Bible, Romans 3:23) In order to be free from sin's

2 Courses of action to be cleansed from sin

afflications, man faces two courses of action. The Savior said: "And surely every man must repent or suffer . . ." (D&C 19:4)

1. *Repentance*

As one knows the depth of misery and pain that will be experienced by those who choose to "suffer," Jesus commanded and pleaded for mankind to choose "repentance." This command is repeated often in this revelation.

Those who are wise enough to follow the admonition of the Savior and be obedient to His command will avoid the degree of suffering for sins experienced by Jesus.

> For behold, I, God, have suffered these things for all, that they might not suffer if they would repent; But if they would not repent they must suffer even as I; Which suffering caused myself, even God, the greatest of all, to tremble because of pain, and to bleed at every pore, and to suffer both body and spirit—and would that I might not drink the bitter cup, and shrink—Nevertheless, glory be to the Father, and I partook and finished my preparations unto the children of men. Wherefore, I command you again to repent, lest I humble you with my almighty power; and that you confess your sins, lest you suffer these punishments of which I have spoken, of which in the smallest, yea, even in the least degree you have tasted at the time I withdrew my Spirit. (D&C 19:16-20)

In speaking of that withdrawal of spirit, Brigham Young said:

> . . .the Father withdrew His spirit from His Son, at the time he was to be crucified.
> . . .at the hour when the crisis came for him to offer up his life, the Father withdrew Himself, withdrew His Spirit, and cast a vail over him. That is what made him sweat blood. If he had had the power of God upon him, he would not have sweat blood; but all was withdrawn from him, and a veil was cast over him . . .(JD, Vol. 3, p. 206)

Elder Joseph Fielding Smith also explained:

> Now, when he [Jesus Christ] said that if we do not repent we will have to suffer even as he did, he had no reference to being nailed to a cross, but it was the torment of mind, of spirit, that he had reference to, before he ever got to the cross, and if men will not repent, they will have to suffer even as he suffered. (CR, October 1947, p. 148)

To the sinner who follows the Savior's counsel and truly repents there will certainly come a remission of sins. Such a remission is accompanied by a healing of the spiritual wounds and a peace of conscience conveyed by the Holy Spirit. Elder Marion G. Romney has commented on such a joyful condition and the healing process that makes it possible.

> . . .the remittance of sins which attends divine forgiveness heals the spirit.
> . . .by the power of the Holy Spirit his soul is healed. When this occurs, he will recognize it by the way he feels, for he will feel as the people of Benjamin felt when they received remission of sins. The record says, " . . .the spirit of the Lord came upon them, and they were filled with joy, having received a remission of their sins, and having peace of conscience . . ." (B. of M. Mosiah 4:3) (CR, October 1963, p. 25)

2. *Suffering*

The second course of action one may choose to be cleansed from sin is to pay the penalty himself. If one chooses this course he certainly ought to be aware of the position he will be in after departing from mortal life. The Lord describes this state as Eternal Punishment. It is not to be understood that such eternal punishment is to last forever for each unrepentant sinner. (see D&C 19:6-12) Only sons of perdition will share such a fate. But it does mean that the individual sufferer will be required to suffer sufficiently long in order to obtain a healing of his spirit wounds. Only then is he cleansed and able to be admitted to a degree of glory.

The place where such individuals suffer for their own sins is referred to scripturally, as Hell. There is in reality, such a place. But those who enter will also exit. Elder James E. Talmage taught:

> Hell is no place to which a vindictive judge sends prisoners to suffer and to be punished principally for his glory; but it is a place prepared for the teaching, the disciplining of those who failed to learn here upon the earth what they would have learned. True, we read of everlasting punishment, unending suffering, eternal damnation. That is a direful expression; but in his mercy the Lord has made plain what those words mean. "Eternal punishment" he says, is God's punishment, for he is eternal; and that condition or state or possibility will ever exist for the sinner who deserves and really needs such condemnation; but this does not mean that the individual sufferer or sinner is to be eternally and everlastingly made to endure and suffer. No man will be kept in hell longer than is necessary to bring him to a fitness for something better. When he

reaches that stage, the prison doors will open and there will be rejoicing among the hosts who welcome him into a better state. The Lord has not abated in the least what he has said in earlier dispensations conerning the operation of this law and his gospel, but he has made clear unto us his goodness and mercy through it all, for it is his glory and his work to bring about the immortality and eternal life of man. (CR, April 1930, p. 97)

President Brigham Young also taught this principle:

How long the damned remain in hell, I know not nor what degree of suffering they endure. If we could by any means compute how much wickedness they are guilty of, it might be possible to ascertain the amount of suffering they will receive. They will receive according as their deeds have been while in the body. God's punishment is eternal, but that does not prove that a wicked person will remain eternally in a state of punishment. (JD, Vol. 9, pp. 147-148)

President John Taylor discussed eternal punishment and explained the nature of hell:

...the wicked shall be turned into hell, with all the nations that forget God. Do you believe that? "Certainly I do." I remember a minister once asking me a question upon this subject. Says he, "Do you believe in eternal punishment?" "O yes, I believe the wicked will be turned into hell, with all the nations that forget God." "Do you believe they will stay there?" "O no." "Why do you not?" "Because it is not according to Scripture." "But if they all be turned into hell, who forget God, and will go away into everlasting punishment, will they not stay there forever?" "Yes," I said, "they will go into everlasting punishment, but they will come out again." "How is that?" "Why the Scriptures declare that death and hell will deliver up their dead, and the sea deliver up the dead that is in it; and all nations will stand before God, to be judged according to the deeds done in the body." So you see they have got to come out to be judged according to their works, whether they be good or evil. Suppose we have a State prison, for instance, in this place, a transgressor of the laws of the land is put in for a certain time, according to the deeds which he has done, and the evidence and circumstances of the case. After he has suffered according to law, he is set at liberty, but, mark you, the prison still remains, which may be compared to eternal punishment, or God's punishment. Who will go there? The wicked, for the punishment of their sins, and to teach them a useful lesson . . . (JD, Vol. 1, pp.158-159)

Summary and Conclusion

The doctrines taught and emphasized by the Savior in Section 19 are vitally important. An understanding and application of these truths is critically serious to the eternal welfare and destiny of all of Father's children. Every person must decide for himself whether to receive the healing benefits of the atonement of the Savior through sincere repentance, or suffer for his own sins until all wounds of his spirit are healed. The atoning act of Jesus Christ is the most important event of the earth's history. To focus once again on the importance of making the proper choice, we should listen to the words of two special witnesses, even apostles, of the Lord Jesus Christ.

Elder Bruce R. McConkie has written:

Nothing in the entire plan of salvation compares in any way in importance with that most transcendent of all events, the atoning sacrifice of our Lord. It is the most important single thing that has ever occurred in the entire history of created things; it is the rock foundation upon which the gospel and all other things rest. (MD, pp.57-58)

In his closing address of the general conference of the Church, President Spencer W. Kimball counseled:

You have heard the Brethren speak with great strength of the principles of the gospel. You heard Brother Benson in his inspired sermon tell us that the immutable laws of God remain steadfast in the heavens above; when men and nations refuse to abide by them, the penalty must follow. They will be wasted away. Sin demands punishment . . .

. . .this is the gospel of Jesus Christ and to all who are listening in, we haven't been fooling. What we have said to you in these three days is truth, downright truth, and it has a definite bearing upon the salvation and exaltation of every soul that could listen and hear.

This is the gospel of Christ. He is our Lord. This is a Christian church. We follow him. We love him. We praise him. We glorify him. And now we must go forward and follow him in every detail. The gospel has been restored. It is here for us in all its fulness. Never before has it been so full and so complete, so comprehensive, never before that we know of in the world. And here it is, available to us and available to millions of people, some of whom are

listening. We hope they will not make the mistake of casting it aside
or ignoring it . . . (CR, October 1974, pp. 165-166)

Chapter 12

Doctrine and Covenants Section 20

Suggested Title

Church Organization and Government

Overview of Section Content

1. Introduction (vs. 1-7)
2. Book of Mormon testifies of God's work in the latter days (vs. 8-16)
3. Highlights of significant doctrinal principles from the Book of Mormon (vs. 17-36)
4. Qualifications for making baptismal covenant (vs. 37)
5. Duties of elders, priests, teachers and, deacons (vs. 38-59)
6. Law of common consent (vs. 60-67)
7. Duties of members, mode of baptism, sacramental prayers and records of membership (vs. 68-84)

Historical Setting

Joseph Smith, Jun.

In this manner [referring to the contents of section 18] did the Lord continue to give us instructions from time to time, concerning the duties which now devolved upon us; among many other things of the kind, we obtained of Him the following, by the spirit of prophecy and revelation; which not only gave us much information, but also pointed out to us the precise day upon which, according to His will and commandment, we should proceed to organize His Church once more here upon the earth. (HC, Vol. 1, p. 64.)

Joseph Fielding Smith

...The Prophet states that after he and Oliver Cowdery received the Priesthood they continued to receive instructions from the Lord and they waited for the fulfillment of the promise made by John for the organization of the Church. In the meantime they had received several revelations. This revelation (Sec. 20), instructing the Prophet and his brethren to organize the Church was given either on or a very short time before the sixth day of April, 1830. (CHMR, Vol. 1, p. 85.)

Sacred Truths

Introduction

As Joseph Smith informed us in the historical setting for this revelation, the time was at hand for the Lord to organize His church once more upon the earth. This revelation provided Joseph with basic fundamentals of doctrines and organizational principles essential for him to be able to organize and administer the affairs of the Lord's kingdom. We should keep in mind that the Lord brought about the restoration line upon line, precept upon precept, and did not at any one time reveal all things pertaining to His church. However, this revelation provided a basic foundation upon which the Lord would build and restore His latter-day kingdom. In many respects this section could be called a constitutional document.

In this chapter we will divide the content of Section 20 into two major categories:

1. Constitutional doctrines
2. Constitutional duties

Consitutional Doctrines

In preparation for the establishing and organizing of His church, the Lord provided an opportunity for His prophet to be prepared for his duties. From the time of the First Vision in 1820, Joseph Smith was schooled and trained by the Savior. One of the primary means used to help him develop the spiritual areas of his life was the translation of the Book of Mormon. That experience gave him opportunity to grow in his understanding and in his spiritual relationship with Jesus Christ. In this revelation (Section 20), the Lord reviews that developmental process:

And gave him power from on high, by the means which were before prepared, to translate the Book of Mormon;
Which contains a record of a fallen people, and the fulness of the gospel of Jesus Christ to the Gentiles and to the Jews also; (D&C 20:8-9)

The Lord gave Joseph an assignment to translate the Book of Mormon. This could not have been accomplished except that he searched the plates for their meaning in order to accurately convey the same in the translation. The Lord emphasized the importance of this phase of his preparation when he told Joseph:

And you have a gift to translate the plates; and this is the first gift that I bestowed upon you; and I have commanded that you should pretend to no other gift until my purpose is fulfilled in this; for I will grant unto you no other gift until it is finished. (D&C 5:4)

In other words, the searching and understanding of scriptures became the key to Joseph's preparation and spiritual growth. The Lord called attention to the fruits of that scriptural search. We read: "By these things [Book of Mormon teachings] we know..." (D&C 20:17) What had the prophet come to know during this preparatory period that would enable him to be an instrument in the hands of the Lord in organizing and directing the Church of Jesus Christ? Several things are mentioned:

1. There is a God in heaven (vs. 17-19)
2. Jesus Christ atoned for fallen man (vs. 20-25)
3. The Holy Ghost testifies of the Father and the Son (vs. 26-28)
4. All mankind must repent (vs. 5-6, 29)
5. Principles of justification and sanctification (vs. 30-31)
6. Man must endure to the end in faith (vs. 25, 29, 32-34)
7. God is unchangeable, the holy scriptures are true and men will be judged thereby (vs. 11-15, 35)

The importance and value of these revealed truths was emphasized by Elder Bruce R. McConkie:

The greatest truth known to man is that there is a God in heaven who is infinite and eternal; that he is the creator, upholder, and preserver of all things; that he created us and the sidereal heavens and ordained and established a plan of salvation whereby we might advance and progress and become like him. The truth pertaining to him is that he is our Father in heaven, that he has a body of flesh and bones as tangible as man's, that he is a literal person, and that if we believe and obey his laws we can gain the exaltation that he possesses . . .

The second greatest truth in all eternity pertains to the divine sonship of the Lord, Jesus Christ. It includes the eternal verity that he was foreordained in the councils of eternity to come to earth and be the Redeemer of men, to come and ransom men from the temporal and spiritual death brought upon them by the fall of Adam. This second greatest truth is that Christ worked out the infinite and eternal atoning sacrifice because of which all men are raised in immortality and those who believe and obey are raised also unto eternal life.

The third greatest truth known to mankind is that the Holy Spirit of God is a revelator and a sanctifier, that he is a personage of spirit, that his assigned ministry and work in the eternal Godhead is to bear record of the Father and of the Son, to reveal them and their truths to men. His work is to cleanse and perfect human souls, to burn dross and evil out of human souls as though by fire. We call that the baptism of fire. (BYU Speeches of the Year, 1980, p. 79)

Also commenting on this subject, Elder Marion G. Romney not only stressed the importance of knowing the true and living God, but explained how such knowledge would have meaningful and eternal application in our lives:

The church's doctrine of the living and true God is based upon the experiences and teaching of its prophet founder, Joseph Smith, Jun. Speaking on this most important subject he once said: [Quotes D&C 20:17-19]

This scripture was given in 1830. It is, therefore, modern scripture. However, the teachings in it are not new. That there is a God in heaven who created the heaven and the earth is taught in the first verse of the first chapter of the first book in the Bible. That he created man, male and female, in his own image is taught in the same chapter. That men should love and serve him and that he should be the only being whom they should worship is the substance of the first of the Ten Commandments. "Thou shalt have no other gods before me." (Exod. 20:3)

What is new and distinctive in this modern scripture is the knowledge claimed by Joseph Smith for himself and for them for whom he spoke. " . . .we know," said he, "that there is a God in heaven..." (D&C 20:17. Underlining added) In making this declaration the Prophet spoke from personal experience.

The Prophet Joseph considered a knowledge of God to be of such importance that, in setting forth the beliefs of the Church, he placed it at the head of the list—"We believe in God, the Eternal Father, ..." (Articles of Faith)

One with such knowledge is in the way of eternal life, for, according to the teachings of Jesus, "...this is life eternal, that they might know thee the only true God, and Jesus Christ, whom thou hast sent." (John 17:3) Having such knowledge, one is assured that God, although infinite and eternal, the framer of heavens and the earth and all things that in them are, being the possessor of all power, all wisdom, and all understanding, being more intelligent than all other beings, is, nevertheless, an individual—an understanding, kind, and loving parent ready to hear and minister to the needs of his children—that he is not merely some unthinkable, unknowable, indefinable, far-off, distant force. When one with such a knowledge prays, he knows that he is praying to some one and not just to some thing. (CR, October 1964, pp. 49-51)

Constitutional Duties

As before noted, the restoration did not come all at once, but rather came line upon line. The latter portion of this revelation describes some of the basic duties and practices of the church membership. Such description includes information concerning our covenant relationship with the Lord, duties of various priesthood officers, common consent, and some duties of members of the Church after their baptism.

Volumes could be written and endless sermons could be delivered upon the limitless meanings that could be extracted from these verses. The Lord expects the members of His church to make a careful analysis of these expectations and conform their lives to these fundamental priniples. For instance, a regular review of verse 37 could serve as a constant reminder of our responsibilities as pertaining to our covenants with the Savior.

A home teacher would be wise to analyze the meaning of verse 53. He would discover that he is to "strengthen" the membership. Pondering such a duty, he would realize that he can only strengthen people when he knows their needs. In order to know those needs he must "be with" them. Regular association with assigned families and attention to their needs would enable him to fulfill his divine calling.

In reflecting upon verse 75, all covenant members of the Church will realize the Lord expects them to meet often with the Church and thereby receive the privilege of renewing their covenants with the Lord. It cannot be done outside the Lord's authorized church meetings. What a blessing it is to be able to re-read the sacramental prayers and not depend only upon hearing them read at the time of administering the sacrament.

Summary and Conclusion

Thus we can see that this revelation fulfills the function of a constitutional document. Though it is not exhaustive in content, it serves as a basic foundation upon which members of the Savior's church can begin to build. Herein we are taught the fundamental doctrines and essential duties that will open additional doors to subsequent learning and practices culminating in a Christ-like character for every Latter-day Saint.

Chapter 13

Doctrine and Covenants Section 21

Suggested Title

When My Prophet Speaks

Overview of Section Content

1. Relationship of the Prophet to the Lord (vs. 1-5, 7-8)
2. Relationship of church membership to the Lord's prophet (vs. 4-5)
3. Promises to obedient church membership (vs. 6, 9)
4. The first and second elders of the church (vs. 1, 10-12)

Historical Setting

Joseph Smith, Jun.

Whilst the Book of Mormon was in the hands of the printer, we still continued to bear testimony and give information, as far as we had opportunity; and also made known to our brethren that we had received a commandment to organize the Church; and accordingly we met together for that purpose, at the house of Mr. Peter Whitmer, Sen., (being six in number,) on Tuesday, the sixth day of April, A.D., one thousand eight hundred and thirty. Having opened the meeting by solemn prayer to our Heavenly Father, we proceeded, according to previous commandment, to call on our brethren to know whether they accepted us as their teachers in the things of the Kingdom of God, and whether they were satisfied that we should proceed and be organized as a Church according to said commandment which we had received. To these several propositions they consented by a unanimous vote. I then laid my hands upon Oliver Cowdery, and ordained him an Elder of the "Church of Jesus Christ of Latter-day Saints;" after which, he ordained me also to the office of an Elder of said Church. We then took bread, blessed it, and brake it with them; also wine, blessed it, and drank it with them. We then laid our hands on each individual member of the Church present, that they might receive the gift of the Holy Ghost, and be confirmed members of the Church of Christ. The Holy Ghost was poured out upon us to a very great degree—some prophesied, whilst we all praised the Lord, and rejoiced exceedingly. Whilst yet together, I received the following commandment: (HC, Vol. 1, pp 74-78)

B.H. Roberts

Names of the six members of the Church as they were organized April 6, 1830—
1 Oliver Cowdery
2 Joseph Smith, Jun.,
3 Hyrum Smith, Peter Whitmer, Jun.,
5 Samuel H. Smith,
6 David Whitmer.
(HC, Vol. 1, p. 76 Footnote)

Sacred Truths

Introduction

The very day the Lord established His church in this dispensation, He revealed how He would direct His church. The eternal destiny of each member of the Church depends upon his understanding and application of the principles and laws revealed in this section. The discussion of this section will focus on the first three areas as noted above in the overview.

Relationship of the Prophet to the Lord

The Savior defined the relationship that exists between Him and His prophet. Speaking to Joseph Smith, the Lord said: " . . .thou shalt be called a seer, a translator, a prophet, an apostle of Jesus Christ . . ." (D&C 21:1, underlining added) Joseph's appointment and calling was not of men nor of any organization of men. It was of Jesus Christ. This concept is reinforced in the same verse when the Savior declared that Joseph's calling was the will of the Father as well as the Son. Further, the Lord directed that the prophet's callings should be recorded in the history of the Church. Therefore, every member of the church, from that day forward, should be aware of the relationship existing between the Prophet and the Savior. No one should misunderstand the sacred and responsible calling of the prophet when the Lord declared: "For his word [the prophet] ye shall receive, as if from mine own mouth. "(D&C 21:5) Again, adding further emphasis, the Savior declared: "For thus saith the Lord God: Him [the prophet] have I inspired to move the cause of Zion in mighty power for good . . ."(D&C 21:7)

Joseph Smith was and always will be the first elder of the Church of Jesus Christ. (See D&C 21:1, 11)

Relationship of Church Membership to the Lord's Prophet

The Lord has made it equally clear that a relationship exists between the members of the Lord's church and the Lord's prophet. Explaining that all members are included in that relationship, President Harold B. Lee said:

> So on the day the church was organized, the Lord said this: "Wherefore, meaning the church" [D&C 21:4] and that was addressed not just to the few on that day, but to all who have been or who will be members of this church . . .(*Ensign*, November 1971, p. 11)

The Lord declared His expectations of the membership and their responsibility to follow His prophet, when He delivered the following commandment:

> . . .thou shalt give heed unto all his words [the prophet] and commandments which he shall give unto you as he receiveth them, walking in all holiness before me. (D&C 21:4, underlining added)

When the Lord said "all his words," we are left to conclude there are no exceptions. Any student of the history of the Lord's dealings with His children is aware that the Lord's prophet has spoken on all subjects pertinent to the temporal and spiritual welfare of man.

Further, it should be understood that the prophet does not have to preface his remarks by saying, "thus saith the Lord" in order that the membership should be obligated to give heed to his words. President J. Reuben Clark declared:

> There are those who insist that unless the prophet of the Lord declares, "thus saith the Lord," the message may not be taken as a revelation. This is a false testing standard. For while many of our

modern revelations as contained in the Doctrine and Covenants do contain these words, there are many that do not. (Address to seminary and Institute Personnel, BYU, July 7, 1954)

Members of the Church have no difficulty following and giving heed to the words of the prophet as long as he says that which agrees with their views. The problems arise when the prophet issues statements that conflict with the opinion of some members. They seemingly forget their differences do not lie with the prophet, but rather with the Lord himself. The Savior directed:

> For his word [the prophet] ye shall receive, as if from mine own mouth, in all patience and faith. (D&C 21:5)

When the Lord uses the word "patience," a time period is involved. Though we may not now see the full implications of the prophet's message, time will exonerate his word. In the meantime, while seeking for complete understanding, we are counseled to have "faith" sufficient to act on the Lord's words given through His prophet.

Said President Marion G. Romney:

> It is an easy thing to believe in the dead prophets, but it is a greater thing to believe in the living prophets. I will give you an illustration.
>
> One day when President Grant was living, I sat in my office across the street following a general conference. A man came over to see me, an elderly man. He was very upset about what had been said in this conference by some of the Brethren, including myself. I could tell from his speech that he came from a foreign land. After I had quieted him enough so he would listen, I said, "Why did you come to America?" "I am here because a prophet of God told me to come." "Who was the prophet;" I continued. "Wilford Woodruff." "Do you believe Wilford Woodruff was a prophet of God?" "Yes, I do." "Do you believe that President Joseph F. Smith was a prophet of God?" "Yes, sir."
>
> Then came the sixty-four dollar question. "Do you believe that Heber J. Grant is a prophet of God?" His answer, "I think he ought to keep his mouth shut about old age assistance."
>
> Now I tell you that a man in his position is on the way to apostasy. He is forfeiting his chances for eternal life. So is everyone who cannot follow the living Prophet of God. (CR, April 1953, p. 125)

As we reflect on what the Lord has said, there is a basic underlying principle upon which all of these admonitions are founded. That principle is faith in the Lord Jesus Christ. Would He lead us astray? Could we have faith in Him if He permitted His prophet to lead us astray? He said, "For his word ye shall receive, as if from mine own mouth . . ." (D&C 21:5)

How clearly the Lord's prophets have taught this principle:

> I testify in the name of Israel's God that He will not suffer the head of the Church, him whom He has chosen to stand at the head, to transgress His laws and apostatize; the moment he should take a course that would lead to it, God would take him away . . . (Joseph F. Smith, J.D., Vol. 24, p. 192)

> I say to Israel, the Lord will never permit me or any other man who stands as president of this Church to lead you astray. It is not in the program. It is not in the mind of God. If I were to attempt that the Lord would remove me out of my place, and so he will any other man who attempts to lead the children of men astray from the oracles of God and from their duty. God bless you. Amen. (Wilford Woodruff, DWW, pp. 212-213)

> I remember years ago when I was a bishop I had President Grant talk to our ward. After the meeting, I drove him home. At that time there was a great deal of criticism against the President of the Church because of a front-page editorial some of you may remember. We talked about it. When we got to his home I got out of the car and went up on the porch with him. Standing by me, he put his arm over my shoulder and said: "My boy, you always keep your eye on the President of the Church, and if he ever tells you to do anything, and it is wrong, and you do it, the Lord will bless you for it." Then with a twinkle in his eye, he said, "But you don't need to worry. The Lord will never let his mouthpiece lead the people astray." (Marion G. Romney, CR, October 1960, p. 78)

Promises to Obedient Church Membership

There is always a blessing for those who are obedient to God's laws and commandments. In this revelation the Lord promises the following to those who "do these things" (give heed to His prophet): (See D&C 21:6, 9)

1. The gates of hell shall not prevail against you.
2. The Lord God will disperse the powers of darkness from before you.

3. The Lord God will cause the heavens to shake for your good, and his name's glory.
4. The Lord will give a special witness that the prophet's words are given to him by Jesus Christ.

Speaking of these promises, President Harold B. Lee has said:

To you Latter-day Saints everywhere, that promise will be yours if you will follow the leadership the Lord has placed within the church . . .(*Ensign*, November 1971, p. 12)

Summary and Conclusion

In conclusion, President Harold B. Lee has emphasized the importance and summarized the vital messages of this revelation. He said:

Now the only safety we have as members of this church is to do exactly what the Lord said to the Church in that day when the Church was organized. We must learn to give heed to the words and commandments that the Lord shall give through his prophet, "as he receiveth them, walking in all holiness before me; . . .as if from mine own mouth, in all patience and faith." (D&C 21:4-5) There will be some things that take patience and faith. You may not like what comes from the authority of the Church. It may contradict your political views. It may interfere with some of your social life. But if you listen to these things, as if from the mouth of the Lord himself, with patience and faith, the promise is that "the gates of hell shall not prevail against you; yea, and the Lord God will disperse the powers of darkness from before you, and cause the heavens to shake for your good, and his name's glory." (D&C 21:6) . . .Your safety and ours depends upon whether or not we follow the ones whom the Lord has placed to preside over his church. He knows whom he wants to preside over this church, and he will make no mistake. The Lord doesn't do things by accident. He has never done anything accidentally. And I think the scientists and all the philosophers in the world have never discovered or learned anything that God didn't already know. His revelations are more powerful, more meaningful, and have more substance than all the secular learning in the world.
Let's keep our eye on the President of the Church . . . (CR, October 1970, pp. 152-153)

Chapter 14

Doctrine and Covenants Section 22

Suggested Title

Dead Works

Overview of Section Content

1. Baptism—A new and everlasting covenant (vs. 1, 4)
2. Dead works (vs. 2-3)

Historical Setting

Joseph Smith, Jun.

Revelation to the Church of Christ which was established in these last days, in the year of our Lord, one thousand eight hundred and thirty. Given at Manchester, New York, April, 1830, in consequence of some desiring to unite with the Church without re-baptism, who had previously been baptized. (HC, Vol. 1, p. 79)

Joseph Fielding Smith

. . .Immediately after the Church was organized converts were made. Some of these had belonged to churches which believed in baptism by immersion. In fact, many of the early converts of the Church had previously accepted this mode believing that it was right. The question of divine aurhority, however was not firmly fixed in their minds. When they desired to come into the Church, having received the testimony that Joseph Smith had told a true story, they wondered why it was necessary for them to be baptized again when they had complied with an ordinance of baptism by immersion . . . (CHMR, Vol. 1, p. 101)

Sacred Truths

Introduction

The need for this revelation is described in the historical setting. The Savior's house is a house of order and it became necessary to teach the people in the infant days of the Church that certain principles and practices are eternal and cannot be bypassed. In this chapter we will discuss the two subject areas as noted in the overview of section content.

Baptism—A New and Everlasting Covenant

Speaking of baptism, the Lord referred to the ordinance as "a new and an everlasting covenant." (D&C 22:1) This is not to be confused with the term "the new and everlasting covenant." The Lord has revealed that the new and everlasting covenant is "the fulness of my gospel." (D&C 66:2) Explaining the relationship of these two terms. Elder Bruce R. McConkie has said:

> The gospel is the everlasting covenant because it is ordained by Him who is Everlasting and also because it is everlastingly the same. In all past ages salvation was gained by adherence to its terms and conditions, and that same compliance will bring the same reward in all future ages. Each time this everlasting covenant is revealed it is new to those of that dispensation. Hence the gospel is the new and everlasting covenant.
>
> All covenants between god and man are part of the new and everlasting covenant. (D&C 22; 132:6-7) Thus celestial marriage is "a new and everlasting covenant" (D&C 132:4) or the new and everlasting covenant of marriage. (*Doctrines of Salvation*, vol. 1, pp. 152-166) Some covenants, however, have force and validity in all dispensations; baptism is one of these. (D&C 22) (MD, p. 479)

Dead Works

The Lord referred to unauthorized baptisms as "dead works." (D&C 22:2-3) Any ordinance performed without the Lord's authority is invalid. No covenant is established. This condition is described by the Savior as follows:

For they have strayed from mine ordinances, and have broken mine everlasting covenant. (D&C 1:15, see also Bible, Isa. 24:5)

One might ask the question, why are these works called "dead"? The obvious conclusion is that there is no life. And what gives life to anything? All things are dependent upon the presence of the spirit for life. As pertaining to the ordinances of the gospel the Holy Ghost must ratify or seal every ordinance in order for it to be valid or a living covenant. (See D&C 132:7) Two conditions may prevent the sealing of the spirit:

1. Lack of authority to bind men to God in the covenant relationship.
2. Unworthiness on the part of the covenant maker.

President Anthon H. Lund has stressed the need for divine authority and the presence of the Holy Spirit in the ordinances of the true Church. Commenting on these subjects, he said:

The true Church must be established by authority of God, and there must be the life of the Holy Spirit in it. The Holy Ghost must be conferred upon the members by the ordinance ordained for its bestowal, and when the Spirit is received it will testify unto the recipients that they have obeyed the demands of the true Gospel. (CR, October 1915, p. 10)

Summary and Conclusion

For each of us there is a vital question to be asked: Are our works and covenants dead or alive? Have they been performed by proper authority and have we so lived that the Holy Ghost can continue to testify that we meet the demands of the true gospel?

Chapter 15

Doctrine and Covenants Section 23

Suggested Title

Specific Duties: Oliver Cowdery, Hyrum Smith, Samuel H. Smith,
Joseph Smith, Sr., Joseph Knight, Sr.

Overview of Section Content

1. Specific duties—Oliver Cowdery (vs. 1-2)
2. Specific duties—Hyrum Smith (vs. 3)
3. Specific duties—Samuel H. Smith (vs. 4)
4. Specific duties—Joseph Smith, Sr. (vs. 5)
5. Specific duties—Joseph Knight, Sr. (vs. 6-7)

Historical Setting

Joseph Smith, Jun.

The following persons being anxious to know of the Lord what
might be their respective duties in relation to this work, I enquired
of the Lord, and received for them the following: (HC, Vol. 1, p. 80)

Hyrum M. Smith and Janne M. Sjodahl

The brethren here mentioned being anxious to learn the mind
and the will of the Lord concerning them, this Revelation was

given. It is perfectly clear that these intimate friends and close associates of the Prophet were fully convinced that God spoke through him. If not, they would not have asked him to inquire of the Lord for them. (DCC, p. 119)

Sacred Truths

Introduction

As can be seen in the historical setting, these five men were anxious to know what their respective duties might be in relation to the work of the Lord. It should be noted that these men had sought similar instruction through the prophet on previous occasions. Since then, however, the Lord's church had been organized and now they were seeking to know how they could assist in the work of the newly-established kingdom.

All of these brethren, except Joseph Knight, Sr., had been baptized and were in a covenant relationship with the Savior. Each of the four church members were told by the Lord they were "under no condemnation" at that time. (See D&C 23:1, 3-5) This statement does not suggest that they were without responsibility to maintain that status in the future. They had done all that the Lord required of them up to that time. Speaking on this principle, President Brigham Young has said:

> If a person with an honest heart, a broken, contrite, and pure spirit, in all fervency and honesty of soul, presents himself and says that he wishes to be baptized for the remission of his sins, and the ordinance is administered by one having authority, is that man saved? Yes, to that period of time. Should the Lord see proper to take him then from the earth, the man has believed and been baptized, and is a fit subject for heaven—a candidate for the kingdom of God in the celestial world, because he has repented and done all that was required of him to that hour . . . (JD, Vol. 8, p. 124)

To each of these inquirers, the Lord responded and gave specific instruction.

Oliver Cowdery

The Lord instructed Oliver to make his calling known to the Church and the world. He was to bear testimony that he had a divine calling of Jesus Christ, even that of an apostle and second elder of the Church. (See D&C 18:9 and 20:3) He was also to preach the principles of the restored gospel of Jesus Christ " . . .henceforth and forever." (D&C 23:2)

Furthermore, he was counseled to " . . .beware of pride, lest thou shouldst enter into temptation." (D&C 23:1)

In this personal revelation, Oliver was instructed in matters that, had he been careful to observe, he could have been more fruitful in his calling in the Church and kingdom forever.

As with Oliver Cowdery, so it is that every member of the Church has an opportunity to receive a personal revelation through the inspiration given to ordained patriarchs of the Church. In his blessing, each member is counseled and instructed on matters pertaining to his weaknesses, strengths and callings. If each of us give heed, we will be more fruitful in our individual callings within the Lord's kingdom.

Hyrum Smith

When Hyrum inquired previously of the Lord as to his duties, he was instructed as follows:

> Seek not to declare my word, but first seek to obtain my word, and then shall your tongue be loosed ...(D&C 11:21, underlining added)

We learn that he was obedient to this instruction. Nearly one year later he was told:

> ...thy heart is opened, and thy tongue loosed ... (D&C 23:3, underlining added)

His calling was to exhort and teach the Church continually. His attitude and the spirit of his heart was open and acceptable to the Lord. He remained as such for in 1841 the Lord declared:

> ...blessed is my servant Hyrum Smith; for I, the Lord, loveth him because of the integrity of his heart, and because he loveth that which is right before me, saith the Lord. (D&C 124:15)

Pertaining to Hyrum's duty unto the church because of his family, Elder Joseph Fielding Smith has written:

> ...There is another thing of great significance in this brief blessing to Hyrum Smith (Sec. 23:3) which is: "Wherefore thy duty is unto the church forever, and this because of thy family. Amen." It is doubtful if the Prophet Joseph fully understood the meaning of this expression when this revelation was given. In later years it was made clear. Evidently it has reference to the office of Patriarch and in this office, it was his duty and that of his family forever. (CHMR, Vol. 1, p. 113)

Samuel H. Smith

Indeed, Samuel did fulfill his calling to exhort and " . . .strengthen the church, . . ." (D&C 23:4) He labored throughout his life to be obedient to this instruction. His faithfulness is evidenced in a blessing given to him by his father:

> *Samuel*, you have been a faithful and obedient son. By your faithfulness you have brought many into the Church. The Lord has seen your diligence, and you are blessed, in that he has never chastised you, but has called you home to rest; and there is a crown laid up for you, which shall grow brighter and brighter unto the perfect day.
>
> When the Lord called you, he said, "Samuel, I have seen thy suffering, and heard thy cries, and beheld thy faithfulness; thy skirts are clear from the blood of this generation." Because of these things I seal upon your head all the blessings which I have heretofore pronounced upon you; and this my dying blessing, I now seal upon you. Even so. Amen. (*History of Joseph Smith by His Mother, Lucy Mack Smith*, p. 310)

The following excerpt from his obituary notice appearing in the Times and Seasons brings to our attention the quality of devotion and attributes of character of this good man.

> The exit of this worthy man, so soon after the horrible butchery of his brothers, Joseph and Hyrum, in Carthage Jail, is a matter of deep solemnity to the family, as well as a remediless loss to all. If ever there lived a good man upon the earth, Samuel H. Smith was that person. His labors in the Church from first to last; carrying glad tidings to the Eastern cities, and finally his steadfastness as one of the Witnesses to the Book of Mormon, and many saintly traits of virtue, knowledge, temperance, patience, godliness, brotherly kindness and charity, shall be given of him hereafter, as a man of God. (*LDS Biographical Encyclopedia* Vol. 1, p. 282)

(Roy W. Doxey, *The Doctrine and Covenants Speaks*, Vol. 1, p. 141)

Joseph Smith, Sr.

This portion of the revelation is very similar to that which was spoken to Hyrum as discussed above. In comparing the two, an interesting perspective is provided in the following comment:

The Revelations to Joseph Smith, Sr., and Hyrum Smith contained an identical prediction to the effect that it was their calling to strengthen the church forever. This could not refer to their personal ministry on earth, but it has been fulfilled in the ministry of their descendants, and will, no doubt, come true, as the Revelations say, "forever." (DCC, p. 122)

Joseph Knight, Sr.

As before stated, Joseph Knight Sr. was the only one of the five men who had not entered into a covenant relationship with the Savior at that time.

One of the reasons for this negligence was described by the Savior:

> . . .you must take up your cross, in the which you must pray vocally before the world as well as in secret, and in your family, and among your friends, and in all places. (D&C 23:6)

The Lord would not violate Joseph Knight's agency in bearing witness to his soul of the divinity of His work until requested to do so through prayer. A testimony does not come from man but only from the Lord. Though Joseph Knight had been associated with Joseph Smith and worked closely with him, still it remained for him to seek a personal witness from the Lord.

Furthermore, there was no hesitation in the Lord's instruction as He defined Joseph Knight's duty " . . .to unite with the true church, and give your language to exhortation continually, that you may receive the reward of the laborer." (D&C 23:7) The Lord made plain to a non-member that there is a "true church." Well might we follow this pattern of the Lord and likewise bear testimony and invite others to unite with the Lord's true church. Only through our affiliation with and labor within the Lord's church can there be a reward for us, as laborers.

It is interesting to note that this instruction was given in April 1830 and in June of that same year, Joseph Knight Sr. was baptized and united with the true church of Jesus Christ. From that time forward his life was that of a faithful laborer in the kingdom. Commenting on his faithfulness, Joseph Smith later recorded:

> . . .I am now recording in the Book of the Law of the Lord,—of such as have stood by me in every hour of peril, for these fifteen long years past,—say, for instance, my aged and beloved brother, Joseph Knight, Sen., who was among the number of the first to administer to my necessities, while I was laboring in the com- mencement of the bringing forth of the work of the Lord, and of laying the foundation of the Church of Jesus Christ of Latter-day

Saints. For fifteen years he has been faithful and true, and even-handed and exemplary, and virtuous and kind, never deviating to the right hand or to the left. Behold he is a righteous man, may God Almighty lengthen out the old man's days; and may his trembling, tortured, and broken body be renewed, and in the vigor of health turn upon him, if it be Thy will, consistently, O God; and it shall be said of him, by the sons of Zion, while there is one of them remaining, that this man was a faithful man in Israel; therefore his name shall never be forgotten. (HC, Vol. 5, pp. 124-125)

Summary and Conclusion

When a person is a recipient of divine truth, he is obligated to conform his life to that truth. By so doing, that individual is approved of the Lord. When a person knowingly lives contrary to the Lord's will he is under condemnation in the sight of the Lord.

Chapter 16

Doctrine and Covenants Section 24

Suggested Title

Magnify Thine Office—Joseph Smith, Jun.

Overview of Section Content

1. Joseph Smith's calling is reaffirmed and expanded (vs. 1-9)
2. Oliver Cowdery's calling is reaffirmed and emphasized (vs. 10-12)
3. Additional counsel in the callings of Joseph Smith and Oliver Cowdery (vs. 13-19)

Historical Setting

After the Church was organized, the Prophet Joseph Smith visited groups of friends in Manchester, Fayette and Colesville, New York. While in Colesville, Joseph was engaged in teaching the gospel to a number of people who were anxious to be baptized. However, their interest in the Church created feelings of opposition among the sectarian priests who feared the loss of their followers. A number of people were stirred up in mob action and persecution became very intense. Joseph was arrested on trumped up charges of disorderly conduct and setting the country in an uproar by preaching the Book of Mormon. This resulted in a trial and eventual acquittal, though he experienced much harassment throughout the proceedings. After the trial, Joseph and Oliver Cowdery returned to the

Prophet's home in Harmony, Pennsylvania. While there, Joseph informs us that he received the three revelations, known as sections 24, 25, and 26. (For further information see HC, Vol. 1, pp. 86-104 and CHMR, Vol. 1, p. 114)

Sacred Truths

Introduction

Reflecting upon Joseph's busy schedule we note how heavily committed his time had been to the completion of the Book of Mormon translation and publication, the organizing of the Lord's church, and missionary endeavors amongst the Saints and others. He had not had sufficient time to provide for all the temporal requirements of his family. It was late in the growing season (July) and he had not yet had time to plant his acreage upon which he was so dependent for his necessities of life.

Knowing Joseph's needs and concerns, the Lord counseled him as follows:

> Magnify thine office; and after thou hast sowed thy fields and secured them, go speedily unto the church which is in Colesville, Fayette, and Manchester, and they shall support thee; and I will bless them both spiritually and temporally. (D&C 24:3)

Joseph's Calling

The Lord also told Joseph:

> ...thou shalt devote all thy service in Zion; and in this thou shalt have strength.
> And in temporal labors thou shalt not have strength, for this is not thy calling. Attend to thy calling and thou shalt have wherewith to magnify thine office ... (D&C 24:7, 9 Underlining added)

The instructions given to the prophet, as quoted in these verses, can be conveniently separated into two subject areas:

1. *Full-time service*

For the first time in this dispensation, the Lord restored and activated a principle of the gospel: The laborer is worthy of his hire. (See Bible, Luke 10:7) This principle applies to a spiritual laborer as well as to those engaged in temporal labors. When the Lord called the prophet to full-time service, He directed the church members to provide him with his temporal necessities of life, and promised the Church blessings both temporally and spiritually for so doing. If they failed to heed this instruction, they could expect a cursing instead of a blessing. (See D&C 24:3-4) This principle that was explained to the prophet was later given as a law to the Church. (See D&C 42:70-73)

When the Lord calls certain people to fulltime service in His kingdom, He provides for their physical needs while so engaged in His work. This principle is of the Lord and makes it possible for His servants to accomplish what the Lord calls them to do.

2. Magnifying One's Calling

What does it mean to "magnify" one's calling? The word magnify is commonly interpreted to mean "enlarge." In order for an enlargement to take place, one needs to gather the powers of the existing resources and focus them on a given point. This is illustrated in the process by which a magnifying lens enlarges by focusing the powers of the available light.

Joseph Smith was to concentrate and focus all his energies and talents to the calling given him by the Lord at that time. He was to pray, write, expound the scriptures, exercise patience and administer the affairs of the Church. (See D&C 24:5-9) As he utilized all of his available resources in the magnifying of his calling, the Lord would then give the increase and enlarge his abilities and the fruits of his labors.

Summary and Conclusion

As unto Joseph Smith and Oliver Cowdery, so also to us has the Lord given instructions to magnify our callings.

We, as members of the Church, have opportunity to receive many callings from time to time: home teacher, class advisor, parent, priesthood leader, etc. Many illustrations could be given as to how one might magnify his calling in these various opportunities. For instance, a home teacher trying to assist in strengthening an assigned family might not be able to accomplish the desired results through his efforts alone. However, he might reach out and tap some of the available resources in the ward and thereby gain access to the combined strength and powers that are available to him. Quorum involvement, youth peers, activity programs, class instruction, special program, etc. might all serve as component parts of a combined program that will focus on the needs of the concerned family. By reaching out and focusing all of these resources, the home teacher is doing all he can to magnify his calling concerning his assigned family. Then, as he seeks the Lord's help, he does so with the conviction he is doing what he can and is entitled to the Lord's assistance.

Chapter 17

Doctrine and Covenants Section 25

Suggested Title

An Elect Lady

Overview of Section Content

1. Emma Smith—An elect lady with specific responsibilities (vs. 1-3, 7-12)
2. The Lord's instruction and counsel to Emma Smith and other sisters (vs. 4-6, 13-15)
3. Principles of this revelation applicable to all women (vs. 16)

Historical Setting

Section 25 was one of three revelations given to Joseph Smith after he returned to his home in Harmony, Pennsylvania. (See Historical Setting in Chapter 16.)

Joseph Fielding Smith

...This revelation was given to Emma Smith, wife of Joseph Smith. She was the daughter of Isaac and Elizabeth Lewis Hale, and was born July 10, 1804. She was married to the Prophet in 1827, while he was under the tutelage of the Angel Moroni. She believed in the Prophet although her parents did not, and she was baptized by Oliver Cowdery in June, 1830. Her life from that time on was a very trying one due to constant persecution and mobbings. She passed through these trials with her husband and shared them, as did the faithful wives of other leaders of the Church. The calling given to Emma Smith in this revelation was an important one, and was fulfilled. (CHMR, Vol. 1, p. 117)

Sacred Truths

Introduction

This revelation contains information and counsel that was specifically directed to Emma Smith. It also contains instructions, though given to Emma, that are appropriately applied to all women:

And verily, verily, I say unto you, [Emma] that this is my voice unto all. Amen. (D&C 25:16)

For the purposes of this lesson, we will discuss the contents of this section as outlined in the Overview of Section Content, items 1 and 2.

Emma Smith—An Elect Lady With Specific Responsibilities

The Lord referred to Emma as " . . .an elect lady, whom I have called." (D&C 25:3) We see two meanings to this statement.

1. Emma Smith was the first president of the Female Relief Society organization in the Church. At the time she was called to that assignment, the Prophet Joseph Smith said:

I assisted in commencing the organization of "the Female Relief Society of Nauvoo" in the Lodge Room. Sister Emma Smith, President, and Sister Elizabeth Ann Whitney and Sarah M. Cleveland, Counselors. I gave much instruction, read in the New Testament, and Book of Doctrine and Covenants, concerning the Elect Lady, and showed that the elect meant to be elected to a certain work, &c., and that the revelation was then fulfilled by Sister Emma's election to the Presidency of the Society, she having previously been ordained to expound the scriptures. (HC, Vol. 4, pp. 552-553)

2. Emma heeded the Lord's call and came into His church and kingdom and would always be considered an elect lady as long as she would hear the Lord's voice and harden not her heart. (See D&C 29:7) The Lord said to her:

a. She was His daughter because she had received His gospel.

b. She was promised blessings if she remained faithful. (See D&C 25:1-2)

Every woman who makes and keeps covenants with the Lord in His kingdom is appropriately described as "an elect lady." This title is not reserved exclusively for any one person. Each covenant daughter of God is promised many blessings but they are all conditioned upon faithfulness.

The Lord also said to Emma that she would "...be ordained...to expound scriptures, and to exhort the church, ..." (D&C 25:7). In explanation of the use of the term "ordained," Elder Joseph Fielding Smith explained:

> The term "ordain" was used generally in the early days of the Church in reference to both ordination and setting apart, and too, correctly according to the meaning of the word. Men holding the Priesthood were said to have been "ordained" to preside over branches and to perform special work. Sisters also were said to have been "ordained" when they were called to some special duty or responsibility. In later years we developed a distinction between ordain and setting apart. Men are ordained to offices in the Priesthood and set apart to preside over stakes, wards, branches, missions, and auxiliary organizations. The sisters are set apart— not ordained—as presidents of auxiliary organizations, to missions, etc. This saying that Emma Smith was "ordained" to expound scripture, does not mean that she had conferred upon her the Priesthood, but that she was set apart to this calling, which found its fulfillment in the Relief Society of the Church. (CHMR, Vol. 1, p. 118)

Emma was also directed to make a selection of sacred hymns for use in the worship services of the Church (See D&C 25:11-12). The Lord used the term "sacred." Some hymns would not be sacred and thus not appropriate for His purposes.

Additional insights to this important subject have been given as the Lord has counseled us through His authorized representatives. Several of them are included herein:

> Since singing is pleasing to the Lord and a prayer unto him when it is "sacred" and a song of the heart, Latter-day Saints should endeavor always to sing in harmony with the Spirit and with understanding. Frequently the spirit of a meeting is hampered by improper music and singing...Our songs should be always in keeping with the Gospel truth. False doctrine is discovered fre-

quently in sectarian hymns. Beautiful melody cannot compensate for false sentiment, yet we have this to contend with constantly in the services of the Church . . .Choir leaders should endeavor to be prepared with songs which will harmonize perfectly with the theme of the meeting . . .(Joseph Fielding Smith, CHMR, Vol. 1, p. 119)

My experience of a lifetime, and particularly the last thirty-two years as a General Authority, convinces me that the most effective preaching of the gospel is when it is accompanied by beautiful, appropriate music . . .(Harold B. Lee, CR, April 1973, p. 181)

In our day music itself has been corrupted. Music can, by its tempo, by its beat, by its intensity, dull the spiritual sensitivity of men . . .
There is so much wonderful, uplifting music available that we can experience to our advantage. Our people ought to be surrounded by good music of all kinds . . .we encourage parents to include musical training in the lives of their children. (Boyd K. Packer, CR, October 1973, pp. 21, 23)

The Lord's Instruction and Counsel to Emma Smith and Other Sisters

This discussion will consider only six areas of counsel from the Lord in this revelation:

1. *Murmur not*

In explanation of the Lord's use of this phrase to Emma, Elder Joseph Fielding Smith has said:

. . .Emma Smith was human, possessing many of the characteristics which are found in most of us. Being the wife of the man whom the Almighty had blessed, she felt, as most women would have felt under like circumstances, that she was entitled to some special favors. It was difficult for her to understand why she could not view the plates, the Urim and Thummim, and other sacred things, which view had been given to special witnesses. At times this human thought caused her to murmur and ask the questions of the Prophet why she was denied this privilege. In this revelation the Lord admonishes her and tells her that it is for a wise purpose to be made known in time to come, why she and the world were deprived of this privilege. (CHMR, Vol. 1, p. 117)

Many Latter-day Saint women are placed in situations where husbands are called to serve and must retain a certain confidentiality to the affairs of their callings. At such times, it is not uncommon for wives to have feelings of being "left out." It is a natural reaction and comes because of the human nature of the individual. Like Emma, most wives are interested in their husbands' activities and are used to sharing in his interests and responsibilities. To be separated from such sharing experiences often produces these feelings. To every woman in such situations, the word of the Lord is given:

> Murmur not because of the things which thou hast not seen, for they are withheld from thee and from the world, which is wisdom in me in a time to come. (D&C 25:4)

2. Office of thy calling

The Lord emphasized and allowed us to recognize that women are expected to be a source of strength as they give comfort. Specifically, He addressed a wife and said to her:

> And the office of thy calling shall be for a comfort unto my servant, Joseph Smith, Jun., thy husband, in his afflictions, with consoling words, in the spirit of meekness. (D&C 25:5)

The office of Emma's *calling* was to comfort Joseph in his two roles:

   a. The Lord's servant
   b. Her husband

As with Emma, so each wife, whose husband also serves the Lord, is called by the Lord to support, sustain and be a strength to him. Her assistance will be a comfort to him in his efforts to be a profitable servant of the Lord. Likewise, as she comforts him in his role as a husband, will she strengthen him and their family through her obedience to this injunction of the Lord. She will thus strengthen her own relationship with the Lord as she performs this role in conjunction with her servant husband.

3. Go with thy husband

Throughout his lifetime, Joseph would be directed by the Lord to go to various places in the performance of his duties. At this time (July 1830), Joseph had been commanded to go to New York and administer to the needs of the Church there. (See D&C 24:3) Emma is also commanded to go with him.

> And thou shalt go with him at the time of his going . . .(D&C 25:6)

When the Lord placed man upon the earth, He said " . . .it is not good that the man should be alone, . . .[so He] formed . . .a woman, and brought her unto the man." (P. of G.P., Abraham 5:14, 16)

The entire purpose of mortality is focused on the bringing together of a man and a woman in an eternal husband and wife relationship. It is of extreme importance that they both strive to develop a relationship and a oneness that will endure forever. That can only be accomplished by being together whenever possible. There are many ways to be together and they all require effort to accomplish: rearing of children, budgeting, worship experience, church callings, recreational activities, custodial and main- tenance requirements of home and property, etc. In fact, very little of life's experience needs to be done alone.

In this regard, however, we must not overlook the fact that both callings of husband and wife are from the Lord. Therefore, a righteous husband and wife would strive to do only that which pleases the Lord. Neither would expect a companion to *"go with them"* in unrighteousness.

President Harold B. Lee has said:

> . . .the wife is to obey the law of her husband only as he obeys the laws of God. No woman is expected to follow her husband in disobedience to the commandments of the Lord. (Ensign, February 1972, p. 50)

President Spencer W. Kimball also emphasized:

> A woman need have no fear of being imposed upon or being subject to any dictatorial measures or improper demands when her husband is thoughtful, self-sacrificing, and worthy. One would think that no intelligent woman would hesitate to submit herself to her own truly righteous husband in everything... ("Men of Example," Address to Religious Educators, Assembly Hall, September 12, 1975)

4. *Lay aside things of the world*

This directive of the Lord would include at least the following two considerations:

a. Tangible things of the world, which would include possessions and properties. We should not assume the Lord does not want us to have an abundance of things of the world that would provide for our comforts and enjoyment. The earth and all things therein have been provided for the benefit of man as he learns to develop and subdue his surroundings. However, the acquiring of these "things" must not become goals in and of themselves. They are to aid us in our seeking the kingdom of God and His righteousness and if necessary, we should be willing to sacrifice and " . . .lay aside the things of the world, . . ." (D&C 25:10) for the building of the Lord's kingdom and our own eternal exaltation.

b. Intangible things of the world would include philosophies and fashions of worldliness. Elder David O. McKay has described this state of worldliness we should avoid as follows:

> Now, what do we mean by the world? It is sometimes used as an indefinite term. I take it that the world refers to the inhabitants who are alienated from the Saints of God. They are aliens to the Church, and it is the spirit of this alienation that we should keep ourselves free from. We are told by Paul not to conform to the fashions of the world. Titus was warned not to partake of those things, the evils of the world, and to "flee also youthful lusts: but follow righteousness, faith, charity, peace, with them that call on the Lord out of a pure heart." (II Tim. 2:22) Purity of heart—Zion is the pure in heart, we have been told, and the strength of this Church lies in the purity of the thoughts and lives of its members, then the testimony of Jesus abides in the soul, and strength comes to each individual to withstand the evils of the world. (Gospel Ideals, p. 153)

Wise are the sisters who remain free of the evil practices and ideas of the world. Such women will never be involved in the worldly ways of immorality, abortion, immodesty, sabbath-day breaking, etc. Rather, the faithful and obedient sisters are able to respond to the Lord when He said:

> Wherefore, lift up thy heart and rejoice, and cleave unto the covenants which thou hast made. (D&C 25:13)

5. *Seek for the things of a better world*

There is only one power that transcends the limitations of this world—the power of Jesus Christ. He has counseled the women to " . . .seek for the things of a better [world]." (D&C 25:10) She can only accomplish such by establishing and keeping a covenant relationship with the Lord. He said:

> Keep my commandments continually, and a crown of righteousness thou shalt receive. And except thou do this, where I am you cannot come. (D&C 25:15)

6. *Delight in thy husband*

The Lord directed the sisters to:

Continue in the spirit of meekness, and beware of pride. Let thy soul delight in thy husband, and the glory which shall come upon him. (D&C 25:14)

In this counsel, the Lord stresses the need for a wife to restrict her interests and attentions to her husband and not any other man. She should delight in her husband. She should be happy and content with him with whom she has covenanted for an eternal marriage relationship. She must never forget that her exaltation and glory will come in conjunction with the merits of a righteous husband. This is the " . . .glory which shall come upon him." (D&C 25:14)

It is likewise imperative that the husband should remember the source and nature of the glory he can obtain. We recall the Lord's word to Oliver Cowdery:

In me he shall have glory, and not of himself, whether in weakness or in strength, whether in bonds or free. (D&C 24:11)

When a husband is engaged in seeking to know and do the will of the Lord, he will seek the blessings of God for his wife and family. As he seeks to provide for them the necessities of life; as he strives to teach them the gospel of the Master; as he presides in his family in righteousness; as he blesses them through keeping his own covenants with the Savior, he will attain unto and share with them the glory of Jesus Christ. Who could ask for more?

Summary and Conclusion

The world has long been struggling to define the role of women. In July 1830, in 16 scriptural verses, the Lord resolved it all. He has taught each sister:

1. Her true identity as a daughter of God
2. Her true destiny as a wife and mother
3. The ways by which she should order her life in covenant and marriage relationships. (Six areas of this counsel have been discussed in this chapter.)

President Harold B. Lee emphasized these important teachings in several addresses to the sisters of the church:

To be what God intended you to be as a woman depends on the way you think, believe, live, dress, and conduct yourselves as true examples of Latter-day Saint womanhood, examples of that for which you were created and made. To be thus merits the deepest respect of your sweetheart and your husband. (Ensign, February 1972, p. 48)

Now, just a word to women students, in this day, when so much is being said about the prime role of the woman. We say the prime role in life for a woman is to become a wife and a mother. (BYU Speeches of the Year, 1973, p. 93)

You must understand that your husbands hold the priesthood of God and they have the key to the effectual door to a celestial home in the eternities for you and your children; and if they do not honor and magnify the priesthood they hold, you and your families will suffer thereby, even to the point of being deprived of that celestial home.

I shall never forget a lovely mother of five children whose husband had recently become active in the Church. They had gone to the temple for that glorious experience of having the whole family sealed together. After she had related this experience, she expressed great joy. She looked over the pulpit to her husband who was sitting in one of the front seats and said to him, "Daddy, I don't know how the girls and I can tell you how much we appreciate what you have done for us, because you see except for you, our daddy who holds, the priesthood, neither the girls nor I would be able to be together in a home beyond this life." (Area Conference, Munich, Germany, August 1973, p. 55)

Chapter 18

Doctrine and Covenants
Section 26

Suggested Title

All things by Common Consent, Prayer, Faith

Overview of Section Content

1. The brethren are instructed to study scriptures, preach, and administer to the church (vs. 1)
2. Law of common consent reaffirmed (vs. 2)

Historical Setting

Section 26 was one of three revelations given to Joseph Smith after he returned to his home in Harmony, Pennsylvania. (See Historical Setting in Chapter 16)

Sacred Truths

Introduction

This discussion will focus on the law of common consent as revealed in verse two of the revelation. We will discuss two aspects of this law:

Responding to the Voice of the Lord

Joseph Smith learned that common consent was a vital part of the operations and functions of the Lord's kingdom. Prior to the time he and

Oliver Cowdery received the Melchizedek Priesthood he was instructed
by the Lord as follows:

> . . .the word of the Lord came unto us in the chamber, [Peter
> Whitmer home] commanding us that I should ordain Oliver
> Cowdery to be an Elder in the Church of Jesus Christ; and that he
> also should ordain me to the same office; and then to ordain others,
> as it should be made known unto us from time to time. We were,
> however, commanded to defer this our ordination until such times
> as it should be practicable to have our brethren, who had been and
> who should be baptized, assembled together, when we must have
> their sanction to our thus proceeding to ordain each other, and have
> them decide by vote whether they were willing to accept us as
> spiritual teachers or not, . . .(HC, Vol. 1, pp. 60-61, underlining
> added)

At the time of the organization of the Church, Joseph received a
revelation which included the following:

> No person is to be ordained to any office in this church, where
> there is a regularly organized branch of the same, without the vote
> of the church; (D&C 20:65)

Obedient to the above instructions, Joseph recorded the proceedings
associated with the organization of the Church, April 6, 1830:

> Having opened the meeting by solemn prayer to our Heavenly
> Father, we proceeded, according to previous commandment, to call
> on our brethren to know whether they accepted us as their teachers
> in the things of the Kingdom of God, and whether they were
> satisfied that we should proceed and be organized as a Church
> according to said commandment which we had received. To these
> several propositions they consented by a unanimous vote. (HC,
> Vol. 1, p. 77, underlining added)

Emphasizing the privilege the Lord extends to His people to respond to
His will and the importance of the law of common consent. Elder Orson F.
Whitney Said:

> Obedient to the divine mandate spoken to them in Father
> Whitmer's humble home, Joseph and Oliver took steps to ascertain
> whether or not their brethren would sanction their ordination as
> Elders of the Church and were willing to come under their spiritual
> tutelage.

What!—exclaims one. After these men had communed with heavenly beings and received from them commandments for their guidance; after receiving divine authority to preach the Gospel, administer its ordinances, and establish once more on earth the long absent Church of Christ! After all this must they go before the people and ask their consent to organize them and preside over them as a religious body? Yes, that was precisely the situation. Notwithstanding all those glorious manifestations, they were not yet fully qualified to hold the high positions unto which they had been divinely called. One element was lacking—the consent of the people. Until that consent was given, there could be no church with these people as its members and those men as its presiding authorities. The Great Ruler of all never did and never will foist upon any of his people, in branch, ward, stake or Church capacity, a presiding officer whom they are not willing to accept and uphold.

Happily for all concerned, the brethren associated with Joseph and Oliver on that memorable sixth of April of the year 1830, did sanction their ordination, did "Decide by vote" to accept them as their "spiritual teachers."

But suppose it had been otherwise. Suppose the brethren in question had not been willing to accept the men whom the Lord had chosen, but had lifted their hands against instead of for them. What would have been the result? Would such action have taken from Joseph and Oliver their Priesthood or their gifts and powers as seers, prophets and revelators of the Most High? No. Any more than it would have blotted out the fact that Joseph had seen God, and that he and Oliver had communed with angels sent from Heaven to ordain them. Their brethren had not given them the Priesthood, had not made them prophets and seers, and they would have remained such regardless of any adverse action on the part of their associates. The Gospel, the Priesthood, the keys of the Kingdom of Heaven are not within the gift of the membership of the Church. They are bestowed by the Head of the Church, Jesus Christ, in person or by proxy, and without his consent no power on earth or under the earth could take them away.

But if the vote had been unfavorable, this would have resulted: The brethren and sisters who were waiting to be admitted into the Church would have closed the door in their own faces, would have cut themselves off from a most precious privilege, would have deprived themselves of the inestimable benefits flowing from the exercise of the gifts and powers possessed by the men divinely commissioned to inaugurate this great Latter-day Work; and they could have gone elsewhere, and, under divine direction, have

organized the Church of Christ among any people worthy to constitute its membership and willing that these men should be their
leaders. But the vote was in their favor, thank the Lord! and we who
are here today are among the beneficiaries of that act of faith and
humility. (CR, October 1930, pp. 45-46)

The privilege of responding to the Lord's voice is also emphasized by
Elder Charles W. Penrose:

It may seem rather a dry and formal matter to some of the people to
come together and lift up their hands to sustain the authorities of
the Church, but it is a necessary duty and, if we look at it properly,
we shall take pleasure therein. It may seem a little monotonous,
but, as I have said, it is necessary, for it was designed by the
Almighty in the organization of this Church, that the voice of the
people should respond to the voice of the Lord. It is the voice of the
Lord and the voice of the people together in this Church that
sanctions all things therein. In the rise of the Church the Lord gave a
revelation which said that "all things shall be done by common
consent." And the Lord designs that every individual member shall
take an interest therein, shall bear a part of the responsibility, and
shall take upon him or her the spirit of the Church, and be an active
living member of the body. It is designed that this Church shall be
alive in its parts; that every individual particle shall be influenced
by the spirit thereof . . . (JD, Vol. 21, pp. 45-46)

The opportunity to exercise one's agency is manifested in the application of the law of common consent. The following illustrates this
principle:

In the Church of Christ where the government is that of the
Kingdom of Heaven, neither autocracy nor deomocracy obtains,
but government by Common Consent. That is to say, the initiative
in all that pertains to the government of the Church rests with the
Head of the Church, even our Lord Jesus Christ, and He exercises
this sovereign function through his authorized servants, upon
whom He has bestowed the Holy Priesthood; but it is the privilege
of the people to accept, or reject, His laws and ordinances, for God
has given every individual free agency. Obedience must be
voluntary. The government of the Church has been called a
Theodemocracy. It is the form of government that will be general
during the Millennium. (DCC, pp. 131-132)

Protection Against Deception

From time to time, various people have represented themselves to members of the Church as authorized representatives of the Lord. Often they claim to have been ordained in some secret meeting. They sometimes claim to have received a calling or revelation under circumstances that are unknown to church authorities.

According to what the Lord has revealed, such things are not possible. He said:

> And all things shall be done by common consent in the church . . . (D&C 26:2, underlining added)

If any person is authorized to function in the name of the Lord on any level in the Lord's church, such a person will have been sustained in a proceeding wherein the membership will have had the opportunity to respond to his calling. If any revelation has been given by the Lord to His church, and the members are expected to accept the contents thereof as church doctrine, such a revelation will likewise be presented to the membership for their sustaining vote.

It is clear that one of the reasons for the law of common consent is to protect the Lord's people from being deceived. No one is authorized to preside in the Church except authority for such representation has been obtained and sustained in the church. It cannot be otherwise. The Lord has made it clear.

> Again I say unto you, that it shall not be given to any one to go forth to preach my gospel, or to build up my church, except he be ordained by some one who has authority, and it is known to the church that he has authority and has been regularly ordained by the heads of the church. (D&C 42:11)

Elder Joseph Fielding Smith has emphasized this principle and practice:

> No man can preside in this Church in any capacity, without the consent of the people. (CR, June 1919, p. 92, underlining added)

Summary and Conclusion

It is important to note that the Lord gave every individual the opportunity to know for himself of the source of callings and actions within the Church. The Lord said the implementation of the Law of Common Consent shall be accompanied " . . .by much prayer and faith, for all things you shall receive by faith." (D&C 26:2)

Chapter 19

Doctrine and Covenants Section 27

Suggested Title

The Sacrament-Whole Armor of God

Overview of Section Content

1. Sacramental emblems (vs. 1-4)
2. Purpose of sacrament (vs. 2, 5-14)
3. The armor of God (vs. 15-18)

Historical Setting

Joseph Smith, Jun.

Early in the month of August Newel Knight and his wife paid us a visit at my place in Harmony, Pennsylvania; and as neither his wife nor mine had been as yet confirmed, it was proposed that we should confirm them, and partake together of the sacrament, before he and his wife should leave us. In order to prepare for this I set out to procure some wine for the occasion, but had gone only a short distance when I was met by a heavenly messenger, and received the following revelation, the first four paragraphs of which were written at this time, and the remainder in the September following. (HC, Vol. 1, p. 106)

Sacred Truths

Introduction

From this revelation, we learn several things pertaining to the partaking of the sacrament of the Lord's supper:

1. Emblems that can be used for the sacrament
2. Appropriate attitude while partaking of the sacrament
3. Purpose of the sacrament
   a. In remembrance
   b. In anticipation

Sacramental Emblems

One of Joseph Smith's first experiences with the subject of the sacrament came as part of the revelation instructing him how to organize the Church. He learned that sacramental emblems represent the body and blood of the Savior. (See D&C 20:40, 77, 79) He was instructed further:

> . . .it mattereth not what ye shall eat or what ye shall drink when ye partake of the sacrament . . . (D&C 27:2)

However, this statement did not allow for the use of strong drinks, meaning alcoholic beverages. (See D&C 27:3-4) Through instructions of the First Presidency, the Church has been directed to use water and bread as emblems of this special and sacred ordinance.

Appropriate Attitude

As important as it is to have the proper emblems to represent the Savior's atoning sacrifice, it is also essential and vital that partaking of the emblems should be done with the proper attitude and for the right reason.

The act of partaking of the emblems of the sacrament is an opportunity for the individual to further strengthen his covenant relationship with the Father and the Son. (See D&C 27:2) Elder Melvin J. Ballard described that relationship as follows:

> The sacred covenant of the sacrament with its attendant blessings, which we repeat as we consecrate the emblems of the broken body and the spilt blood of the Lord, has been especially revealed to the Latter-day Saints by the Lord himself, so that we have the very words of the covenant as they were formulated by our Redeemer, with its promised blessings. I appreciate, I believe, to some extent, the sacredness of the covenant which we, as members of the Church, enter into when we partake of the sacred emblems. I realize that each time we partake of these emblems, we manifest

before the Father that we do remember His Son; and by the act of partaking of the bread and the water, we make a solemn covenant that we do take upon us the name of our Redeemer, and that we do, further, make a pledge and an agreement by that act that we will keep His commandments. (Crusader for Righteousness, p. 131)

Purpose of the Sacramant

As we partake of the physical emblems of the sacrament, our minds should concentrate on two great events—the Savior's atonement and His future coming.

The Savior spoke of this two-fold purpose in this revelation as follows:

> For, behold, I say unto you, that it mattereth not what ye shall eat and what ye shall drink when ye partake of the sacrament, if it so be that ye do it with an eye single to my glory—remembering unto the Father my body which was laid down for you, and my blood which was shed for the remission of your sins.
>
> Behold, this is wisdom in me; wherefore, marvel not, for the hour cometh that I will drink of the fruit of the vine with you on the earth, and with Moroni, whom I have sent unto you to reveal the Book of Mormon, containing the fulness of my everlasting gospel, to whom I have committed the keys of the record of the stick of Ephraim. (D&C 27:2, 5)

Elder Charles W. Penrose has called our attention to these two events:

> We are partaking of the emblems of the body and blood of Jesus Christ, the Redeemer of the world. We do this in remembrance of him, in remembrance of the atonement which he wrought for us and for all mankind who will listen to his voice and obey his commandments, and also to direct our thoughts to another great event in connection with the history of our Lord and Savior Jesus Christ, which is yet to take place. We take this sacrament this afternoon not only in remembrance of the past, but to direct our minds to the future. We partake of it to witness that we believe in the atonement wrought out by the Lord Jesus on the Mount of Calvary, and also that we expect his reappearance on the earth. We expect that he will come again not the next time as the babe of Bethlehem, not the next time to be despised and rejected of men, a man of sorrows and acquainted with grief, but as the Lord of life and glory, as the King of Israel to sit upon the throne of his father David, to rule from the rivers to the ends of the earth; not to be brought unto the subjection of men, but to have all things made

subject to him; not to bear his cross up the side of Calvary, but to come as a monarch, as a ruler of men, as the rightful Lord and King of this earth upon which we live. In partaking of these emblems this afternoon, then, our minds are carried back to the past, and carried forward to the future, and when we hold a piece of bread, blessed by the servants of God, in our hands, we take it in token and witness to God that we believe in him of whom this piece of bread is a representative. This bread is to us a representation of the body of Christ broken for us. When we drink of the cup we do so in remembrance of his blood and as a witness to God and to each other, that we believe in Jesus Christ. Not only that, but we also bear testimony before the heavens and one another, that we are willing to take upon us the name of Jesus Christ, and remember him, and keep the commandments which he has given unto us. So that in our public assemblies on Sunday afternoon—or the Sabbath day if you please to call it so—we come together to renew our covenants, to make manifest before God and one another our feelings and desires in relation to these matters, to witness to the heavens and the earth that we are called to be Saints, that we have come out of the world, that we have separated our selves from that which is evil, and dedicated and consecrated ourselves to the service of God, to carry out his purposes on the earth, to be guided by his Spirit, to be prompted by the same motives that actuated our Lord and Savior Jesus Christ, when he was a man among men, to renew our covenants before God, that we will serve him in all things, and that we will prefer the truth as it is in Christ Jesus, that we will prefer the kingdom of God as He has set it up on the earth in the latter days above all other things; that we will place in our estimation first the Kingdom of God and his righteousness with the hope and belief that if we do this all other things shall be added unto us as we need them. (J.D., Vol. 22, pp. 82-83)

Regarding the above references to the partaking of the sacrament and looking forward to the future coming of the Savior, it should be noted that the Savior will hold a great sacrament meeting at that time with those who are worthy. Speaking of that great sacrament meeting, Elder Joseph F. Smith has said:

...in revelation given September, 1830, referring to Joseph and Oliver, the Lord said in reference to partaking again of the Sacrament on the earth, that "the hour cometh that I will drink of the fruit of the vine with you on the earth, and with Moroni, *** and also with Elias, *** and also John the son of Zacharias, *** which

John I have sent unto you, my servants, Joseph Smith, Jun., and Oliver Cowdery, to ordain you unto this first Priesthood which you have received, that you might be called and ordained even as Aaron; and also Elijah, *** and also with Joseph and Jacob, and Isaac, and Abraham, your fathers, by whom the promises remain; and also with Michael, or Adam, the father of all, the prince of all, the ancient of days. And also with Peter, and James, and John, whom I have sent unto you, by whom I have ordained you and confirmed you to be apostles, and especial witnesses of my name, and bear the keys of your ministry, and of the same things which I revealed unto them; unto whom I have committed the keys of my kingdom, and a dispensation of the gospel for the last times; and for the fulness of times, in the which I will gather together in one all things, both which are in heaven and which are on earth." (*Doc. and Cov.* 27:5-13) (G.D., p. 194)

In addition to those mentioned by name who will be in attendance at the sacrament meeting, the Savior said:

And also with all those whom my Father hath given me out of the world. (D&C 27:14)

Who are the people who are given to the Savior and are "out of the world"? To be given to the Savior connotes an act of covenant making. To be out of the world is to fully observe and keep one's covenants with the Lord. In other words, every Latter-day Saint has the potential opportunity to meet with the Savior in a sacrament meeting experience at the time of His coming.

To assist us in our efforts to remain free of the world of wickedness, the Lord instructed us as follows:

Wherefore, lift up your hearts and rejoice, and gird up your loins, and take upon you my whole armor, that ye may be able to withstand the evil day, having done all, that ye may be able to stand.

Stand, therefore, having your loins girt about with truth, having on the breastplate of righteousness, and your feet shod with the preparation of the gospel of peace, which I have sent mine angels to commit unto you;

Taking the shield of faith wherewith ye shall be able to quench all the fiery darts of the wicked;

And take the helmet of salvation, and the sword of my Spirit, which I will pour out upon you, and my word which I reveal unto you, and be agreed as touching all things whatsoever ye ask of me, and be faithful until I come, and ye shall be caught up, that where I am ye shall be also. Amen. (D&C 27:15-18)

As an explanation of how the specific parts of the Lord's armor can assist us in our battles with the powers of darkness, Elder Harold B. Lee taught:

We have four parts of the body that . . . [are] the most vulnerable to the powers of darkness. The loins, typifying virtue, chastity; the heart, typifying our conduct; our feet, our goals or objectives in life; and finally, our head, our thoughts . . .

We should have our loins girt about with truth. What is truth? Truth, the Lord said, is knowledge of things as they are, things as they were, and things as they are to come. (D&C 93:24) What is going to guide us along the path of proper morals or proper choices? It will be the knowledge of truth. There must be a standard by which we measure our conduct, else how shall we know which is right? How do we know it is wrong to lie? How do we know it is wrong to kill, unless we have a knowledge of the truth . . . Our loins should be girt about with truth, the Prophet said.

And the heart, what kind of breastplate shall protect our conduct in life? We shall have over our hearts a breastplate of righteousness. Well, having learned truth we have a measure by which we can judge between right and wrong, and so our conduct will always be gauged by that thing which we know to be true. Our breastplate to cover our conduct shall be the breastplate of righteousness.

By what shall we protect our feet, or by what shall we gauge our objectives or goals in life? . . . "Your feet shall be shod with the preparation of the gospel of peace." (Ephesians 6:15) Interesting? What is the gospel of peace? The whole core and center of the gospel of peace was built around the person of him who was cradled in the manger, of whom on that night the angels sang, "Glory to God in the highest, and on earth, peace, good will to men." Or to put it even more correctly, "on earth peace to men of good will." Our feet should be shod with the preparation of the gospel of peace to them of good will . . .

And then finally the helmet of salvation. Did you ever hear of that kind of helmet? The helmet of salvation . . . Salvation is to be saved. Saved from what? Saved from death and saved from sin . . .

A helmet of salvation shall guide our thinking all through our days. Well, as we think that through, let me review again for just a moment, to get the full significance. Truth to safeguard our virtue; righteousness to keep our conduct right; the preparation of the gospel of peace to guide our course and to set our standards and aims in life; salvation, a return back to the presence of the Lord, shall be the inhibiting promise and a motivating objective to guide us on to the victory of life over death. That is what it means . . .

. . .[The] armoured man holds in his hand a shield and in his other hand a sword, which were the weapons of those days. The shield was the shield of faith and the sword was the sword of the spirit, which is the Word of God. I can't think of any more powerful weapons than faith and a knowledge of the scriptures, in which are contained the Word of God. One so armoured and one so prepared with those weapons is prepared to go out against the enemy that is more to be feared than the enemies that strike in the darkness of the night, that we can't see with our eyes. *(Speeches of the Year,* B.Y.U., November 9, 1954., Underlining added)

Summary and Conclusion

In retrospect, we have learned several important truths pertaining to our sacramental worship experience. We have learned that the emblems themselves can assist in strengthening our understanding of the covenant relationship with the Lord. We have learned that we should not only mentally reflect upon the Savior's atonement but we should also anticipate the great opportunity that lies ahead for those who are prepared to meet Him at the time of His second coming. We have also learned that our preparation for such a glorious experience is made possible by taking upon ourselves the whole armor of Jesus Christ.

Chapter 20

Doctrine and Covenants
Section 28

Suggested Title

Revelation for the Church-One at the Head

Overview of Section Content

1. Only the prophet receives revelation for the Church (vs. 1-7)
2. Oliver Cowdery called to serve a mission to the Lamanites (vs. 8-10, 14-16)
3. Hiram Page was deceived by Satan (vs. 11-12)
4. All things must be done in order in the Church (vs. 13)

Historical Setting

Joseph Smith, Jun.

   ...Brother Knight [Joseph Knight, Sr.] had come with his wagon, prepared to move my family to Fayette, New York. Mr. Whitmer, having heard of the persecutions against us at Harmony, Pennsylvania, had invited us to go and live with him; and during the last week in August we arrived at Fayette, amidst the congratulations of our brethren and friends.

   To our great grief, however, we soon found that Satan had been lying in wait to deceive, and seeking whom he might devour.

Brother Hiram Page had in his possession a certain stone, by which he had obtained certain "revelations" concerning the upbuilding of Zion, the order of the Church, etc., all of which were entirely at variance with the order of God's house, as laid down in the New Testament, as well as in our late revelations. As a conference meeting had been appointed for the 26th day of September, I thought it wisdom not to do much more than to converse with the brethren on the subject, until the conference should meet. Finding, however, that many, especially the Whitmer family and Oliver Cowdery, were believing much in the things set forth by this stone, we thought best to inquire of the Lord concerning so important a matter; and before conference convened, we received the following. (HC, Vol. 1, pp. 109-110)

Joseph Fielding Smith

. . .Hiram Page was born in Vermont in 1800. He joined the Church five days after its organization and was baptized by Oliver Cowdery in Seneca Lake. Previously he had become one of the Eight Witnesses of the Book of Mormon. Soon after his baptism he obtained a stone by means of which he received certain spurious revelations, at variance with the principles of the Gospel and the revelations received by Joseph Smith. Among other things he claimed to have received a revelation making known the place where the City of Zion would be built. In reading the Book of Mormon (Ether 13) it was discovered that Zion, or the New Jerusalem, was to be built upon this continent. This prediction caused some speculation at that early day and Hiram Page endeavored to settle the question by means of revelation received through his stone. As it was but a few months after the organization of the Church the members had not learned that there was but one appointed of the Lord to receive revelations for the Church, and several others thought that Hiram Page or Oliver Cowdery could receive revelation, just as well as Joseph Smith. Oliver Cowdery and the members of the Whitmer family were deceived by these false declarations of Hiram Page. This caused serious trouble and Oliver Cowdery took the Prophet to task for not accepting what Hiram Page had given. Finally the prophet persuaded Oliver Cowdery that these things were wrong, and later the whole membership renounced the revelation given through this stone, but this did not come until the Lord had given to the Church the revelation known as section twenty-eight. (CHMR, Vol. 1, p. 125)

Sacred Truths

Introduction

This section teaches us about revelation. We learn there are two sources—the Lord and Lucifer. Very often people do not distinguish between them. In this chapter we will discuss revelation as it comes from both sources.

Revelation From Lucifer

Hiram Page received revelation. What he and others did not know was that Lucifer was the revelator to them. One of the lessons we learn from this section is that sincere people can be mislead and misguided if they interpret satanic promptings as being revelation from the Lord. To clearly identify the source of Hiram Page's so-called relevation, the Lord instructed Oliver Cowdery:

> ...thou shalt take thy brother, Hiram Page, between him and thee alone, and tell him that those things which he hath written from that stone are not of me and that Satan deceiveth him. (D&C 28:11)

Revelation From the Lord

The Lord taught Oliver Cowdery and the entire church membership that revelation for the Lord's church will be given to and through only one man, the Lord's prophet.

> But, behold, verily, verily, I say unto thee, no one shall be appointed to receive commandments and revelations in this church excepting my servant Joseph Smith, Jun., for he receiveth them even as Moses. (D&C 28:2)

There is order in the Lord's church and all things must be done according to that order.

> For all things must be done in order, and by common consent in the church, by the prayer of faith. (D&C 28:13)

Revelation for the Lord's church is no exception to the established order. According to the Lord that order is as follows:

1. The Lord reveals His mind and will to His appointed mouthpiece, the prophet. (See D&C 28:2)

2. All revelations that are binding upon the church membership will be presented to the Church for their sustaining vote. This is done in compliance with the Law of Common Consent. (See D&C 28:13)
3. Officers and members of the Church, who are authorized to teach, are charged with the responsibility to stay within the guidelines the Lord gave to Oliver Cowdery:

> Behold, I say unto thee, Oliver, that it shall be given unto thee that thou shalt be heard by the church in all things whatsoever thou shalt teach them by the Comforter, concerning the revelations and commandments which I have given.
> And thou shalt not command him who is at thy head, and at the head of the church. (D&C 28:1, 6)

Summary and Conclusion

Members of The Church of Jesus Christ should all be aware that all teachings must be in accord with the revelations and commandments the Lord has given through His prophets, those who are at the head of His church.

No one need ever be led astray by teachings that are not of the Lord. In this section, the Lord revealed His order as a protection against deception.

Chapter 21

Doctrine and Covenants Section 29

Suggested Title

The Spiritual Gathering of Mine Elect

Overview of Section Content

1. The gathering of the Lord's elect (vs. 1-8)
2. The Lord's Second Coming (vs. 9-11)
3. The Twelve Apostles to judge Israel (vs. 12-13)
4. Signs, plagues, etc. prior to the Lord's Second Coming (vs. 14-21)
5. Events following the millennium (vs. 22-29)
6. All things are spiritual unto the Lord (vs. 29-35)
7. Lucifer cast out of Heaven (vs. 36-39)
8. Adam, the fall, and the atonement (vs. 40-45)
9. Children and the redemption (vs. 46-50)

Historical Setting

Joseph Fielding Smith

. . .In these early days of the Church the Lord revealed to the Prophet for the benefit of the members, line upon line and precept upon precept, thus unfolding to them the great truths of the Gospel. This revelation was given a few days before the conference of September 26, 1830, and in anticipation of that gathering. The Lord had commanded Oliver Cowdery to tarry (Sec. 28:10) until after this conference should be held, before departing on his mission to the Lamanites. The wonderful doctrines explained in this revelation were of such importance that it was well for Oliver and his companions to know them that they might teach the people on their way, and to the Lamanites when they arrived at their destination, with a more complete comprehension of the plan of Salvation than they otherwise would have had. This revelation is very comprehensive . . . (CHMR, Vol. 1, p. 130)

Sacred Truths

Introduction

In this section, the Lord reveals to us that all things have a spiritual meaning to Him. He said:

> Wherefore, verily I say unto you that all things unto me are spiritual, and not at any time have I given unto you a law which was temporal; neither any man, nor the children of men; neither Adam, your father, whom I created. (D&C 29:34)

Our goal is to become Christ-like. Therefore, all things need to have a spiritual meaning to us as we struggle through the temporal and physical environments of mortality. President David O. McKay discussed this principle and explained as follows:

> Indeed, man's earthly existence is but a test, whether he will concentrate his efforts, his mind, his soul upon things which contribute to his comfort and gratification of his physical instincts and passions, or whether he will make as his life's purpose and aim the acquisition of spiritual qualities . . .
> Spirituality, our true aim, is the consciousness of victory over self and of communion with the Infinite . . .
> Being "honest, true, chaste, benevolent, virtuous, and in doing good to all men" are attributes which contribute to spirituality, the highest acquisition of the soul. It is the divine in man, the supreme, crowning gift that makes him king of all created things.
> The spiritual life is the true life of man. It is what distinguishes him from the beasts of the forests. It lifts him above the physical, yet he is still susceptible to all the natural contributions that life can give him that are needful for his happiness or contributive to his advancement. (CR, October 1956, pp. 5-6)

Our discussion of this section will be an attempt to relate its contents to the principle stated by the Lord—"All things unto me are spiritual." (D&C 29:34) We will discuss the following topics:

1. The Gathering of the Lord's Elect
2. The Lord's Second Coming
3. Spiritual Laws
4. The Fall and the Atonement
5. Children and the Redemption

The Gathering of the Lord's Elect

In every dispensation, the Lord has given an opportunity to the people to be gathered. This dispensation is no exception, for the Lord has said:

> Listen to the voice of Jesus Christ, your Redeemer, the Great I Am, whose arm of mercy hath atoned for your sins.
>
> Who will gather his people even as a hen gathereth her chickens under her wings, even as many as will hearken to my voice and humble themselves before me, and call upon me in mighty prayer. (D&C 29:1-2)

We note that those gathered will be those who hearken to the Lord's voice. He refers to such as "mine elect":

> And ye are called to bring to pass the gathering of mine elect; for mine elect hear my voice and harden not their hearts. (D&C 29:7)

Where does one hear the voice of the Lord? The Lord leaves no doubt where His voice can be heard. In His preface to His own book, the Lord said:

> What I the Lord have spoken, I have spoken, and I excuse not myself; and though the heavens and the earth pass away, my word shall not pass away, but shall all be fulfilled, whether by mine own voice or by the voice of my servants, it is the same. (D&C 1:38)

And again, on the day the Lord organized His church upon the earth in this dispensation, He said, concerning His prophet:

> Wherefore, meaning the church, thou shalt give heed unto all his words and commandments which he shall give unto you as he receiveth them, walking in all holiness before me;
>
> For his word ye shall receive, as if from mine own mouth, in all patience and faith. (D&C 21:4-5)

Speaking to the future Quorum of Twelve Apostles the Lord emphasized the importance of hearing His voice through His scriptures. He said;

> These words are not of men nor of man, but of me; wherefore, you shall testify they are of me and not of man;
> For it is my voice which speaketh them unto you; for they are given by my Spirit unto you, and by my power you can read them one to another; and save it were by my power you could not have them;
> Wherefore, you can testify that you have heard my voice, and know my words. (D&C 18:34-36)

In summary, the voice of the Lord may be received as one listens to the Living Prophets, studies the messages of the scriptures, and is prompted through the inspiration of the Holy Ghost. And to those who not only hear but also hearken to the Lord's voice, the Lord gives the distinguished honor of being called "His elect."

The gathering, then, is a spiritual one, and depends upon the spiritual responsiveness of the people to the voice of the Lord.

The Lord's Second Coming

In verses 9-21, the Lord describes events and conditions surrounding the time of His second coming. He particularly identifies a number of events that will serve as signs of His coming. Though they will be physical phenomena, it remains for the spiritually-minded to be able to recognize them. Commenting on the need for spiritual orientation in order to discern these signs, Elder LeGrand Richards has said:

> If the world could discern the signs of the times, it would not be difficult for them to understand that the God of Israel has set his hand to do a marvelous work and a wonder among his people in the earth and that there is a kingdom established that is ultimately destined to fill the whole earth. And it will do it because it is God's work and not the work of man.
> While I was president of the Southern States Mission, one of our missionaries wrote in from Florida and said, "President Richards, I have been reading about the signs of the coming of the Lord." He said, "When the sun darkens and the moon ceases to give its light and the stars fall from heaven, everybody will know that he is coming."
> And I wrote back and said, "Probably they will know. The newspapers might announce some great phenomenon in the

heavens, misplacement of planets, that have caused this consternation, and scientists will have their explanation to make of it, and unless they have faith in the Living God, unless as Jesus said, they can read the signs of the times, they may not know anything about what is going on in the world."

"Why," I said, "if the inhabitants of this earth had the ability and the power to read the signs of the times, they would know that already the Lord has given far more than the darkening of the sun or obscuring the light of the moon or causing the stars to fall from heaven, for what he has accomplished in the establishment of his kingdom in the earth in these latter days, and the unseen power operating in the world for the accomplishment of his purposes, are greater signs than any of these phenomena that we read about—the signs of his coming." (CR, April 1951, pp. 40-41)

Inasmuch as Section 45 of the Doctrine and Covenants speaks further of the second coming of the Savior and signs in connection therewith, additional discussion will be forthcoming in Chapter 35 of this volume.

Spiritual Laws

The Lord informs us that all things unto Him are spiritual, even the commandments and laws He has given. (See D&C 29:34-35) Every law has a spiritual dimension. One who is obedient to the Savior's commandments with a desire to grow spiritually will attain unto that spiritual growth and power.

To illustrate: When we remember the purpose of the Sabbath is to provide opportunity to worship and give reverence to God, then our observance of the Sabbath brings us closer in our spiritual relationship with the Lord.

We ought not to look at the Word of Wisdom as a law of health only—rather it is a principle of obedience. Therefore, the breaking of the law results in spiritual degeneracy and a loss of personal spiritual power.

Keeping the moral law allows us to retain our spiritual sensitivity. Payment of tithing carries its own spiritual satisfaction. Responding to the injunction to "pray always" (See D&C 20:33) provides for us an edifying experience. Properly partaking of the sacrament touches the spiritual fibers of our souls.

Then our Church activity becomes more than just perfunctory performances—more than outward occurrences—more than mechanical motions. Instead it becomes the opportunity for divine development of spiritual strength. Since God does not create man's moral nature, it is our inherent responsibility to prepare ourselves to receive eternal inheritance and enjoy eternal lives.

Thus the spiritual keeping of the law becomes the way by which we come to know the Master.

The Fall and The Atonement

We learn from the Lord, that the fall of Adam and its subsequent effects upon all mankind resulted in our becoming subject to both physical and spiritual death. (See D&C 29:40-45) We are also taught that through the atonement of Jesus Christ, the effects of the physical death have been overcome and resurrection is provided for all mankind. As to the spiritual death, each person has an opportunity, through the atonement, to overcome the effects of sin through repentance and be glorified with the Savior.

As we consider the effects of the fall, our real concern is the spiritual results of transgressing God's laws. To overcome this spiritual death, we must enter into and keep the spiritual dimensions of our covenants with the Lord.

Children and The Redemption

Little children are not subject to spiritual death until they become accountable before the Lord. (See D&C 68:25, 27) Because of the Savior's atonement, children remain free from sin and are heirs of the celestial kingdom. (See D&C 29:46-47; 137:10)

There are a great number of parents who find peace knowing that their children who die in their infancy are saved through the powers of the atonement. Their salvation is assured. The promises for the children become, then, the challenges for the parents, that there can be a reuniting of loved ones in eternal family relationships. Elder Wilford Woodruff taught these principles and explained as follows:

> The question may arise with me and with you—"Why has the Lord taken away my children?" But that is not for me to tell, because I do not know; it is in the hands of the Lord, and it has been so from the creation of the world all the way down. Children are taken away in their infancy, and they go to the spirit world. They come here and fulfill the object of their coming, that is, they tabernacle in the flesh. They come to receive a probation and an inheritance on the earth; they obtain a body or tabernacle, and that tabernacle will be preserved for them, and in the morning of the resurrection the spirits and bodies will be reunited, and as here we find children of various ages in a family, from the infant at the mother's breast to manhood, so will it be in the family organization in the celestial world. Our children will be restored to us as they are laid down if we, their parents, keep the faith and prove ourselves worthy to

obtain eternal life; and if we do not so prove ourselves our children will still be preserved, and will inherit celestial glory.

. . .and all parents who have received children here according to the order of God and the holy priesthood, no matter in what age they may have lived, will claim those children in the morning of the resurrection, and they will be given unto them and they will grace their family organizations in the celestial world.

. . .it is sufficient for me to know that our children are saved, and that if we ourselves keep the faith and do our duty before the Lord, if we keep the celestial law, we shall be preserved by that law, and our children will be given unto us there, as they have been given here in this world of sorrow, affliction, pain and distress. (J.D., Vol. 18, pp. 31-32)

As it is with children in their infancy, so it is with children who are retarded in their understanding. (See D&C 29:50) Neither of them are accountable before the Lord and both come under the protective powers of the atonement of Jesus Christ. Speaking about these special children, Elder Joseph Fielding Smith has said:

The Lord has made it known by revelation that children born with retarded minds shall receive blessings just like little children who die in infancy. They are free from sin, because their minds are not capable of a correct understanding of right and wrong. Mormon, when writing to his son Moroni on the subject of baptism places deficient children in the same category with little children who are under the age of accountability, they do not require baptism, for the atonement of Jesus Christ takes care of them equally with little children who die before the age of accountability, as follows:

For behold that all little children are alive in Christ, and also all they that are without the law. For the power of redemption cometh on all them that have no law; wherefore, he that is not condemned, or he that is under no condemnation, cannot repent; and unto such baptism availeth nothing. [B. of M., Moroni 8:22]

Again the Lord has stated:

And again, I say unto you, that whoso having knowledge, have I not commanded to repent?

And he that hath no understanding, it remaineth in me to do according as it is written . . . [D&C 29:49-50]

Therefore the Church of Jesus Christ of Latter-day Saints considers all deficient children with retarded capacity to understand, just the same as little children under the age of accountability. They are redeemed without baptism and will go to the celestial kingdom of God, there, we believe, to have their faculties or other deficiencies restored according to the Father's mercy and justice. (AGQ, Vol. 3, pp. 20-21)

Once again, we see that all things are spiritual unto the Lord. Though a child loses its physical body in death or is encumbered with physical deficiency in understanding, still his spirit is pure. His spiritual relationship with the Lord is certain; his salvation is assured.

Summary and Conclusion

There are temporal dimensions to many aspects of the practices and principles of the kingdom of God-payment of tithes, meeting attendance, chapel and temple construction, welfare programs, etc. However, these endeavors are not terminal projects, but serve as means to an end. The purpose of the work of the kingdom is to develop the spiritual qualities and strengths in the individual that are essential to his enjoyment and participation in the glories of a life with God.

Chapter 22

Doctrine and Covenants Section 30

Suggested Title

Whitmer Brothers—Obedience

Overview of Section Content

1. Chastisement of David Whitmer for disobedience (vs. 1-4)
2. Peter Whitmer called to serve a mission to the Lamanites (vs. 5-8)
3. John Whitmer called to preach the gospel (vs. 9-11)

Historical Setting

Joseph Smith, Jun.

At length our conference assembled. The subject of the stone previously mentioned was discussed, and after considerable investigation, Brother Page, as well as the whole Church who were present, renounced the said stone, and all things connected therewith, much to our mutual satisfaction and happiness. We now partook of the Sacrament, confirmed and ordained many, and attended to a great variety of Church business on the first and the two following days of the conference, during which time we had much of the power of God manifested amongst us; the Holy Ghost came upon us, and filled us with joy unspeakable; and peace, and faith, and hope and charity abounded in our midst.

Before we separated we received the following: [Section 30 and 31 follow] (HC, Vol. 1, p. 115)

Sacred Truths

Introduction

This revelation is addressed to the three Whitmer brothers, David, Peter Jr., and John. In this chapter we will discuss the message given to David only. The Lord's instructions to Peter Jr. will be a part of our discussion in Chapter 24. John's missionary call is self-explanatory.

The Lord's counsel to David Whitmer will be discussed in the following two areas:

1. David's disobedience
2. Pre-requisites to obedience

David's Disobedience

We recall that in Chapter 20 of this volume, we discussed the involvement of the Whitmer family in their acceptance of a false revelation. As noted in the Historical Setting of this chapter, the false revelation was denounced at the conference of the Church. Then, the Lord gave David Whitmer this revelation through the Prophet Joseph Smith, pointing out the fallacy of his having given heed to directions coming from an unauthorized source.

There were several contributing factors that culminated in this act of disobedience. Those factors were identified by the Lord as follows: (See D&C 30:1-3)

1. His fear of man
2. His concentrating on things of the earth more than on the Lord
3. His failure to heed the promptings of the Spirit
4. His failure to follow the Lord's authorized leadership

Had David not failed to be spiritually sensitive in these four areas, he would not have been deceived and would have avoided the consequences of disobedience. One of the results of that disobedience was the Lord's directive, recorded as follows:

Wherefore, you are left to inquire for yourself at my hand, and ponder upon the things which you have received.

And your home shall be at your father's house, until I give unto you further commandments. And you shall attend to the ministry in the church, and before the world, and in the regions round about. Amen. (D&C 30:3-4)

Pre-Requisites to Obedience

Obedience to Jesus Christ includes, but is more than, covenant-making or verbally giving commitments to principles. It is an act or series of acts or conditions that are consistent with His prescribed patterns of behavior. Some of these essential conditions are brought to our attention in these instructions the Lord gave to David Whitmer:

1. Recognition of and reliance upon the only true source of strength—Jesus Christ
2. Emphasis on things of God *more* than on the things of the earth
3. Giving heed to the Lord's spirit
4. Giving heed to the Lord's authorized representatives

As we ponder the above-mentioned items, we wonder what one might do to develop himself in each of these areas. One suggested course of action that is vital to such personal development is an immersion of self in the revelations given by the Lord as scriptural standard works of the Church. President Spencer W. Kimball has stressed the importance of such a scriptural immersion. He said:

> There are blessings that come from immersing ourselves in the scriptures. The distance narrows between ourselves and our Father in heaven. Our spirituality shines brighter. We love more intensely those whom we should love. It is much easier to follow counsel. The lessons of life are learned more readily and surely. ("Men of Example"—Address given to Religious Educators, September 12, 1975, p. 2)

Summary and Conclusion

We have learned from this revelation to David Whitmer, that we cannot be passive in our covenant relationship with the Savior. We must be actively involved in growing spiritually. Scripture study, meeting attendance, acts of kindness, service to others, prayer and fasting, etc. all serve the same purpose—we can become more capable of obedience to the Savior.

Chapter 23

Doctrine and Covenants Section 31

Suggested Title

Thomas B. Marsh—Follow Counsel

Overview of Section Content

1. The Lord's promise to Thomas B. Marsh (vs. 1-2)
2. The Lord identifies ecclesiastical responsibilities of Thomas B. Marsh at that time (vs. 3-8, 10)
3. The Lord identifies some personal responsibilities of Thomas B. Marsh (vs. 9, 11-13)

Historical Setting

This revelation was received at the conference of the Church September 26, 1830, at Fayette, New York. (See Historical Setting for Section 30.) It was addressed to Thomas B. Marsh nearly five years before he would be called as the President of the first Quorum of Twelve Apostles in this dispensation.

Sacred Truths

Introduction

The Lord's counsel to Brother Marsh can be grouped and will be discussed in two major categories:

1. Ecclesiastical responsibilities
2. Personal responsibilities

Ecclesiastical Responsibilities

It would be well to remember what the Lord had made perfectly clear to Oliver Cowdery prior to this conference; that there is only one man in His church appointed by Him to receive and write revelations for the entire church. That man is the President of the Church. (See D&C 28:1-6)

Brother Marsh is here reminded of this eternal principle and divine law. He was told:

> You shall declare the things which have been revealed to my servant Joseph Smith, Jun. You shall begin to preach from this time forth, yea, to reap in the field which is white already to be burned. (D&C 31:4)

The counsel which he was given is of universal application to every member of this Church. When we are called upon to explain the gospel, our answers must always be based on those teachings that "...have been revealed to my servant, Joseph Smith, Jun." (D&C 31:4) Of course, this principle applies to the teachings declared by each of his successors, as Presidents of the Church.

Personal Responsibilities

The other portion of the Lord's counsel gave direction to Brother Marsh personally and could be summarized as follows:

1. Be patient
2. Revile not
3. Govern your house in meekness, be steadfast
4. Be guided by the Comforter
5. Pray always
6. Be faithful unto the end

For the purpose of this discussion, we will recall an incident that became a turning point in his life. In an address delivered in Salt Lake City, April 6, 1855, Elder George A. Smith described the events as follows:

> ...When the Saints were living in Far West, the wife of Marsh and Sister Harris agreed to exchange milk in order to enable each of them to make a larger cheese than they could do separately. Each was to take the other the "strippings" as well as the rest of the milk. Mrs. Harris performed her part of the agreement, but Mrs. Marsh kept a pint of "strippings" from each cow. When this became

known the matter was brought before the Teachers, and these decided against Mrs. Marsh. An appeal was taken to the Bishop. He sustained the Teachers. If Marsh had obeyed the Revelation and governed his house in humility with steadfastness, he would have righted the wrong done, but, instead of doing so, he appealed to the High Council. Marsh, who at the time was President of the Twelve, possibly thought that the Council would favor him, but that body confirmed the Bishop's decision. He was not yet satisfied, but appealed to the First Presidency, and Joseph, the Prophet, and his two counsellors consented to review the case. They approved the finding of the High Council. Was Marsh satisfied then? No. With the persistency of Lucifer himself, he declared that he would uphold the character of his wife, "even if he had to go to hell for it." Elder George A. Smith observes:

> The then President of the Twelve Apostles, the man who should have been the first to do justice and cause reparation to be made for wrong, committed by any member of his family, took that position, and what next? He went before a magistrate and swore that the "Mormons" were hostile to the State of Missouri. That affidavit brought from the government of Missouri an exterminating order, which drove some 15,000 Saints from their homes and habitations, and some thousands perished through suffering the exposure consequent to this state of affairs. (J.D., Vol. 3, p. 284) (DCC, p. 167)

It is not our purpose to judge Thomas B. Marsh—we leave that in the hands of our Eternal Judge. However, there is a lesson for all of us in the counsel given by the Lord to this man.

From the above story comes the vivid realization that the Lord had foreseen these potential problems and had given pertinent counsel by way of revelation years before. Had that counsel been heeded, the problem would have been averted.

Had Brother Marsh followed the Lord's counsel, he would have been patient with the decisions of priesthood leaders. He would not have reviled against them. Instead, he would have set his own house in order and governed it in meekness. Thus he would have been faithful to the end as he sought guidance and received direction from the Lord.

The sad commentary which followed his unwise action was excommunication from the Church. He lost immediate opportunities and severed his relationship with his greatest source of counsel. To see how far one can remove himself from the Lord, let us observe an event of his later life:

One cold, rainy, disagreeable evening about the last of February or first of March, 1857, just after candle light, our family was seated around the table for supper when a stranger knocked at the door and I bade him come in. An old man, carrying a satchel and wearing a black waterproof coat, opened the door and inquired if this was where Brother Mace lived. I told him that was my name. With his hand still on the door knob holding it open, he said, "I must introduce myself. I am Thomas B. Marsh, the Mormon apostate." He said he left the Church in 1838, but had never written anything or done anything to hinder the progress of the Church, but just left it. Now he wished to return and spend the rest of his days with the Saints.

He said he had walked all the way from his home in Missouri and the night before he had stopped with George W. Harris in Kanesville and this morning had been directed to come to me at Florence. This announcement of himself produced a singular sensation in each one present and a feeling of sorrow and pity took possession of each as they gazed upon a man who had fallen from so high a position as a President of the Quorum of the Twelve Apostles. I had never seen this man before but had heard many reports that he was an enemy to Joseph and the Church. On that account I had long been prepared to meet him and when I did to have a sharp controversy. But this sorrowful countenance, the palsied frame and above all, his humble manner and speech disarmed me so that I felt more like weeping than anything else. I invited him to take supper with us and assisted him to remove his coat but when he was seated I found he was unable to cut his food. I assisted him in this. After supper was finished he gave the cause which led him to apostatize. He now acknowledged his folly but at the time had thought Joseph was wrong in his decision . . .He said that during the previous summer he was taken with a stroke of palsy which paralyzed him to the extent that he had been unable to keep himself for a period of six weeks. As soon as he recovered sufficiently to help himself he decided to return to the Church, and as soon as he was able to travel he left his wife, children and friends taking only what he could carry in a satchel. When he reached Kanesville he found George W. Harris, whose wife had died, and stayed with him over night. They had talked over their past quarrel, made things right with each other, and separated friends. That night he had another stroke.

A bed was prepared for him and I assisted him in undressing and getting into bed. He then stated that he was placing himself in my charge because he felt that his condition might grow worse, leaving him as last year, practically helpless. In that case he desired of me to get some Elders to help me take him out and baptize him even if we had to use a sheet to carry him because he was so anxious to die in the Church. However, the next morning he was no worse, and I invited him to stay with us until his condition improved. In conversing with him I was astonished at his ignorance of the principles which he had once taught. I endeavored to explain to him many of these principles which now seemed entirely new to him. As fast as he could understand them he was anxious to learn them. (Biography of Wandle Mace, pp. 31-32)

Brother Marsh was subsequently rebaptized into the Church and later died in Ogden, Utah.

Summary and Conclusion

If we can learn anything from this revelation, it is that the Lord counsels in two areas—Ecclesiastical and Personal responsibilities. There are no issues we face in life upon which we have not been given direction. The question is: Are we responsive to the Lord's counsel? Will we give heed to his instructions by being patient, or will we be found reviling? Are we struggling to govern our homes in meekness and steadfastness as guided by the Holy Spirit? Do we pray always that we may be obedient and faithful unto the end? Are prayers offered in our families for strength and commitment to follow the brethren who lead the Savior's Church as they counsel us on pertinent issues?

For example, in April 1972, the Lord's prophet, Joseph Fielding Smith, opened General Conference and addressed the Latter-day Saints and Father's children everywhere. He pleaded with them to heed the counsel given at the conference. he then proceeded to address himself to the following people:

1. All of Father's children
2. Honest in heart in all nations
3. Those who have received the gospel
4. Families
5. Parents
6. Fathers
7. Mothers
8. Youth of Zion
9. Those called to positions of trust in the Church

(See CR, April 1972, pp. 12-14)

We call attention to the inclusiveness of the above list of people. He has left no one out. It might be well to ask ourselves the following vital questions: Are we aware of the counsel given in that conference? If not, how can we give heed to what was said? Do we attend these and other meetings; are we reading and reviewing the material when it is printed? How do we respond to the counsel when we hear it? Do we understand the serious nature of counsel when it is given? Listen to the following as said by Elder Wilford Woodruff:

> We, as a people, should not treat lightly this counsel, for I tell you in the name of the Lord—and I have watched it from the time I became a member of this Church—there is no man who undertakes to run counter to the counsel of the legally authorized leader of this people that ever prospers . . .you will find that all persons who take a stand against this counsel will never prosper.
>
> We have been governed by counsel instead of commandment in many things, which has been a blessing to the saints . . .(JD, Vol. 14, pp. 33, 36)

President Stephen L. Richards commented on counsel:

> . . .a moment's reflection will convince you of the rather serious regard in which we hold counsel. While it is true that we characterize infraction of the law as sin, and we do not apply quite that drastic a terminology to failure to follow counsel, yet in the Church, under the priesthood, counsel always is given for the primary purpose of having the law observed, so that it does occupy a place of standing and importance, almost comparable to that law of the gospel. (BYU Speeches of the Year, February 26, 1957)

Knowing that the Lord counsels his children through his servants, do we have faith enough in the Savior to heed his instructions? What if that counsel is contrary to our own predetermined course of action? Is there ever a problem giving heed when we are counseled to do that with which we are not already in agreement?

Might each of us "Pray always, lest you enter into temptation and lose your reward." (D&C 31:12)

Chapter 24

Doctrine and Covenants Section 32

Suggested Title

First Lamanite Mission

Overview of Section Content

1. The Lord called Parley P. Pratt and Ziba Peterson to a Lamanite mission (vs. 1-3)
2. The Lord's counsel to the Lamanite missionaries (vs. 4-5)

Historical Setting

Joseph Smith, Jun.

During the conference, which continued three days, the utmost harmony prevailed, and all things were settled satisfactorily to all present, and a desire was manifested by all the Saints to go forward and labor with all their powers to spread the great and glorious principles of truth, which had been revealed by our Heavenly Father. A number were baptized during the conference, and the word of the Lord spread and prevailed.

At this time a great desire was manifested by several of the Elders respecting the remnants of the house of Joseph, the Lamanites, residing in the west—knowing that the purposes of

God were great respecting that people, and hoping that the time had come when the promises of the Almighty in regard to them were about to be accomplished, and that they would receive the Gospel, and enjoy its blessings. The desire being so great, it was agreed that we should inquire of the Lord respecting the propriety of sending some of the Elders among them, which we accordingly did, and received the following . . .(HC, Vol. 1, p. 118)

Sacred Truths

Introduction

Previous to this revelation, the Lord had called Oliver Cowdery and Peter Whitmer, Jr. to serve as the first missionaries of this dispensation to teach the gospel to the Lamanites. (See D&C 28:8; 30:5) Now the Lord called two additional brethren to accompany these missionaries. (See D&C 32:1-3)

In this chapter we will discuss the following two areas pertaining to this first Lamanite mission:

1. The Lord's counsel to the missionaries
2. Some results of the mission

The Lord's Counsel to the Missionaries

The Lord made it very plain what He intended the missionaries should teach and how they should function in their calling. He said:

> And they shall give heed to that which is written, and pretend to no other revelation; and they shall pray always that I may unfold the same to their understanding.
> And they shall give heed unto these words and trifle not, and I will bless them. Amen. (D&C 32:4-5)

The importance of this counsel cannot be minimized. It takes on increasingly important proportions as we recognize how frequently the Lord has stressed this concept in the preceding revelations. Beginning with the day the Church was organized, the Lord emphasized the channel through which His directions will be given and made known to His Church. Only the Lord's prophet is authorized by Him to speak as His mouthpiece. (See D&C 21:4-5) Prior to the conference of the Church in September 1830, the Lord proclaimed His prophet to be the only channel through which the Lord would speak to the entire membership of the Church. No one else is authorized by the Lord to so speak. (See D&C 28:2) While the conference was assembled, the Lord gave three revelations and in each one of them, He stressed the need to follow His instructions as given to the Church through His prophet and rely upon no other source of information. (See D&C 30:2; 31:4; 32:4)

It would be well to be reminded that all of these instructions are recorded in the Lord's book and are intended for all men. (See D&C 1:2) Nothing has changed. We are still obligated to " . . .give heed to that which is written, and pretend to no other revelation . . ." (D&C 32:4) Such is the Lord's direction pertaining to revelation for the entire Church. Members and officers are obviously entitled and responsible to seek and obtain revelation in their individual callings. But, only the prophet has been authorized by the Lord to receive revelation for the membership of the Church.

Some Results of the Lamanite Mission

After the prophet Joseph received this revelation, he recorded the following:

> Immediately on receiving this revelation, preparations were made for the journey of the brethren therein designated, to the borders of the Lamanites . . .(HC, Vol. 1, p. 120)

This missionary journey extended from Fayette, New York through Kirtland, Ohio to the western borders of the state of Missouri. (See accompanying map in this chapter) Upon arrival in Missouri, they attempted to proselyte among the Lamanite people but their efforts met with much opposition due to restrictions placed upon them by Indian agents. This journey was no small undertaking—the distance was great and most of the journey was accomplished during winter months which created many hardships for these brethren. (For an account of this experience, see Autobiography of Parley P. Pratt, pp. 47-62)

Even though their labors were limited among the Lamanite people, yet the efforts of these missionaries brought many converts into the Church in the Kirtland area. Parley P. Pratt, one of these missionaries, had formerly been affiliated with the Campbellites or Disciples in and around Kirtland, Ohio. Sidney Rigdon was a pastor associated with this group and was a close friend and associate of Elder Pratt. While on the way to Missouri, Elder Pratt responded to a strong desire to stop in Kirtland and share the message of the newly-restored gospel with his former friends and acquaintances. As a result of his efforts, along with those of his missionary companions, several people were baptized, including Sidney Rigdon and Frederick G. Williams who were to play prominent roles in the Church. Later, Edward Partridge and many more were added to the growing list of members in Ohio. By the time Joseph Smith moved to Ohio (February 1831) this group numbered nearly one hundred members. (See HC, Vol. 1, p. 146)

In retrospect, this Lamanite mission provides us with a view of some of the Lord's purposes at this early age of the Church. These missionaries served as forerunners for the Lord to establish His church as a base of operations in Ohio. Ultimately, He would direct His saints to assemble there. From Ohio, the Lord would also direct the Church to continue its movement west to the revealed land of Zion, the New Jerusalem, in Missouri.

Though these missionaries may not have realized the full import of their calling, it is thrilling for us to see some of the benefits of their experience. The following would need to be included:

1. The Church had its first experience with proselyting among the Lamanites and learned what great effort would be required to take the gospel to these descendants of Joseph.
2. The Lord established an area as a place to gather His saints and restore many important keys pertaining to the salvation of man.
3. The Lord sent forerunners to Missouri where He would later gather the members of the Church.
4. Many prominent and faithful leaders of the Church were brought into the Church at this time.
5. The importance of missionary work was emphasized as the Lord called these men to serve under difficult and adverse conditions.

Overall, this Lamanite mission bore rich fruit that is still providing benefits to the Church today.

Summary and Conclusion

The Lord directs the missionary efforts of His church. Ultimately, His gospel is to go to all of His children throughout the earth. The place, the means or the method by which the missionary work is to be accomplished may vary according to time and circumstances. The course to be followed in the missionary effort will be defined and described by the Lord through his living prophets.

FIRST LAMANITE MISSION

Chapter 25

Doctrine and Covenants Section 33

Suggested Title

The Eleventh Hour-Oil For Our Lamps

Overview of Section Content

1. A missionary call to preach the gospel in the eleventh hour (vs. 1-4)
2. The Church is established to gather the elect, teach the gospel, and prepare mankind for the Savior's second coming (vs. 5-18)

Historical Setting

Joseph Smith, Jun.

The Lord, who is ever ready to instruct such as diligently seek in faith, gave the following revelation at Fayette, New York . . . .(HC, Vol. 1, p. 126)

Joseph Fielding Smith

. . .Ezra Thayer and Northrop Sweet came in the Church at the time of the preaching of the Lamanite missionaries. In October, 1830, they were called by revelation to enter the ministry and hearken to the voice of the Lord . . . .(CHMR, Vol. 1, p. 141)

Sacred Truths

Introduction

In the missionary call of Ezra Thayer and Northrop Sweet the Lord revealed the reason for the restoration of His Church and described the mission of that church in the last days. We will discuss these two concepts in this chapter.

Restoration of the Lord's Church

We learn from the Lord that His vineyard (the earth) "...has become corrupted..." (D&C 33:4) Though the Lord established His church in the meridian of time with His powers and principles of truth, there had been a falling away since then. His church no longer existed. He explained that because of "priestcrafts," the people were led astray and the earth was corrupted with many false teachings. (See D&C 33:4)

By way of explanation of the use of the term "corrupt," Elder Hyrum M. Smith has said:

> ...I would not have you understand me as believing all mankind, Christian or otherwise, have turned away entirely from thoughts of God and from the hope of salvation. The very image of God is impressed upon the children of men. They belong to him; He owns them, and he will never rest until he has brought them into a condition where they gladly and voluntarily render unto God that which belongs to God. They have been deceived and are deceived by corrupt professors, corrupt ministers.
>
> Let me explain, when I use the term "corrupt" with reference to these ministers of the gospel, that I use it in the same sense that I believe the Lord used it when he made that declaration to Joseph Smith, the prophet, in answer to the prophet's prayer. He did not mean, nor do I mean, that the ministers of religion are personally unvirtuous or impure. I believe as a class they, perhaps, in personal purity, stand a little above the average order of men. When I use the term "corrupt" I mean, as I believe the Lord meant, that they have turned away from the truth, the purity of the truth, the beauty of the truth, and have turned to that which is false. A false doctrine is a corrupt doctrine; a false religion is a corrupt religion; a false teacher is a corrupt teacher. Any man who teaches a false doctrine, who believes in and practices and teaches a false religion is a corrupt professor, because he teaches that which is impure and not true. (CR, October 1916, pp. 42-43)

Because of this condition of darkness upon the earth, the Lord restored

His church, or in other words called it forth " . . .out of the wilderness." (D&C 33:5, also see Bible, Revelation chapter 12)

Describing the time of this restoration, the Lord used the phrase "the eleventh hour." (See D&C 33:3) Explaining the use of this term, Elder Joseph Fielding Smith has said:

> This is "the eleventh hour." The time in which we live is compared to the eleventh hour, and so it is in the Lord's reckoning, for we are in the closing scenes of the present world. Elder Orson F. Whitney referred to our dispensation as the "Saturday night" of time. And according to the parable of the men employed in the vineyard, we who labor in this hour will be rewarded if we are faithful with equal compensation with those who labored in the previous hours, or dispensations, in the history of mankind. (CHMR, Vol. 1, p. 142)

The Lord also said that the restoration in this dispensation was "the last time" that He would call laborers. (D&C 33:3, see also D&C 43:28; 95:4) His church will never again be taken from the earth. The restored kingdom of God " . . .shall never be destroyed: . . .it shall stand forever." (Bible, Daniel 2:44)

Mission of the Lord's Church

We learn from this revelation that the mission of the Lord's church is to gather the Lord's elect who will hearken to His voice and prepare them for His second coming. (See D&C 33:6-18) The Lord explained that such a mission will be accomplished only as the Church takes the message of the gospel to all of Father's children everywhere. That is our missionary responsibility.

As the saints are gathered into the Church through the covenant making process, they begin to build upon the rock of the gospel of Jesus Christ. This process of building is likened unto the parable of the ten virgins. The Lord directed His saints to have their " . . .lamps trimmed and burning, and oil with you that you may be ready at the coming of the Bridegroom—." (D&C 33:17)

What is the oil the Lord said we must have to prepare us for His coming? Elder Spencer W. Kimball has explained as follows:

> In the parable, oil can be purchased at the market. In our lives the oil of preparedness is accumulated drop by drop in righteous living. Attendance at sacrament meetings adds oil to our lamps, drop by drop over the years. Fasting, family prayer, home teaching, control of bodily appetites, preaching the gospel, studying the

scriptures—each act of dedication and obedience is a drop added to our store. Deeds of kindness, payment of offerings and tithes, chaste thoughts and actions, marriage in the covenant for eternity—these, too, contribute importantly to the oil with which we can at midnight refuel our exhausted lamps. (*Faith Precedes the Miracle*, p. 256)

Summary and Conclusion

We must all realize that oil of spiritual preparedness must be acquired and retained by each individual. One cannot share such spiritual conditions with another. Speaking of this individual preparation, Elder Kimball has taught:

> The foolish asked the others to share their oil, but spiritual preparedness cannot be shared in an instant. The wise had to go, else the bridegroom would have gone unwelcomed. They needed all their oil for themselves; they could not save the foolish. The responsibility was each for himself.
>
> This was not selfishness or unkindness. The kind of oil that is needed to illuminate the way and light up the darkness is not shareable. How can one share obedience to the principle of tithing; a mind at peace from righteous living; an accumulation of knowledge? How can one share faith or testimony? How can one share attitudes or chastity, or the experience of a mission? How can one share temple privileges? Each must obtain that kind of oil for himself. (*Faith Precedes the Miracle*, pp. 255-256)

Chapter 26

Doctrine and Covenants Section 34

Suggested Title

Orson Pratt's Mission—Our Relationship with the Savior

Overview of Section Content

1. Orson Pratt's relationship to the Savior (vs. 1-4)
2. Orson Pratt's mission (vs. 5-12)

Historical Setting

Joseph Smith, Jun.

In the fore part of November, Orson Pratt, a young man nineteen years of age, who had been baptized at the first preaching of his brother, Parley P. Pratt, September 19th (his birthday), about six weeks previous, in Canaan, New York, came to inquire of the Lord what his duty was, and received the following answer... (HC, Vol. 1, pp. 127-128)

Joseph Fielding Smith

Orson Pratt, one of the most capable among the many capable men who came into the Church in the early days, was born September 19, 1811, in Hartford, New York. He was the younger brother of Parley P. Pratt, and when his brother Parley returned to his home with the message of the gospel, Orson believed him and was baptized, September 19, 1830, on his birthday. In the following months he traveled two hundred miles to see Joseph Smith in Fayette, and on the 4th of November received this revelation. He was ordained an elder December 1, 1830, by the Prophet and went on his first mission to Colesville. In the early part of 1831, he went on foot to Kirtland, a distance of about three hundred miles. He filled several short missions to various parts of the Eastern States. He was a member of Zion's Camp and was chosen and ordained an Apostle in 1835. He was one of the greatest mathematicians of modern times and one of the clearest and most logical defenders of the Church and the mission of Joseph Smith that the Church has produced. His mathematical ability was a great asset to the Pioneers when they were crossing the plains and mountains from Winter Quarters to the Salt Lake Valley, and with Erastus Snow he blazed the way into the Salt Lake Valley arriving on the 21st day of July, three days before the arrival of the main body of pioneers. (For a full biographical sketch, see Jenson's "Biographical Encyclopedia," Vol. 1:87-91) (CHMR, Vol. 1, pp. 143-144)

Sacred Truths

Introduction

In this section the Lord revealed several important things to Orson Pratt. We will discuss two of these subjects in this chapter.

Orson Pratt's Relationship to the Savior

Orson Pratt was but nineteen years old and had been a member of the Church less than two months when this revelation was given to him. The Savior addressed Orson and said:

> My son Orson, hearken and hear and behold what I, the Lord God, shall say unto you, even Jesus Christ your Redeemer. (D&C 34:1)

Here the Lord referred to Orson as His son. This relationship, of course, is descriptive of the covenant kinship that comes to individuals through the spiritual rebirth. Because of the covenants we make with the Savior, we are called His children. Through the change of our hearts, we are spiritually begotten of Him. (See B. of M., Mosiah 5:7)

The Savior spoke further to this nineteen-year-old boy, and explained who it was that was giving this revelation. Orson was being addressed by the Redeemer, the light and life of the world. Without him, there could not even be life—mortal or immortal. Everyone is dependent upon Jesus Christ. Our relationship with Him is one of total dependency. (See D&C 34:2)

Next, the Lord taught Orson Pratt how this whole relationship came to be. It was born in the love of the Lord. His love for Orson and all others was beautifully expressed by the Savior when He explained that He:

> . . .so loved the world that he gave his own life, that as many as would believe might become the sons of God. Wherefore, you are my son. (D&C 34:3)

It is worth noting that love is giving not taking. One can give without loving, but one cannot love without giving. We recall that God so loved the world that He gave. (See Bible, John 3:16) In this revelation, the Savior declared that He so loved the world that He also gave.

How does such love come to be? How do we develop this Christ-like love for others? The answer is found in the words of the Savior, when He declared:

> This is my commandment, that ye love one another, <u>as I have loved you</u>. (Bible, John 15:12, underlining added)

The question we need to ask is: How did Jesus love that we might do the same? As we study the ministry of the Savior, we discover that His whole life was one of serving and sacrificing in behalf of other people. The result of such selflessness is the development of an unparalleled love for the people. In order for us to acquire this divine love for others, we must likewise follow that pattern of service and sacrifice. Many illustrations could be given, but one will be sufficient to include here. Elder Harold B. Lee illustrated this principle as applied in a marriage relationship:

> Our young people come to the marriage altar having been taught in the public schools how important it is to make a certain adjustment in marriage, and many of them are very fearful about that adjustment. If these young people would understand that the application of that principle of sacrifice and service would be the answer to the problem of adjustment, their fears would be subdued. If they would resolve from the moment of their marriage, that from that time forth they would resolve and do everything in their power to please each other in things that are right, even to the sacrifice of their own pleasures, their own appetites, their own desires, the problem of adjustment in married life would take care

of itself, and their home would indeed be a happy home. Great love is built on great sacrifice, and that home where the principle of sacrifice for the welfare of each other is daily expressed is that home where there abides a great love. (CR, April 1947, p. 49)

Orson Pratt's Mission

To this nineteen-year-old son (Orson Pratt), the Savior extended an opportunity to develop Christ-like love for others. He outlined a lifetime mission that would give Orson experiences of service and sacrifice—the two ingredients essential to acquire celestial love. (See D&C 34:5-12)

Summary and Conclusion

From this revelation comes an understanding of how one fulfills his obligation to comply with the two great commandments upon which all else rests: love the Lord and love fellowmen.

Chapter 27

Doctrine and Covenants Section 35

Suggested Title

Sidney Rigdon—A Forerunner—Joseph Smith's Translation of the Bible

Overview of Section Content

1. Introduction by the Savior (vs. 1-2)
2. Sidney Rigdon, a forerunner (vs. 3-5)
3. The Lord's great work among the gentiles (vs. 7-16)
4. Joseph Smith and the keys of the Kingdom (vs. 17-18, 25-27)
5. The Savior's charge to Sidney Rigdon (vs. 6, 19-24)

Historical Setting

Joseph Smith, Jun.

In December Sidney Rigdon came to inquire of the Lord, and with him came Edward Partridge; the latter was a pattern of piety, and one of the Lord's great men. Shortly after the arrival of these two brethren, thus spake the Lord . . . (HC, Vol. 1, p. 128)

Hyrum M. Smith and Janne M. Sjodahl

Sidney Rigdon, who became noted in Church History, was born in Saint Claire, Pa., Feb. 19th, 1793. At the age of 25 years he joined a Baptist church. In 1819 he obtained a license as a minister, and a couple of years later he received a call to take charge of a church at Pittsburg, Pa. While engaged in this ministry, he became convinced that some of the doctrines of the Baptists were not Scriptural, and he resigned his position and joined his brother-in-law in the tanning business. At this time he became acquainted with Alexander Campbell, the reputed founder of the church known as "Disciples," or "Campbellites," and with one Mr. Walter Scott, and these three started that religious movement. Rigdon left Pittsburg and went to Bainbridge, and later to Mentor, preaching faith, repentance, baptism by immersion for the remission of sins, and righteous conduct. He had many adherents.

In the fall of 1830, Parley P. Pratt, Ziba Peterson, Oliver Cowdery, and Peter Whitmer, Jr., who were on their mission to the Lamanites, called at the house of Sidney Rigdon, and Parley P. Pratt, who knew him, presented him a copy of the Book of Mormon and related its story. He believed and was baptized, as were many members of his church in that vicinity. Sidney Rigdon and Edward Partridge shortly afterwards went to Fayette for the purpose of visiting the Prophet and learning something about the will of God concerning them. (DCC, p. 181)

Sacred Truths

Introduction

Sidney Rigdon came to Joseph Smith as a new convert to the Church. This revelation was given to him and identified how he had been and would yet be a meaningful part of the Lord's work among the gentiles in the latter days. For purposes of our discussion, this chapter will be divided into the three following areas:

1. Sidney Rigdon, a forerunner for the Savior
2. The Savior's charge to Sidney Rigdon
3. The Lord's work among the gentiles

Sidney Rigdon, A Forerunner for the Savior

We learn from the prophet Mormon, that the Lord works through people in various nations of the world, whether or not they have embraced the fulness of the everlasting gospel. (See B. of M., Alma 26:37; Alma 29:8) Such is the case with Sidney Rigdon. Prior to his acceptance of the gospel as taught him by the Lamanite missionaries, he was a forerunner for the Savior while serving as a minister for another faith, and he knew it not. The Savior informed him:

> Behold, verily, verily, I say unto my servant Sidney, I have looked upon thee and thy works. I have heard thy prayers, and prepared thee for a greater work.
>
> Thou art blessed, for thou shalt do great things. Behold thou wast sent forth, even as John, to prepare the way before me, and before Elijah which should come, and thou knewest it not.
>
> Thou didst baptize by water unto repentance, but they received not the Holy Ghost;
>
> But now I give unto thee a commandment, that thou shalt baptize by water, and they shall receive the Holy Ghost by the laying on of the hands, even as the apostles of old. (D&C 35:3-6)

The scope of the Lord's work is beyond man's comprehension. Our vision and understanding is often improved as we look back and see the patterns of the Lord's involvement in the affairs of man for the salvation of their souls. Speaking to this topic, Elder Orson F. Whitney has taught:

> All down the ages men bearing the authority of the Holy Priesthood—patriarchs, prophets, apostles and others, have officiated in the name of the Lord, doing the things that he required of them; and outside the pale of their activities other good and great men, not bearing the Priesthood, but possessing profundity of thought, great wisdom, and a desire to uplift their fellows, have been sent by the Almighty into many nations, to give them, not the fulness of the Gospel, but that portion of truth that they were able to receive and wisely use. Such men as Confucius, the Chinese philosopher; Zoroaster, the Persian sage; Guatama or Buddha, of the Hindus; Socrates and Plato, of the Greeks; these all had some of the light that is universally diffused, and concerning which we have this day heard. They were servants of the Lord in a lesser sense, and were sent to those pagan or heathen nations to give them the measure of truth that a wise Providence had allotted to them.
>
> And not only teachers—not poets and philosophers alone; but inventors, discoverers, warriors, statesmen, rulers, et al. These also have been used from the beginning to help along the Lord's work—mighty auxiliaries in the hands of an Almighty God, carrying out his purposes, consciously or unconsciously. (CR, April 1921, pp. 32-33)

It would be well to point out that we ought not to judge the actions and affairs of others. The Lord may be doing His work through means we know not of. Suffice it to say that many people in many lands under many circumstances may now be working, at least in part, to bring about the Lord's holy purposes.

The Savior's Charge to Sidney Rigdon

The Savior's charge to Sidney Rigdon can be grouped into three areas as follows:

1. Use of correct authority

As a Campbellite minister, Sidney Rigdon had been teaching some true principles of the gospel from the Bible, such as faith, repentance, baptism, etc. He had been baptizing according to his knowledge, though he lacked proper authority to perform the ordinance properly. Following his entrance into the Lord's church, he was given the proper authority by ordination and then was given a commission by the Savior to use that priesthood authority to bless the lives of others who come unto the Savior. (See D&C 35:5-6)

2. Sidney Rigdon's relationship to the Prophet Joseph Smith

Sidney Rigdon was reminded that though he held the priesthood and power of Jesus Christ, still Joseph Smith held the power and right to direct the use of that priesthood. Joseph held the keys of the kingdom and was the Lord's presiding authority. It was through Joseph, the Savior would save Israel and lead them out of obscurity into the light of the gospel. (See D&C 35:17-18, 25-27)

To assist the prophet in the fulfillment of his great calling, Sidney was counseled to watch over Joseph, tarry with him, journey with him, forsake him not and bear testimony of the prophet's calling by teaching the messages of the scriptures. (See D&C 35:19, 22-23)

3. Sidney Rigdon to be a scribe for Joseph Smith

Sometime after the Church was organized in 1830, Joseph Smith commenced a translation of the King James Bible. In December of that year, Sidney Rigdon was given the assignment to write for Joseph. (See D&C 35:20) This project continued to occupy much of Joseph's time and attention until 1833 during which time Sidney provided much help as a scribe.

A significant contribution of this translation process is related to the development of some portions of the Doctrine and Covenants. Discussing this contribution, Robert J. Matthews has said:

> Many of the revelations that comprise the Doctrine and Covenants have a direct relationship to the translation of the Bible which the Prophet Joseph was making at the time the revelations were received. They consist of two kinds: (1) directions or instructions to the Prophet about the Bible translation and (2) doctrinal revelations given to the Prophet while he was engaged in the translation process. The first kind were usually brief and direct, and

can be understood only in the historical context in which they were given. That is, unless one knows the background from which they came and that they refer to the New Translation, these passages fail to convey much meaning to the reader. In revelations of this category the Prophet was instructed about the following:

1. The appointment of scribes (D&C 25:6; 35:20; 47:1)
2. To cease translating while moving from New York to Ohio (D&C 37:1)
3. To begin the translation of the New Testament (D&C 45:60-61)
4. To hasten to complete the translation (D&C 93:53)
5. Not to translate the Apocrypha (D&C 91:1-6)
6. To establish a house for printing the translation (D&C 41:7; 94:10; 104:58; 124:89)
7. Other related instructions (D&C 26:1; 42:56-61; 90:13)

In the second category are revelations on doctrinal subjects that grew out of, or came as a result of, the translation but are more or less self-contained and can be understood quite well apart from their historical context. In other words, it is not essential for one to know that these revelations were given during the translation in order to understand their basic message. In this category we find the vision of the degrees of glory (section 76), an explanation of the book of Revelation (section 77), and probably much of the information in sections 74, 84, 86, 88, 93, 102, 104, 107, 113, and 132.

The Prophet was actively engaged in making the translation of the Bible from June 1830 until July 1833. Examination of the chronological table in the forepart of the Doctrine and Covenants will quickly show that most of the doctrinal revelations were received during this period. I believe this is not a <u>coincidence</u> but a <u>consequence</u>. It was Joseph Smith's study and translation of the Bible that set the stage for the reception of many revelations on the doctrines of the gospel. There is an inseparable connection between the New Translation of the Bible and many of the revelations that constitute the book of Doctrine and Covenants. (*Joseph Smith's Translation of the Bible*, pp. 255-256)

The Lord's Work Among the Gentiles

The Lord told Sidney Rigdon of His plans to do His work among the gentiles and His intentions to work through servants who would be considered weak and unlearned in the eyes of the world. (See D&C 35:7, 13) Many times the Lord calls people who are not already schooled in the teachings of the world and imbued with the philosophies of men. They don't have to unlearn incorrect doctrines in order to teach and present the

Lord's principles. Speaking of the Lord's calling and sending forth servants who may appear to the world as weak and unlearned, Elder Joseph Fielding Smith has said:

> Never in the history of the world has this truth been so greatly manifest as in the preaching of the Gospel by the weak and humble Elders of the Church. They have gone forth into strength which the Lord promised them and they have confounded the wisdom of the wise and the understanding of their prudent men has been hid. (Isa. 29:14) Think of the Prophet Joseph Smith, who was without training or education, only in the simple grades, so far as the learning of the world is concerned. Yet the Lord called him and educated him and he has confounded the entire religious world and brought to naught their false doctrines. (CHMR, Vol. 1, p. 149)

Those who are empowered by the Lord and called to do His work are to have the power to thrash the nations by the Lord's spirit. (See D&C 35:13-14) The use of the term "thrash" calls to mind the process of separating grain from chaff. The Lord reminded Sidney Rigdon that the people of the earth would be separated according to their receptiveness to the things of the spirit.

As the Lord sends forth His servants with the message of truth, they proclaim it with the accompanying witness of the Holy Ghost as to its truthfulness. Those who are able to feel that spiritual witness have the opportunity to respond to the message. Others not spiritually responsive will likely reject it. Thus the world is separated or "thrashed" by the spirit.

The Lord said:

> And there are none that doeth good except those who are ready to receive the fulness of my gospel, which I have sent forth unto this generation. (D&C 35:12)

Summary and Conclusion

Good works in social environments are admirable. Sidney Rigdon had done many good things and had taught many truths. His endeavors assisted many people to be better prepared to receive the fulness of the gospel. However, the restored gospel includes more than good works. It also provides the ordinances by proper authority that are necessary for individual salvation.

Chapter 28

Doctrine and Covenants Section 36

Suggested Title

Edward Partridge—Recognition of the Lord's Authorized Representatives

Overview of Section Content

1. Calling of Edward Partridge (vs. 1-3)
2. Calling of all others who accept the gospel (vs. 4-8)

Historical Setting

Edward Partridge accompanied Sidney Rigdon from Ohio to Fayette, New York for the purpose of visiting Joseph Smith. (See chapter twenty-seven, Historical Setting) During this visit, the Lord gave a revelation to Edward Partridge through His prophet. Referring to this revelation, Joseph recorded:

"And the voice of the Lord to Edward Partridge was: . . .[D&C Section 36 follows]." (HC, Vol. 1, p. 131)

Joseph Fielding Smith

[Edward Partridge] . . .was baptized by the Prophet [Joseph Smith] in December 1830, while on the visit to Fayette. (CHMR, Vol. 1, p. 150)

Sacred Truths

Introduction

In this revelation the Lord extended a calling to Edward Partridge to preach the Lord's gospel. (See D&C 36:1-3) However, in doing so, the Lord made it clear that there were two basic requirements associated with this call.

Worthiness

At the time of his call, Edward Partridge was privileged to have the Lord say to him:

> . . .your sins are forgiven you, and you are called to preach my gospel as with the voice of a trump. (D&C 36:1)

Every call from the Lord is a personal call. Each individual so called, becomes an authorized representative of the Lord. Is there a greater personal relationship than that? To properly function in such a calling and relationship requires a worthiness level that exists with those who become free from their sins. Edward Partridge had the joy of knowing that he was embarking on his call under these favorable conditions.

The Lord's Authorized Representatives

Everyone who serves in the Lord's kingdom does so under or in conjunction with, the jurisdictional and presiding authority of others who are authorized representatives of the Lord. As a new convert coming into the Lord's church, Edward Partridge was taught this important fundamental principle when the Lord said:

> And I will lay my hand upon you <u>by the hand of my servant Sidney Rigdon</u>, and you shall receive my Spirit, the Holy Ghost, even the Comforter, which shall teach you the peaceable things of the kingdom. (D&C 36:2, underlining added)

Summary and Conclusion

It is worthy to note that every baptized member of the Lord's church is capable of having this sacred relationship with the Lord. This relationship is experienced in two ways:

1. Each person can enjoy a one-to-one kinship directly with the Lord. This is realized through prayer, fasting, proper repentance, personal revelation, personal covenants, etc. In this regard, no one stands between the individual and the Lord.

2. As a person labors within his calling in helping to build the Lord's

kingdom, he works with the Lord through his authorized representatives. The authorities of the Church are not bypassed by either the laborer in the kingdom or the Lord as He directs the labor.

Thus, in conclusion, the calling of Edward Partridge symbolizes the calling of all others:

> And now this calling and commandment give I unto you concerning all men—
>
> That as many as shall <u>come before my servants</u> Sidney Rigdon and Joseph Smith, Jun., embracing this calling and commandment, <u>shall be ordained</u> and sent forth to preach the everlasting gospel among the nations—
>
> Crying repentance, saying: Save yourselves from this untoward generation, and come forth out of the fire, hating even the garments spotted with the flesh.
>
> And this commandment shall be given unto the elders of my church, that <u>every man which will embrace it with singleness of heart may be ordained</u> and sent forth, even as I have spoken. (D&C 36:4-7, underlining added)

Chapter 29

Doctrine and Covenants Sections 37 and 38

Suggested Titles

Section 37—The Church to Assemble in Ohio
Section 38—The Great I Am—His Concern For His People

Overview of Section Content

Section 37

1. Joseph Smith is to temporarily cease translation work on the Bible, move to Ohio and strengthen the Church before he leaves (vs. 1-2)
2. The Church is commanded to assemble in Ohio (vs. 3-4)

Section 38

1. The omnipotence of the Great I AM (vs. 1-8)
2. Promise and counsel to the saints (vs. 9-10, 14-22, 34-42)
3. Wicked conditions of the world (vs. 11-13)
4. Saints to be unified (vs. 23-27)
5. Reasons for saints to assemble in Ohio (vs. 13, 28-33)

Historical Setting

This chapter will be a discussion of both of these sections. In section 37, the Lord gave a commandment to all of His saints. In section 38, He reiterated the commandment and gave directions that would assist the saints to be obedient.

Setting For Section 37

Joseph Fielding Smith

. . .Section thirty-seven, is a revelation given to Joseph Smith and Sidney Rigdon in Fayette while Sidney Rigdon was visiting the Prophet in December, 1830: It seems that in keeping with the commandment previously given Sidney Rigdon had commenced to write for the Prophet in his "translation" or revision of the Scriptures. The Lord now commands them to cease for a season and prepare to go to the Ohio because of their enemies and for their sakes. . . .The call to the Ohio was for two reasons. The opposition to the Church in and around Fayette had become bitter. There had been many converts made among the followers of Sidney Rigdon in Kirtland, and the spirit there was friendly. The trend of the Church was ever westward; as persecution arose, and it became necessary to seek protection the Church moved farther and farther west. The Lord had a design in this. The place of the City Zion was west and it was necessary that eventually the Church be located there. Although it would not be a permanent residency, until Zion is redeemed. Not only was Joseph Smith and Sidney Rigdon commanded to go to Ohio, but this came as a command to the entire Church . . . (CHMR, Vol. 1, pp. 150-151)

Setting For Section 38

Joseph Smith, Jun.

The year 1831 opened with a prospect great and glorious for the welfare of the kingdom; for on the 2nd of January, 1831, a conference was held in the town of Fayette, New York, at which the ordinary business of the Church was transacted; and in addition, the following revelation was received . . . (HC, Vol. 1, p. 140)

Sacred Truths

Introduction

In Section 37, the Lord instructed Joseph Smith to temporarily cease the translation work on the Bible. (See D&C 37:1) (For an explanation of Joseph Smith's translation of the Bible, see Chapter 27 of this text) The reason for this cessation is indicated in the same verse when the Lord said:

Behold, I say unto you that it is not expedient in me that you should translate any more until ye shall go to the Ohio, and this because of the enemy and for your sakes. (D&C 37:1)

Not only was Joseph instructed to move to Ohio, but the Lord also commanded the Church membership in the New York area to "...assemble at the Ohio..." (D&C 37:3)

One of the reasons for this move and the gathering of the saints in Ohio was because enemies of the Church were plotting the deaths of the members. (See D&C 37:1; 38:13, 28, 31-32) — *secret combinations*

Shortly after Section 37 was given, a conference of the Church was convened. At this conference, the Lord gave a revelation (Section 38) in which He reaffirmed the importance of the Church's move to the Ohio. (See D&C 38:31-32) This revelation also contained counsel and instructions that would assist the saints to make this move with a greater faith and confidence in the Savior who led them.

The concepts to be discussed in the remainder of this chapter will fall into three categories:

1. The Great I AM
2. The Savior's love and concern for His people
3. The promised blessings for the saints in Ohio

The Great I AM

This was the first time in this dispensation that the Lord's people were asked to gather. It would be natural for many of them to have feelings of hesitancy about moving from already-established homes and leave friends and families in order to be obedient to the Lord's commandment.

In this revelation, the Lord gave the saints sufficient reason to dispel doubt and place their confidence and trust in Him and His judgment. What did He say that gave them assurance that they could place implicit trust in Him? He explains who He is and why He is able to give them and all others correct counsel and direction. In the first eight verses of this section we learn the following truths about Jesus Christ:

1. He is the Great I AM, the Jehovah of the Old Testament people (vs. 1, 4)
2. He knows all things (vs. 2)
3. He made the world (vs. 3)
4. He has power and control over the wicked (vs. 5-6)
5. He presides in the midst of the saints and the righteous will see Him in due time (vs. 7-8)

The words "I AM" constitute a title that was another name for Jehovah, the God of the Old Testament people. (See Bible, Exodus 3:14) The beautiful truth revealed in Section 38 is that Jesus Christ is the same God that has directed the affairs of Father's kingdom since the world began. He is the Great Jehovah, the Great I AM.

Another beautiful truth revealed by the Lord about Himself is that He knows all things. All that God has ever revealed to His people is supportive of this declaration. There is a multitude of scriptural references that declares this same doctrine. (See B. of M., II Nephi 9:20; Ether Chapter 3; P. of G.P. Moses 1:8-28; D&C 88:41, etc) There is no doubt that the Savior and His prophets have declared and taught the omniscience of the Great I AM. Why is it necessary that He knows all things? And why does it matter that we know that He does? As an answer for both of these questions, the Prophet Joseph Smith taught:

> The great Jehovah contemplated the whole of the events connected with the earth, pertaining to the plan of salvation, before it rolled into existence, or ever "the morning stars sang together" for joy; the past, the present, and the future were and are, with Him, one eternal "now;" He knew of the fall of Adam, the iniquities of the antediluvians, of the depth of iniquity that would be connected with the human family, their weakness and strength, their power and glory, apostasies, their crimes, their righteousness and iniquity; He comprehended the fall of man, and his redemption; He knew the plan of salvation and pointed it out; He was acquainted with the situation of all nations and with their destiny; He ordered all things according to the council of His own will; he knows the situation of both the living and the dead, and has made ample provision for their redemption, according to their several circumstances, and the laws of the kingdom of God, whether in this world, or in the world to come. (HC, Vol. 4, p. 597)

> By a little reflection it will be seen that the idea of the existence of these attributes in the Deity is necessary to enable any rational being to exercise faith in him; for without the idea of the existence of these attributes in the Deity, man could not exercise faith in him for life and salvation; seeing that without the knowledge of all things, God would not be able to save any portion of his creatures; for it is by reason of the knowledge which he has of all things, from the beginning to the end, that enables him to give that understanding to his creatures by which they are made partakers of eternal life; and if it were not for the idea existing in the minds of men that God had all knowledge, it would be impossible for them to exercise faith in him. (Lectures on Faith, Lecture Fourth, Para. 11)

From what we learn out of the scriptures and from the above-quoted statement concerning the attributes and powers of the Savior, we can see that not only the early saints, but every saint that has ever lived or will ever yet live, can and should place their lives in the hands of the Savior. All of Father's children can know that their destiny will be determined by their willingness to place their faith in Jesus Christ and therefore their actions and behavior should be compatible with His counsel and commandments.

The Savior's Love and Concern For His People

From the remaining verses of Section 38, we learn there are several dimensions of the Lord's love and concern for His people:

1. Their temporal welfare and salvation (vs. 16-20, 34-38)
2. Just laws and a free people (vs. 21-22)
3. Unity of the Lord's people (vs. 23-27)
4. Intent of the hearts of men (vs. 29-30)
5. Obtaining and properly using riches (vs. 39)

We will not discuss all of the above areas, we will focus on only one—the Lord's desire for unity amongst His people.

In one very brief statement, the Lord declared His desire for unity. He also identified the real problem that exists whenever His people fail to achieve harmonious relationships among themselves. He said:

> ...I say unto you, be one; and if ye are not one ye are not mine.
> (D&C 38:27) *Pres. Benson abt. how pride divides people / ranks them*

The significance of this principle is emphasized by Elder Harold B. Lee who said:

> If we are not united, we are not his. Here unity is the test of divine ownership as thus expressed. If we would be united in love and fellowship and harmony, this Church would convert the world, who would see in us the shining example of these qualities which evidence that divine ownership. Likewise, if in that Latter-day Saint home the husband and wife are in disharmony, bickering, and divorce is threatened, there is an evidence that one or both are not keeping the commandments of God.
>
> If we, in our wards and our branches, are divided, and there are factions not in harmony, it is but an evidence that there is something wrong. If two persons are at variance, arguing on different points of doctrine, no reasonable, thinking persons would say that both were speaking their different opinions by the Spirit of the Lord . . .

If it is so important, then, that this people be united people, we might well expect that upon this principle the powers of Satan would descend for their greatest attack. We might well expect, also, that if there be those of apostate mind among us, they would be inclined to ridicule and to scorn this principle of oneness and unity as being narrow-minded or as being unprogressive. We would likewise expect that those who are enemies would also seek to fight against that principle . . .

May I test your unity as Latter-day Saints? Have you received a witness of the Spirit to your souls testifying that this is the truth; that you know this is the Church and kingdom of God, that you have received by baptism and by the laying on of hands the power of the Holy Ghost by which that unity of testimony might be accomplished? Have you that testimony in your souls?

May I ask you another question? Are you living each day so to improve your lives by living the principles and ordinances of the gospel that you are moving toward that day when you will overcome all things? (CR, April 1950, pp. 97-100)

If there is ever a time when people are out of harmony with one another and a spirit of contention exists, they should look to the source of the real problem. Instead of treating symptoms, the cause needs to be identified and treated. The problem is that one or more of them are not in harmony with the Savior's teachings. They are not in tune with Him. They lack unity with Him. They are not His. There is no divine ownership. Might we be wise enough to look beyond surface symptoms and struggle instead to establish and maintain a correct personal relationship with the Lord. The result will be harmony and peace among the people. *we are His who purchased us thru His redeeming blood*

The Promised Blessings For the Saints in Ohio

For every law that is kept, there is a blessing attached that comes from the Lord. Obedience has its own reward. When the saints were commanded to go to Ohio, the Lord promised them that:

> . . .ye might escape the power of the enemy, and be gathered unto me a righteous people, without spot and blameless—
> Wherefore, for this cause I gave unto you the commandment that ye should go to the Ohio; and there I will give unto you my law; and there you shall be endowed with power from on high. (D&C 38:31-32)

Not only would the saints escape their enemies by going to Ohio, but they would be able to be gathered unto the Lord as a righteous people.

Through their obedience to Him, they would establish a relationship of unity with Him.

Furthermore, the Lord promised to give His church additional laws and commandments that were needed in order to properly govern His people and carry out the functions of His kingdom. The fulfillment of that promise was begun in the issuance of the Lord's law as found in Section 42 of the Doctrine and Covenants.

Still further, the Lord promised to endow the saints in His church with power from on high. There are several ways the fulfillment of this promise can be seen in the Ohio history of the Church. A few are listed as follows:

1. The first temple of this dispensation was built in Ohio.
2. Keys of the priesthood were restored by angelic messengers in the temple.
3. The Savior appeared to many of the saints.
4. The offices of Bishop, Quorum of Twelve Apostles, First Presidency, etc. were restored to the Church.

Summary and Conclusion

In retrospect, at least three great messages have been emphasized in this revelation.

First, the Savior's role in the affairs of mankind and His closeness to us is one of the most significant concepts yet revealed to man.

Second, the greatest insight to man's relationship with other men and his relationship with God is given in the Savior's admonition for unity: "...be one; and if ye are not one ye are not mine." (D&C 38:27) – *ownership*

Third, for those who are obedient to the Savior and follow His directions, there have always been and always will be, great promises and blessings that are bestowed by the Lord upon His people.

and because we're His, He can say to the Father — "Let this imperfect, but fully repentant person come back into thy presence." Otherwise the Savior could say — "my atoning sacrifice has no avail in your life because you didn't do your part." — a bit like Wallenberg saying — these people are ours, they're Swedish — get off the train.

Chapter 30

Doctrine and Covenants Sections 39 and 40

Suggested Titles

Section 39—James Covill—My Gospel
Section 40—James Covill—Cares of the World

Overview of Section Content

Section 39

1. How to receive the Savior (vs. 1-6)
2. Opportunity for James Covill to receive the Savior (vs. 7-10)
3. Opportunity for James Covill to assist others to receive the Savior (vs. 11-24)

Section 40

1. James Covill broke his covenant with the Lord (vs. 1, 3)
2. Why James Covill broke his covenant (vs. 2)

Historical Setting

Setting For Section 39

Joseph Smith, Jun.

Not long after this conference of the 2nd of January closed, there was a man came to me by the name of James Covill, who had been a Baptist minister for about forty years, and covenanted with the Lord that he would obey any command that the Lord would give to him through me, as His servant, and I received the following . . . (HC, Vol. 1, p. 143)

Setting For Section 40

Joseph Smith, Jun.

As James Covill rejected the word of the Lord, and returned to his former principles and people, the Lord gave unto me and Sidney Rigdon the following revelation, explaining why he obeyed not the word . . . (HC, Vol. 1, p. 145)

Sacred Truths

Introduction

Because of the relationship these two revelations have to each other, we will discuss the content of both of them in this chapter.

As can be seen from the Historical Setting for Section 39, James Covill had given lengthy service as a Baptist minister. In such a role, he would have taught and emphasized to his people the need for them to come to the Savior as a basis for their hope for salvation. In this revelation, James Covill is assured that such teachings are true, but the way by which one comes to the Lord is more than mere desire or verbal proclamation of one's acceptance of and commitment to the Savior. In this chapter, we will discuss what it means to receive or reject Jesus Christ.

Receiving the Savior

Responding to James Covill's righteous desire to come unto the Savior (See D&C 39:8), the Lord declared the following:

And verily, verily, I say unto you, he that receiveth my gospel receiveth me; and he that receiveth not my gospel receiveth not me.

And this is my gospel—repentance and baptism by water, and then cometh the baptism of fire and the Holy Ghost, even the comforter, which showeth all things, and teacheth the peaceable things of the kingdom. (D&C 39:5-6)

It is vital to understand that to receive the Savior, one must receive His gospel by entering into a covenant relationship with Him. Such a covenant is established through faith, repentance, and baptism by water and the laying on of hands for the gift of the Holy Ghost.

We have seen in the Historical Setting that James Covil had covenanted with the Lord that he would obey any command given by the Lord through His prophet. The Lord told him that the days of his deliverance had come and commanded him to be baptized and establish a covenant with Him. By so doing, he would not only receive, but likewise be able to teach others, the *fulness* of the Lord's gospel, the Lord's covenant. (See D&C 39:10-11)

It is of interest to note that the Lord referred to James Covill's attitude as being right at that time. He also revealed that there had been some previous improper actions and weaknesses in his past. (See D&C 39:9) Such a comment by the Lord should have served as a reminder and a warning to him in order that he might not repeat such mistakes as he contemplated receiving the fulness of the gospel.

What a witness and testimony of the prophetic calling of Joseph Smith! How could he have known of such previous conditions and inherent weaknesses of James Covill except that such was revealed to him by the Savior who knows all things.

Rejecting the Savior

The Lord responded to James Covill's righteous desires and gave him the opportunity to establish a covenant relationship with Him. James Covill broke his original covenant with the Lord. He did not accept and obey the Lord's command as given through the prophet Joseph Smith.

As noted in the Historical Setting, the Lord gave a revelation in which He revealed to Joseph Smith the reasons why James Covill broke his original covenant and failed to establish and keep an eternal covenant relationship with the Savior. He said:

> Behold, verily I say unto you, that the heart of my servant James Covill was right before me, for he covenanted with me that he would obey my word.
>
> And he rceived the word with gladness, but straightway Satan tempted him; and the fear of persecution and the cares of the world caused him to reject the word. (D&C 40:1-2)

At the critical moment when James Covill might have pursued the path leading to eternal life, the evil one attacked and led him away from the very goal he had desired to achieve.

James Covill's experience can be seen as being representative of what happens to many people. Everyone faces critical moments of making decisions, setting goals, and establishing commitments pertaining to future behavior. It is at these critical times that Lucifer enters into the battle to persuade us against pursuing courses of righteousness. He knows we are likely to become spiritually stronger as time goes by as we honor and keep our commitments with the Lord. Consequently, he seems determined to "straightway" tempt us.

Satan employs many methods as deflectors from our true course. Two of such are identified by the Lord in this revelation. Referring to James Covill, the Lord said:

> And he received the word with gladness, but straightway Satan tempted him; and the fear of persecution and the cares of the world caused him to reject the word. (D&C 40:2)

It was very difficult for James Covill to leave friends, associations, professional security, etc., that had long provided him with mortal comforts. When he took time to consider the realities and implications of his decision to forsake it all and enter the Church of the Savior, he weakened. Satan's influence overcame him, he broke his covenant with the Lord, and forsook his opportunity to receive and share the fulness of the gospel of Jesus Christ.

Summary and Conclusion

Eternal opportunities and blessings are sometimes exchanged for the temporary temporal things of the earth. Why would anyone forfeit their day of deliverance for the cares of the world? Why would anyone choose to dishonor their covenants and forfeit a life of peace with the Savior because of Satanic fears?

Might we keep in mind this lesson. When we are tempted to violate any of God's commandments could we just ask ourselves this question: Am I forfeiting the day of my deliverance?

Chapter 31

Doctrine and Covenants Section 41

Suggested Title

A True Disciple of Jesus Christ—First Bishop of the Church

Overview of Section Content

1. The law of the Lord to come forth to His church (vs. 1-4, 12)
2. A true disciple of Jesus Christ (vs. 5-6)
3. Temporal counsel to Joseph Smith and Sidney Rigdon (vs. 7-8)
4. The call of Edward Partridge to be the first bishop of the Lord's church (vs. 9-11)

Historical Setting

Joseph Smith, Jun.

The latter part of January, in company with Brothers Sidney Rigdon and Edward Partridge, I started with my wife for Kirtland, Ohio, where we arrived about the first of February, and were kindly received and welcomed into the house of Brother Newel K. Whitney. My wife and I lived in the family of Brother Whitney several weeks, and received every kindness and attention which could be expected, and especially from Sister Whitney.

The branch of the Church in this part of the Lord's vineyard, which had increased to nearly one hundred members, were striving to do the will of God, so far as they knew it, though some strange notions and false spirits had crept in among them. With a little caution and some wisdom, I soon assisted the brethren and sisters to overcome them. The plan of "common stock," which had existed in what was called "the family," whose members generally had embraced the everlasting Gospel, was readily abandoned for the more perfect law of the Lord; and the false spirits were easily discerned and rejected by the light of revelation.

The Lord gave unto the Church as follows . . .

[Section 41] (HC, Vol. 1, pp. 145-147)

Sacred Truths

Introduction

We would recall that in anticipation of the saints moving to the Ohio, the Lord promised to give them His law. (See D&C 38:32) As noted in the Historical Setting of this chapter, Joseph Smith had arrived in Kirtland, Ohio. Section 41 is the first recorded revelation in the Doctrine and Covenants that was given in Ohio. Contained in this revelation is the Lord's definition of a true disciple and the Lord's calling of Edward Partridge to be the first Bishop of the Church.

A True Disciple of Jesus Christ

Man has his definition of discipleship, such as "a follower," "a student," etc. In this revelation, the Lord reveals His definition of discipleship. He said:

> He that receiveth my law and doeth it, the same is my disciple; and he that saith he receiveth it and doeth it not, the same is not my disciple, and shall be cast out from among you. (D&C 41:5, underlining added)

It is a sacred privilege to be designated as a disciple of the Master. It is likewise a serious and sacred step to enter into covenants with Him. Those who intend to receive the rewards for discipleship need to be aware of His expectations. They need also to be aware that willful failure to comply with the conditions of the covenants is called hypocrisy and brings the displeasure of the Lord and can result in serious consequences.

Speaking of those who have professed the name of the Savior and have wilfully been disobedient, Elder Joseph Fielding Smith has said:

> . . .Because there were those who had professed the name of the Lord and made covenant to serve him, like James Coville, for

instance, and then they showed by their works that they did not act in sincerity, the Lord gave a revelation for the guidance of the members and warning to those who had professed his name who had not obeyed him. This is one of the most solemn and pointed declarations that can be found in any scripture against the hypocrite and the person who professes in sincerity, and apparently accepts in good faith, a covenant, and then departs from the covenant. (CHMR, Vol. 1, pp. 162-163)

Self-inventory of one's discipleship with his Savior is vital in measuring his progress. This inventory would include such interrogatories as follows:

1. Since I have <u>received</u> the Lord's law of tithing, am I <u>doing</u> it?
2. Since I have <u>received</u> the Lord's law of the Sabbath, am I <u>keeping</u> it holy?
3. Since I have <u>received</u> the Lord's law of marriage, am I <u>living</u> it?

There are many areas of our covenant commitments with the Savior that should be evaluated from time to time. Such evaluations will provide us with a barometer of our true discipleship to the Lord.

A Call To Serve In the Lord's Church

In this revelation, Edward Partridge received a call from the Lord to serve as the first bishop of His church in this dispensation. (See D&C 41:9-11) This calling of Bishop Partridge illustrates the process by which people are called to serve in the kingdom. This process involves the following:

1. The Lord calls through His authorized representatives.
2. The individual called is presented to the Church membership for their sustaining vote.
3. The individual called is given the authority to act in the office of his calling.

1.   The Lord Calls

It needs to be emphasized that this process pertains to a calling to serve in the Savior's church, not in any organization of men. Anyone who serves is entitled to know, and should be aware, that he serves not alone, but he can and should rely upon the Lord, from whom the call comes. With such an awareness, one can then go forth and serve with confidence and conviction, being especially careful to be sensitive to the wishes and prompting directions of the Lord. Thus, a sacredness is associated with the call that provides a greater depth of responsibility to the call and serves as a quiet reminder of the sacred responsibility conveyed to those who serve the Lord.

2. Voice of the Church

As revealed in Section 26 and discussed in Chapter 18 of this volume, the Lord's law to His church requires that those who are properly called must be presented to the membership of the Church and sustained by them. For further discussion, the reader is referred to the chapter noted above.

3. Authority to Act

Who has the right to assume authority? Even the laws of man don't permit such an assumption. Yet, some sincere people have mistakenly assumed that a desire to serve the Savior was sufficient authority to act in His name. There is no scriptural support for such course of action.

In this revelation, the Lord revealed the necessity of receiving His authority through His authorized and designated servants. Only through such authority are actions valid in the sight of the Lord.

> We believe that a man must be called of God, by prophecy and by the laying on of hands, by those who are in authority, to preach the Gospel and administer in the ordinances thereof. (P. of G.P., Articles of Faith, Article No. 5)

Summary and Conclusion

A true disciple of Jesus Christ knows there is no presumed authority in the Lord's church. He recognizes and follows those who are properly called and authorized to administer the Lord's laws unto the people. He not only accepts the laws of the Lord, but he also strives to live them and conduct his life in harmony with revealed teachings of truth.

Chapter 32

Doctrine and Covenants Section 42

Suggested Title

The Law of the Lord to His Church

Overview of Section Content

1. The Savior's instructions concerning His law (vs. 1-3)
2. The law of teaching (vs. 4-17)
3. Various moral laws for the members of the Lord's church (vs. 18-29)
4. The law of consecration (vs. 30-41)
5. The law of labor (vs. 42)
6. Laws concerning death and administrations to the sick (vs.43-52)
7. Laws of remuneration for goods and services (vs. 53-55, 70-73)
8. Counsel concerning the Joseph Smith Translation of the Bible and other scriptures (vs. 56-60)
9. Counsel of the Lord concerning the gathering to the New Jerusalem (vs. 61-69)
10. Laws concerning appropriate action pertaining to transgressors in the Lord's church (vs. 74-93)

Historical Setting

Joseph Smith, Jun.

On the 9th of February, 1831, at Kirtland, in the presence of twelve Elders, and according to the promise heretofore made, [see

D&C 38:32 and 41:2-3] the Lord gave the following revelation, embracing the law of the Church: . . . (HC, Vol. 1, p. 148)

Sacred Truths

Introduction

The Lord gave several laws that comprise the law of the Lord to His church. (See Overview of Section Content) He gave the Church this law at that time as a part of the process of establishing His kingdom in this dispensation. Additional laws have been revealed from time to time since this revelation was given. And the Lord may yet reveal additional laws to His church for the benefit of His saints. But the laws recorded in Section 42 are fundamental and have been a basis upon which the affairs of the Kingdom have been administered by the presiding authorities of the Church.

The scope of the law is so broad that it is not possible here to present many of the aspects that would be pertinent to a complete coverage of the subject. Our discussion will give emphasis to the laws as listed in the overview of section content except the law of consecration which will be discussed in Chapter 41 in connection with Doctrine and Covenants Sections 51 and 54.

The Law of Teaching

As we discuss this law and others, it should be emphasized that the principles pertain to the members of the Church who are in a covenant relationship with the Savior. The first part of this law discussed in verses 4-10 pertains to the proselyting mission of the Church and describes the responsibility of the elders to be actively involved in missionary service. Following this commission, the Savior emphasized the requirements He has given to those who represent Him in teaching and administering His gospel in the Church and unto the world. These requirements can be classified into four areas:

1. Called by Correct Authority

The Lord said:

> Again I say unto you, that it shall not be given to any one to go forth to preach my gospel, or to build up my church, except he be ordained by some one who has authority, and it is known to the church that he has authority and has been regularly ordained by the heads of the church. (D&C 42:11)

It should be noted that the Lord declared that <u>no one</u> is authorized to teach <u>His gospel</u> or build up <u>His church</u> unless he is duly called by authority <u>in the Church</u> and his calling is known <u>to the church</u> unit in which he functions through the process of common consent. (See D&C 20:65; 26:2) Only within the Church can such authority be obtained. Anyone professing authority from the Lord must receive it according to the Lord's stipulations described above.

2. *Teaching of Correct Principles*

The Lord said:

> And again, the elders, priests and teachers of this church shall teach the principles of my gospel, which are in the Bible and the Book of Mormon, in the which is the fulness of the gospel. (D&C 42:12)

It should be understood that in February 1831, the Doctrine and Covenants and the Pearl of Great Price had not yet been published. (See CHMR, Vol. 1, p. 168) The spirit of this instruction refers to the scriptures which are the standard works of the Church.

The law of the Savior requires that His authorized teachers should teach His gospel which is contained in and supported by his authorized scriptures. Stressing the importance of obeying this law, Elder Harold B. Lee has said:

> All that we teach in this church ought to be couched in the scriptures. It ought to be found in the scriptures. We ought to choose our texts from the scriptures. If we want to measure truth, we should measure it by the four standard works, regardless of who writes it. If it is not in the standard works, we may well assume that it is speculation, man's own personal opinion; and if it contradicts what is in the scriptures, it is not true. This is the standard by which we measure all truth. (I.E., January 1969, p. 13)

3. *Worthiness of the Teacher*

The Lord said:

> And they shall observe the covenants and church articles to do them, and these shall be their teachings, as they shall be directed by the spirit. (D&C 42:13)

As mentioned earlier, these laws were given to church members who are in a covenant relationship with the Lord. The Lord here reminds the teachers in the church that they are obligated to keep their covenants and abide by the teachings and rules (articles) of the church. As one complies with this requirement, he can effectively teach two ways:

a. By his own exemplary life
b. By teaching what he has experienced in his own life.

4. *Teaching By The Spirit*

The Lord said:

> And the Spirit shall be given unto you by the prayer of faith; and if ye receive not the Spirit ye shall not teach. (D&C 42:14)

The purpose of teaching the Savior's gospel is to change lives of people and bring them to the Lord. Teaching facts and presenting information only will never accomplish such purposes. People don't make changes in their lives based solely on what they know. They change because of what they feel. It has been said that religion is not taught, but caught. People must catch a feeling for truth as it is presented to them. It is the Holy Ghost that bears witness of truth and provides the necessary feeling.

What then are the responsibilities of an authorized teacher to make it possible for teaching to occur "by the spirit"? There are four mentioned by the Lord in this law:

a. He must receive his calling from the church.
b. He must teach correct principles of truth.
c. He must keep his covenants and be obedient to church laws and regulations.
d. He must seek the spirit through the prayer of faith.

It is a great responsibility to be called to teach in the Lord's kingdom. One must not take lightly such an opportunity. Anyone who accepts the call to teach is under an obligation to comply with the Lord's law pertaining to that calling. Elder Joseph Fielding Smith has pointed out some of the consequences of failing to abide by the Lord's law:

> How careful our instructors in our schools, institutes, semi-naries, priesthood classes and auxiliaries should be to guard the revealed truth from heaven! How fearful we should be lest we teach that which is false and thereby lead souls astray, in paths that lead to death and away from the exaltation in the kingdom of God. "And the Spirit shall be given unto you by the prayer of faith; and if ye receive not the Spirit ye shall not teach," the Lord has said. There is no greater crime in all the world than to teach false doctrines and

lead the unsuspecting astray, away from the eternal truths of the gospel.

We are all going to be judged according to our works, every soul. I have often thought of my place and responsibility in this Church. What a dreadful thing it would be to be going forth to teach, to lead men, to guide them into something that was not true. I think the greatest crime in all this world is to lead men and women, the children of God, away from the true principles. We see in the world today philosophies of various kinds, tending to destroy faith, faith in God, faith in the principles of the gospel. What a dreadful thing that is.

The Lord says if we labor all our days and save but one soul, how great will be our joy with him; on the other hand how great will be our sorrow and our condemnation if through our acts we have led one soul away from this truth.

He who blinds one soul, he who spreads error, he who destroys, through his teachings, divine truth, truth that would lead a man to the kingdom of God and to its fulness, how great shall be his condemnation and his punishment in eternity. For the destruction of a soul is the destruction of the greatest thing that has ever been created. (DS, Vol 1, pp. 313-314)

Various Moral Laws

Contained within this revelation are several verses pertaining to some of the Lord's moral laws. (Verses 18-29) He specifically mentioned the following:

1. *Thou Shalt Not Kill*

When a member of the church is guilty of wilfully taking the life of another child of God, the Lord's law specifies three penalties:

a. He shall not obtain forgiveness for his sin in this world or in the world to come. (See D&C 42:18) This means he will not have access to the redeeming powers of the Savior's atonement. He will bear the entire burden of this sin.

b. The murderer shall die. (See D&C 42:19)

c. He shall be delivered to and dealt with by the laws of the land. (See D&C 42:79)

2. *Thou Shalt Not Steal, Lie*

Stealing and lying are forms of dishonesty and the unrepentant church member who engages in such activity can expect two penalties:

a. Excommunication from the Lord's church. (See D&C 42:20-21) Such persons can not expect a Celestial inheritance, but will, instead, receive the Telestial Glory. (See D&C 76:98-109) It is a serious thing to be dishonest in the sight of the Lord. (For additional information on this topic, see CR, October 1977, p. 38; Also CR, October 1976, pp. 7-8)

b. Delivered up and dealt with by the law of the land. (See D&C 42:84-87; See also D&C 134:8) The jurisdiction of the church does not include the inflicting of punishment according to the laws of the land. For civil action, the Lord has directed that members of the church should be dealt with by civil authority.

3. *Thou Shalt Love Thy Wife*

The Lord requires a complete and total commitment of love between husband and wife in their marriage covenant relationships. He commanded:

> Thou shalt love thy wife with all thy heart, and shalt cleave unto her and none else. (D&C 42:22)

The phrase "all thy heart" means that each of the marriage partners is obligated to give total allegiance to, and do all things possible to build and strengthen love for one's companion in marriage. It is intended to be a total giving of self to each other.

The phrase "none else" eliminates any unrighteous interest or involvement with anyone or anything else. It also establishes a priority of interest. One's companion in marriage comes first before all else. Elder Spencer W. Kimball has taught:

> There are those married people who permit their eyes to wander and their hearts to become vagrant, who think it is not improper to flirt a little, to share their hearts, and have desire for someone other than the wife or the husband. The Lord says in no uncertain terms: "Thou shalt love thy wife with all thy heart, and shall cleave unto her and none else." (D&C 42:22)
>
> And, when the Lord says all thy heart, it allows for no sharing nor dividing nor depriving. And, to the woman it is paraphrased: "Thou shalt love thy husband with all thy heart and shall cleave unto him and none else." The words none else eliminate everyone and everything. The spouse then becomes preeminent in the life of the husband and wife, and neither social life nor occupational life nor political life nor any other interest nor person nor thing shall ever take precedence over the companion spouse. We sometimes find women who absorb and hover over the children at the expense

of the husband, sometimes even estranging them from him. The Lord says to them: " . . .thou shalt cleave unto him and none else."

Marriage presupposes total allegiance and total fidelity. Each spouse takes the partner with the understanding that he or she gives self totally to the spouse: all the heart, strength, loyalty, honor, and affection with all dignity. Any divergence is sin—any sharing the heart is transgression. As we should have "an eye single to the glory of God" so should we have an eye, an ear, a heart single to the marriage and the spouse and family.

Home-breaking is sin, and any thought, act, or association which will tend to destroy another's home is a grievous transgression.

Some who marry never cut themselves loose from the apron strings of the parents. The Lord says through his prophets: "For this cause shall a man [or woman] leave his father and mother, and shall be joined unto his wife [or husband], and they *two* shall be one flesh." (Eph. 5:31. italics added.)

Parents who hold, direct, and dictate to their married children and draw them away from their spouses are likely to regret the possible tragedy. Accordingly, when two people marry the spouse should become the confidant, the friend, the sharer of responsibility, and they two become independent. No one should come between the husband and wife, not even parents. (CR, October 1962, pp. 57-60)

4. *Thou Shalt Not Lust Nor Commit Adultery*

It is vital that everyone understands that lust is the catalyst for adultery. Eliminating lust prevents the overt act of adultery. In the Lord's law, the Savior warns against the disastrous results of courting lust and the ultimate consequences of such immoral action. He said:

> And he that looketh upon a woman to lust after her shall deny the faith, and shall not have the Spirit; and if he repents not he shall be cast out. (D&C 42:23)

The most immediate penalty that results from lustful desires is the loss of the spirit of the Lord. So important is it that we understand this concept, that the Lord emphasized it again when He said:

> And verily I say unto you, as I have said before, he that looketh on a woman to lust after her, or if any shall commit adultery in their

hearts, they shall not have the Spirit, but shall deny the faith and shall fear. (D&C 63:16)

He that fails to dispel lust from his soul becomes increasingly vulnerable to involvement in the deadly sin of adultery. The Lord made it very clear that such involvement without complete and total repentance would result in excommunication from the church. (See D&C 42:24-26) (For additional information, see *Miracle of Forgiveness*, Chapter 5.)

5.   *Thou Shalt Not Speak Evil of Thy Neighbor*

Disobedience to this commandment results in at least two consequences:

First, such a person labors under the false assumption that no harm is done to the neighbor as long as the neighbor is not aware of the nature of the conversation. But what about the person who speaks evil? He has yielded to the world's ways and violated the Lord's commandment to "love thy neighbor". Such a violation results in a lack of respect and love for a kindred spirit. Instead of love, concern, and interest in a child of God a satanical spirit develops which, if not eliminated, will destroy one's soul and his relationship with the Lord. The Lord's spirit cannot flow freely and the individual suffers from a retardation of spiritual growth.

Secondly, when one speaks evil of another, the listeners may be and oft times are persuaded to lower their esteem of their neighbor. The damaging result is that the potential impact for good the neighbor might have had is decreased. The opposite is also true. When one speaks well of his neighbor, his ability to influence others for good is enhanced.

The Law of Labor

The Lord expects His children to work. It was made clear to Adam that he would have to labor for his subsistence by the sweat of his brow. (See Bible, Genesis 3:17-19) This concept was echoed on Mount Sinai when the Lord gave the commandment:

Six days shalt thou labor, and do all thy work: (Bible, Exodus 20:9)

In the dispensation of the fullness of times the Lord has given the law unto His church:

Thou shalt not be idle; for he that is idle shall not eat the bread nor wear the garments of the laborer. (D&C 42:42)

On subsequent occasions, and from time to time, the Lord has reminded the saints of their sacred obligation to work. (See D&C 68:30; 75:29; 88:124)

This law of labor was beautifully explained by President J. Reuben Clark as follows:

> We must purge our hearts of the love of ease; we must put out from our lives the curse of idleness. God declared that mortal man should earn his bread by the sweat of his brow. That is the law of this world.
>
> For the decrepit and infirm, from any cause, I have, we all have, the deepest sympathy, as also for those in distress from causes beyond their control. To all such we owe a sacred duty to help. God's law has always been "Thou shalt love thy neighbor as thyself." This we must do. But side by side with this law is that other law, declared from the beginning, that while man can work, he must work. (CR, April 1937, pp. 26-27)

Laws Concerning Death and Administrations to the Sick

In this revelation we are enlightened on several things pertaining to death and illness.

Concerning death we learn:

1. It is appropriate to weep for the loss of a loved one. (See D&C 42:45)
2. Death is sweet to those who die in Christ; it is bitter to those who do not. (See D&C 42:46-47)

These two concepts were vividly illustrated as Mormon described conditions in Alma's day:

> And from the first year to the fifteenth has brought to pass the destruction of many thousand lives; yea, it has brought to pass an awful scene of bloodshed.
>
> And the bodies of many thousands are laid low in the earth, while the bodies of many thousands are moldering in heaps upon the face of the earth; yea, and many thousands are mourning for the loss of their kindred, because they have reason to fear, according to the promises of the Lord, that they are consigned to a state of endless woe.
>
> While many thousands of others truly mourn for the loss of their kindred, yet they rejoice and exalt in the hope, and even know, according to the promises of the Lord, that they are raised to dwell at the right hand of God, in a state of never-ending happiness. (B. of M., Alma 28:10-12)

If man can get the true concept of life he will understand that death is not a fearful end, but rather it becomes an important step in his ad-

vancement to continued life. One who had such perspective was President
Joseph F. Smith. He commented as follows:

> Every man that is born into the world will die. It matters not
> who he is, nor where he is, whether his birth be among the rich and
> the noble, or among the lowly and poor in the world, his days are
> numbered with the Lord, and in due time he will reach the end. We
> should think of this. Not that we should go about with heavy hearts
> or with downcast countenances; not at all. I rejoice that I am born to
> live, to die, and to live again. I thank God for this intelligence. It
> gives me joy and peace that the world cannot give, neither can the
> world take it away. God has revealed this to me, in the Gospel of
> Jesus Christ. I know it to be true. Therefore I have nothing to be sad
> over, nothing to make me sorrowful . . .
>
>   On the contrary, it is cause for joy unspeakable, and for pure
> happiness. I cannot express the joy I feel at the thought of meeting
> my father, and my precious mother, who gave me birth in the midst
> of persecution and poverty, who bore me in her arms and was
> patient, forbearing, tender and true during all my helpless
> moments in the world. The thought of meeting her, who can
> express the joy? The thought of meeting my children who have
> preceded me beyond the veil, and of meeting my kindred and my
> friends, what happiness it affords! For I know that I shall meet them
> there. God has shown me that this is true. He has made it clear to me
> in answer to my prayer and devotion as He has made it clear to the
> understanding of all men who have sought diligently to know Him.
> (CR, October 1899, pp. 70-71)

Pertaining to illness, we learn:

1. The Lord has provided foods and herbs (medicines) for the healing of
   the sick. (See D&C 42:43)
2. The Lord has directed the elders of the church to administer to the sick
   by the laying on of hands. (See D&C 42:44)
3. Faith is essential to our obtaining the blessings of the Lord. (See D&C
   42:48-52)
4. There is a time in life when man is appointed unto death. (See D&C
   42:48)

The inter-relationship of these principles is explained by President
Brigham Young:

> To explain how much confidence we should have in God, were
> I using a term to suit myself, I should say implicit confidence. I have

faith in my God, and that faith corresponds with the works I produce. I have no confidence in faith without works.

You may go to some people here, and ask what ails them, and they answer, 'I don't know, but we feel a dreadful distress in the stomach and in the back; we feel all out of order, and we wish you to lay hands upon us.' 'Have you used any remedies?' 'No. We wish the Elders to lay hands upon us, and we have faith that we shall be healed.' That is very inconsistent according to my faith. If we are sick, and ask the Lord to heal us, and to do all for us that is necessary to be done, according to my understanding of the Gospel of salvation, I might as well ask the Lord to cause my wheat and corn to grow, without my plowing the ground and casting in the seed. It appears consistent to me to apply every remedy that comes within the range of my knowledge, and to ask my Father in heaven, in the name of Jesus Christ, to sanctify that application to the healing of my body; to another this may appear inconsistent.

But supposing we were traveling in the mountains, and all we had or could get, in the shape of nourishment, was a little venison, and one or two were taken sick, without anything in the world in the shape of healing medicine within our reach, what should we do? According to my faith, ask the Lord Almighty to send an angel to heal the sick. This is our privilege, when so situated that we cannot get anything to help ourselves. Then the Lord and his servants can do all. But it is my duty to do, when I have it in my power. Many people are unwilling to do one thing for themselves, in case of sickness, but ask God to do it all. (JD, Vol. 4, pp. 24-25)

Laws of Remuneration for Goods and Services

The Lord has made it clear that the laborer is worthy of his hire. This concept was revealed in Doctrine and Covenants Section 24, and was discussed in Chapter 16 of this text. Now, in this revelation, the Lord gave His law as it pertains to those who labor full-time in church service. (See D&C 42:53-55, 70-73) In subsequent revelations, the Lord also made reference to this principle as it applied to his saints in various circumstances. (See D&C 43:11-14; 70:12; 106:1-3)

Laws Concerning Appropriate Action Pertaining to Transgressors In the Lord's Church

Transgression occurs in many forms. There are varying degrees of seriousness of sin. It is impossible for man to comprehend or legislate all courses of action that should appropriately be taken in dealing with transgressors. Consequently, the Lord has described basic principles and established some fundamental laws by which His kingdom should be administered. He has also charged the officers of His church with the responsibility of seeking the spirit for guidance that they may deal justly with every case.

Some of these fundamental laws are contained in this portion of the revelation (See D&C 42:74-93) Some of these were discussed in relationship to the moral laws presented earlier in this chapter. Time and space prevent commenting on all aspects of these verses, but one area not previously discussed, will receive our attention. We refer specifically to the handling of offenses or differences that arise between the saints.

Commonly, when members of the Church are offended, they alienate themselves from the offender and discuss the issue instead, with others who are not party to the offense. Such behavior is not in keeping with the Lord's instructions. He has specifically instructed that the offended one should go to the offender for the purpose of being reconciled. If reconciliation is not realized, then the course of action should be to seek the counsel and judgment from presiding officers of the church. Such discussions should be held privately with utmost confidence. Any necessary rebuking procedures should be limited to those who are necessarily involved in the case. (See D&C 42:88-92)

If saints would be obedient in following this counsel, vicious rumors would be eliminated, tender hearts would not be bruised, the spiritual welfare of the individual would be uppermost in the minds and hearts of members and love for one another would be the supreme influence in our relationships.

Summary and Conclusion

This revelation is not the end of the Lord's laws to His church. But it is full of fundamental laws upon which the church is still governed.

All laws of God are given in love for the purpose of bringing happiness to the obedient children of God. We are reminded that the Savior identified His disciples as those who receiveth His laws and doeth them. (See D&C 41:5)

Chapter 33

Doctrine and Covenants Section 43

Suggested Title

The Lord's Law of Revelation to His Church—Some Duties of His Saints

Overview of Section Content

1. The Lord's law of revelation to His church (vs. 1-7)
2. Some duties of Church members when assembled together (vs. 8-11)
3. Church members responsible to uphold and support the Lord's prophet (vs. 12-14)
4. Elders of the Church to teach and assist in the preparation for the Savior's second coming (vs. 15-28)
5. Promises and events associated with the millennial period and the end of the earth (vs. 29-33)
6. The Savior's charge (vs. 34-35)

Historical Setting

Joseph Smith, Jun.

Soon after the foregoing revelation was received [Section 42], a woman came making great pretensions of revealing commandments, laws and other curious matters; and as almost every person has advocates for both theory and practice, in the various notions

207

and projects of the age, it became necessary to inquire of the Lord, when I received the following. (HC, Vol. 1, p. 154)

B.H. Roberts

This woman's name, according to the history of the church kept by John Whitmer, was Hubble. "She professed to be a prophetess of the Lord, and professed to have many revelations, and knew the Book of Mormon was true, and that she should become a teacher in the church of Christ. She appeared to be very sanctimonious and deceived some who were not able to detect her in her hypocrisy; others, however, had the spirit of discernment and her follies and abominations were manifest." John Whitmer's *History of the Church*, ch. iii. (HC, Vol. 1, p. 154, Footnote)

Sacred Truths

Introduction

Less than six months had passed since some of the members of the Church had been deceived when they assumed that people, other than the Lord's prophet, could be authorized to receive revelation for the Lord's church. In the revelation when the Lord corrected this false assumption He made it perfectly clear that He only authorizes one man, at any given time, to be His mouthpiece for the Church. (See D&C 28:1-6)

Now at this time (February 1831) a situation arose again wherein some of the saints were deceived by false revelation. The Lord then gave a revelation to the prophet Joseph Smith that further clarified and established the law by which the Lord directs His kingdom. He also specified some of the duties of His saints.

The Lord's Law of Revelation to His Church

The Lord said:

> For behold, verily, verily, I say unto you, that ye have received a commandment for a law unto my church [D&C 42], through him whom I have appointed unto you [Joseph Smith] to receive commandments and revelations from my hand.
>
> And this ye shall know assuredly—that there is none other appointed unto you to receive commandments and revelations until he be taken, if he abide in me.
>
> And this shall be a law unto you, that ye receive not the teachings of any [other than the prophet] that shall come before you as revelations or commandments; (D&C 43:2-3, 5)

Commenting upon this law, Elder Joseph Fielding Smith has said:

> In this heavenly communication, the Lord gives positive instruction to the Church in relation to the order by which revelation is to be received. Common sense should teach us the wisdom of this commandment without it becoming necessary for the Lord to give counsel such as this revelation contains. There is order in the kingdom of God. There could not be order if every man was privileged to give commandments and claim the right to direct by revelation the members of the Church.
>
> This law is given for our government for all time. It is the one who holds the keys and who stands as the Presiding High Priest and President of the Church, who is the spokesman of the Lord for the members of the Church. Individual members may receive the inspiration and revelation for their own guidance, but not for the Church. Moreover, no member of the Church will profess to receive a revelation for his own guidance, that is contradictory of any revelation coming from the President of the Church. (CHMR, Vol. 1, pp. 171-172)

In this revelation the Lord indicated the necessity for His prophet to come through the gate as designated by the Lord. Elder Joseph Fielding Smith described this process as follows:

> . . .Some Latter-day Saints, because of their lack of knowledge, have been deceived into following false teachers and 'prophets' because they have never learned the simple truth which the Lord makes so plain in this revelation;
>
> For verily I say unto you, that he that is ordained of me shall come in at the gate and be ordained as I have told you before, to teach those revelations which you have received and shall receive through him whom I have appointed. (D&C 43:7)
>
> This commandment is the key by which the members of the Church are to be governed and protected from all those who profess to be appointed and empowered to guide the Church.
>
> . . .We frequently hear discussions in our classes and between brethren to the effect that any man could be called, if the authorities should choose him to preside over the Church and that it is not the fixed order to take the senior apostle to preside, and any member of the quorum could be appointed. The fact is that the senior apostle automatically becomes the presiding officer of the Church on the death of the President. If some other man were to be chosen, then the senior would have to receive the revelation setting himself

aside. President John Taylor has made this very plain. (See "Succession In the Priesthood," Chapter 17, "The Gospel Kingdom.") Says President Taylor, speaking of the time following President Young's death: "I occupied the senior position in the quorum, and occupying that position which was thoroughly understood by the quorum of the twelve, on the death of President Young, as the twelve assumed the presidency, and I was their president, it placed me in a position of president of the Church, or, as expressed in our conference meeting; 'As president of the quorum of the twelve apostles, as one of the twelve apostles, as one of the presidency of the Church of Jesus Christ of Latter-day Saints.' In this manner, also, was President Brigham Young sustained, at the general conference held in Nauvoo, in October following the martyrdom of the Prophet Joseph Smith." (Gospel Kingdom, p. 192) The counselors in the presidency cease to be counselors when the President dies and take their regular place among their brethren. (CHMR, Vol. 1, pp. 172-173)

Through the giving of this law, the Lord has established a means of protection for the saints that they might never be deceived. (See D&C 43:6) Any revelation that comes from the Lord to His church will always come through the one man who has come through the gate and is the senior apostle of Jesus Christ. He will be the one who presides over the Lord's kingdom. This is the law of revelation to the Lord's church.

As a most fitting summary, we refer to the words of President George Q. Cannon.

Now, there is only one way in which the commandments of God can be revealed unto us. God has not left this in doubt. He has not left us to grope in the dark respecting His methods of revealing His mind and will unto His children. In the very beginning of the work of God in these last days, to remove all doubt upon this subject, God gave revelations unto this Church in exceeding great plainness, and there was one principle that was emphatically dwelt upon and enforced, namely, that there was but one channel, one channel alone, through which the word of God and the commandments of God should come to this people. The word of God was not to come from the people up. It was not *vox populi, vox dei*, but it was to be *vox dei, vox populi*—that is, the voice of God and then the voice of the People—from God downward through the channel that He should appoint; by the means that He should institute, that word should come to the people, and when obeyed by the people would bring the union and the love and the strength consequent upon union and love. And this has been the peculiarity and the excellence of this work of God thus far in the earth. Its excellence has consisted in this. Its power, its glory, the glory that we have as a people, the glory that belongs to the Church of God consists in this peculiar feature, that the word of God to us comes from God and not from the people. It is received by the people, accepted by the people, submitted to by the people, and this has produced the union and the love, as I have said, that have characterized the work thus far in its progress in the earth. Take away from it this feature and it becomes weak as water that is unconfined. There is no strength to it. There is nothing to be feared about it. There is nothing to excite animosity or hatred. But give it this feature and it becomes a power in the earth. Even if there were only six men it would be a power. Let there be twelve and it is twice the power, and you go on doubling it, and it increases in a proportionate ratio, and it will do so, as long as that principle is maintained and lived up to. God revealed that principle in the beginning. (J.D., Vol. 24, pp. 362-363)   *George Q. Cannon*

Some Duties of the Saints

After the Lord had explained and given His law of revelation to His church in order to prevent deception amongst the membership, He gave, by way of commandment, several instructions for the saints to follow. Those who follow these instructions are not deceived. The Lord gave direction in at least three important areas:

1. *When assembled—instruct and edify* (See D&C 43:8-10)

One has protection from being deceived when he is assembled with the saints under authorized leadership. Part of the reason for such protection is that instructions are given in company with the spirit that edifies and is a sanctifying influence in one's life. It is apparent that anyone who has received the Lord's authority to direct the saints when assembled, is under strict command from the Lord to teach the law and commandments so that the saints are edified and sanctified. Failure to be obedient to this divine commandment results in the loss of spiritual truths and powers. On the other hand, obedience brings glory to the Lord's kingdom. (See D&C 43:10) If the Lord's people are obedient they will avoid travelogs or other presentations as substitutions for the gospel that serve no spiritual purpose.

2. *Uphold and support the Lord's prophet* (See D&C 43:11-14)

Of equal importance for protection against deception and that we might obtain the glories and mysteries of the kingdom, the Lord directed the membership to sustain and support His prophet in two ways:

a. Through the prayer of faith
b. Physical or temporal necessities of life

Failure to comply with this divine directive results in the loss of access to the Lord's instructions as revealed through His mouthpiece, the prophet. Such people are vulnerable to the deceptive powers of Satan. On the other hand, obedience purifies the Saints before the Lord. (See D&C 43:14)

3.   Teach the world—be instructed from on high—prepare for the Savior's Second Coming (See D&C 43:15-28)

One common way by which people are deceived, is for them to receive teachings and philosophies of the world as though they were always in harmony with gospel truths from the Lord. The Lord's church is the depository of all revealed gospel truth. All things pertinent to salvation are found within the scope of Church teachings. These teachings are the standard by which all other things are measured. The Church is the custodian of these divine truths and is responsible to take such teachings to the world to assist in preparing for the Savior's second coming. The Savior has instructed as follows:

> Again I say, hearken ye elders of my church, whom I have appointed: Ye are not sent forth to be taught, but to teach the children of men the things which I have put into your hands by the power of my Spirit;
>
> And ye are to be taught from on high. Sanctify yourselves and ye shall be endowed with power, that ye may give even as I have spoken. (D&C 43:15-16)

Summary and Conclusion

The Lord revealed several things pertaining to His second coming, the millennial period, and the end of the earth. (See D&C 43:29-33) In order that we might not be deceived and thus be prepared for these events yet future, the Lord gave the following charge:

> Hearken ye to these words. Behold, I am Jesus Christ, the Savior of the world. Treasure these things up in your hearts, and let the solemnities of eternity rest upon your minds.
>
> Be sober. Keep all my commandments. Even so. Amen. (D&C 43:34-35)

Chapter 34

Doctrine and Covenants
Section 44

Suggested Title

Elders Summoned to Kirtland—One Reason The Lord Gathers His People

Overview of Section Content

1. Elders to assemble together—A promise (vs. 1-2)
2. Saints to obtain power by organizing according to laws of man (vs. 3-5)
3. Temporary temporal care for the needy in the church until implementation of the law of consecration (vs. 6)

Historical Setting

Joseph Smith, Jun.

The latter part of February I received the following revelation, which caused the Church to appoint a conference to be held early in the month of June ensuing: . . .(HC, Vol. 1, p. 157)

Hyrum M. Smith and Janne M. Sjodahl

In the latter part of February, 1831, the Lord directed that the missionaries who had gone to the various parts of the Country be summoned to Kirtland to meet in a General Conference. Three

Conferences had been held before, viz., one on June 9th, 1830; one
on September 26th, the same year, and one on January 2nd, 1831.
These were all held at Fayette, N.Y. The Conference referred to in
this Revelation convened at Kirtland, June 3rd, 1831. It was the
Fourth General Conference of the Church, and the first gathering of
its kind in Kirtland. (DCC, p. 249)

Sacred Truths

Introduction

As a result of this revelation, the fourth General Conference of the
Church was appointed to be held in June 1831. This conference was held in
Kirtland, Ohio. In this revelation the Lord called the elders from the various
parts of the country to be in attendance. (See D&C 44:1-2)

One Reason The Lord Gathers His People

In this revelation, the Lord revealed one of the reasons why He directs
His saints to gather. As converts come into the Church and congregations
grow in size, they are able to "...organize [themselves] according to the
laws of man;" (D&C 44:4) When the saints are gathered in sufficient
numbers, they are able to register their votes in greater proportion to the
populace. They can participate in municipal government and have a voice
in determining the laws and practices of local organizations.

The blessings derived from such gathering are revealed as follows:

> ...your enemies may not have power over you; that you may
> be preserved in all things; that you may be enabled to keep my
> laws; that every bond may be broken wherewith the enemy seeketh
> to destroy my people. (D&C 44:5)

The history of the Church reveals that when the saints have been able
to follow the pattern of this revelation, their enemies have not been able to
destroy or hamper the work of the Lord through legal means. Denied this
protection, the saints have been subjected, instead, to mobocracy from
their enemies in their efforts to destroy the Lord's work. This was the case
in the Missouri, Illinois, and the early Utah periods.

Though much suffering resulted from mob action, yet the saints were
given a certain amount of time while being shielded by the law before their
enemies resorted to mob actions. This time proved valuable in that they
were able to build temples, print the revelations and to live and be
governed within the framework of the Church.

Saints are wise who can learn from this revelation. When the Lord
directs His people, they need to obey.

Chapter 35

Doctrine and Covenants
Section 45

Suggested Title

The Savior's Second Coming

Overview of Section Content

1. The Lord admonishes His saints to hearken to His voice (vs. 1-15)
2. The Lord to prophesy as in days of old (vs. 15-17)
3. Signs of the Savior's second coming that were fulfilled in the Savior's generation (vs. 18-24)
4. Signs of the Savior's second coming that will be fulfilled in the dispensation of the fulness of times (vs. 25-44)
5. The Savior's appearance to the saints and the first resurrection (vs. 45-46, 54)
6. The Savior's appearance to the Jews at Jerusalem (vs. 47-53)
7. Conditions prior to and during the millennium (vs. 55-59)
8. Instructions concerning the translation of the Bible (vs. 60-61)
9. Prophecy of wars (vs. 62-63)
10. The saints to gather and build the New Jerusalem (vs. 64-73)
11. The Savior's appearance to the world (vs. 74-75)

Historical Setting

In the previous revelation (Section 44) the Lord instructed the Prophet Joseph Smith to summon the elders to Kirtland. The Lord foretold how their labors would result in the conversion of many. Once Lucifer was aware of the Lord's plans he proceeded to poison the minds of as many people as possible before the arrival of the elders. Commenting on this opposition to the Lord's work, the prophet wrote:

Joseph Smith, Jun.

At this age of the Church [i.e., early in the spring of 1831] many false reports, lies, and foolish stories, were published in the news-papers, and circulated in every direction, to prevent people from investigating the work, or embracing the faith. A great earthquake in China, which destroyed from one to two thousand inhabitants, was burlesqued in some papers, as " 'Mormonism' in China." But to the joy of the Saints who had to struggle against every thing that prejudice and wickedness could invent, I received the following: . . .(HC, Vol. 1, p. 158)

B.H. Roberts

This earthquake in China is a matter of some interest in connection with the history of the church, since it was the means of bringing Simonds Ryder, a somewhat noted preacher of the Camp-bellite faith, into the Church. According to *Hayden's History of the Disciples on the Western Reserve* (a Campbellite book), Mr. Ryder was much perplexed over "Mormonism," and for a time was undecided whether to join the Church or not. "In the month of June," (1831), writes Mr. Hayden, "he read in a newspaper an account of the destruction of Peking in China, and he remembered that six weeks before, a young 'Mormon' girl had predicted the destruction of that city." J.H. Kennedy, in his *Early Days in Mormonism* (Scribner's & Sons, 1888), refers to the same thing, and adds: "This appeal to the superstitious part of his nature was the final weight in the balance and he threw the whole power of his influence upon the side of 'Mormonism.' His surrender caused an excitement almost equal to that which followed the fall of Rigdon." (pp. 103-4) It was doubtless this prophecy and the conversion connected with it that led the papers mentioned in the text to refer to it as " 'Mormonism' in China." The discrepancy in dates, Hayden and Kennedy referring to the published accounts of the events as appearing in June, and the Prophet making reference to it previous to the 7th of March, need cause no confusion. It will be seen that the Prophet alludes to it in connection with a number of other things as taking place "at this age of the Church"—a very indefinite reference as to the time in which a thing may have occurred. (HC, Vol. 1, p. 158, Footnote)

Sacred Truths

Introduction

In this chapter, we will discuss the following two topics:

1. Signs of the Savior's second coming
2. The Savior's appearances at His second coming

Inasmuch as section 88 of the Doctrine and Covenants provides additional information pertaining to the first and second resurrections, a discussion of those topics will be deferred and found in Volume II, Chapter 17.

Since information pertaining to the millennial era is provided in additional detail in section 101 of the Doctrine and Covenants a discussion of this subject will also be deferred and will be found in Volume II, Chapter 30.

As noted in the historical setting, the Church was subject to slanderous and false accusations during this period of time. It must have been refreshing to the Saints to know the Lord was conscious of their feelings when He provided this revelation intended for their joy and edification.

Several times in the first fifteen verses of this revelation, the Lord stressed the need for the Church to hearken to His voice. By listening to Him, the Saints are comforted in the midst of satanic efforts to discredit the work.

The content of this revelation can best be understood when one realizes that the Lord is sharing with us, a conversation he had with His disciples at the time of His earthly ministry. (See D&C 45:15-16)

Signs of the Lord's Second Coming

We learn from this revelation that the Savior's disciples were anxious to know more about the signs of the Savior's second coming. (See D&C 45:16) The reason for their anxiety was as follows:

> For as ye have looked upon the long absence of your spirits from your bodies to be a bondage, I will show unto you how the day of redemption shall come, and also the restoration of the scattered Israel. (D&C 45:17)

The following commentaries are particularly helpful in understanding the concerns of the disciples:

> One reason for their anxiety to know the signs is here stated. The separation of the spirits from the bodies is, even to those who

are Christ's own, a "bondage," which is ended only by a glorious resurrection, and they were interested in knowing by what signs they might recognize that their day of redemption was drawing near, when spirit and body should be united. The departed saints are, we may be sure, looking for the signs of the coming of the Lord, with an intense interest as the saints still in mortality. Jesus graciously showed them "how the day of redemption shall come, and also the restoration of scattered Israel." (DCC, p. 259)

When we go out of this life, leave this body, we will desire to do many things that we cannot do at all without the body. We will be seriously handicapped, and we will long for the body; we will pray for the early reunion with our bodies. We will know then what advantage it is to have a body.

Then every man and woman who is putting off until the next life the task of correcting and overcoming the weakness of the flesh are sentencing themselves to years of bondage, for no man or woman will come forth in the resurrection until he has completed his work, until he has overcome, until he has done as much as he can do. (Melvin J. Ballard—Crusader for Righteousness, p. 213)

Responding to the concerns and desires of His disciples, the Savior prophesied of several events. The fulfillment of these events would serve as signs to them of the Lord's approaching second coming. These signs can be categorized into the following two major time periods:

1.   *The Savior's Generation* (See D&C 45:18-24)

Three events are recorded that would take place during the time of the Savior's own generation. He mentioned:

a. Destruction of the temple in Jerusalem
b. Desolation and destruction of the Jewish nation
c. Scattering of the Jews among all nations

It is clear to any student of history that these prophecies were fulfilled to the same detail the Lord described. Yet, at the time of the Lord's utterance, few would have thought it possible for such dramatic events to ever take place. There is a lesson to be learned. Just as surely as there was a fulfillment of these signs, even so certainly shall there be a fulfillment of the signs predicted to take place in this last dispensation.

2.   *The Dispensation of the Fulness of Times* (See D&C 45:25-44)

Contained in this revelation, as well as in a number of other scriptural sources (such as D&C section 29), are many signs that are now being and will yet be fulfilled. We must not forget the purpose of these signs. He who recognizes them has added assurance of the imminence of the return of the Savior to the earth. A reflection on these signs brings a witness of the reality of the second coming of Jesus Christ.

We will discuss a few of these signs:

The Lord said a remnant of the Jews would be gathered back to Jerusalem (See D&C 45:25) They are there. Is this not a witness?

An event coinciding with the return of the Jews is the restoration of the fulness of the gospel. (See D&C 45:25, 28) It has been restored. Is this not a witness?

There will be wars and rumors of wars and the whole earth will be in commotion. (See D&C 45:26) This describes conditions now. Is this not a witness?

Love of men will wax cold and iniquity shall abound. (See D&C 45:27) In light of the murders, abortions, and other evil practices, again we see a description of current conditions. Again: Is this not a witness?

There will be disciples of Christ who shall stand in holy places (standing firm in covenant commitments) and will not be moved (standing apart from the evil practices of the world). (See D&C 45:32) Many saints are firm in their faith. And is this not a witness?

To the honest in heart who read by the spirit the signs are clear. There is no doubt. Jesus Christ lives and is coming.

The Savior's Appearances At His Second Coming

We learn from this revelation that the Savior's second coming includes at least three general appearances:

1. *To the saints* (See D&C 45:45-46, 56-57)

We would make a few brief observations concerning these appearances. Referring to the saints receiving the Savior, it should be noted that these are people who have made and kept covenants with the Lord. They are referred to as "children of light" (D&C 106:5) These are they who have heeded the counsel of the Lord to:

> Gird up your loins and be watchful and be sober, looking forth
> for the coming of the Son of Man, for he cometh in an hour you
> think not. (D&C 61:38)

These saints received the truth, received the Holy Ghost, and were not deceived, thus fulfilling the parable concerning the five wise virgins. (See D&C 45:56-57)

2. *To the Jews at Jerusalem* (See D&C 45:47-53)

The Lord's appearance to the Jews will take place at a time when they will be engaged in a battle for their survival. When the Savior intervenes in their behalf, He will be recognized and acknowledged as the Messiah and Savior of the world.

3. *To the world* (See D&C 45:74-75)

The Lord's appearance to the world will not be to a select group of people. This appearance will be of such magnitude that the wicked will be destroyed and the remaining righteous will see, know, and dwell with Him upon the earth for a millenial period.

Summary and Conclusion

We remember the words of the Savior in His preface to His book:

> Search these commandments, for they are true and faithful, and the prophecies and promises which are in them shall all be fulfilled. (D&C 1:37)

One of the great revelations containing prophecies and promises is D&C Section 45. There is one major conclusion to be drawn from that which is recorded in this revelation. There is sufficient evidence that the signs foretold by Jesus Christ have been, are now being, and will yet be fulfilled. They all bear witness that Jesus lives and He will return to reign upon the earth.

Chapter 36

Doctrine and Covenants Section 46

Suggested Title

Public Church Meetings—Guidance by the Holy Spirit—
Gifts of the Holy Spirit

Overview of Section Content

1. Church meetings are to be conducted by the spirit (vs. 1-2)
2. No one who earnestly seeks the kingdom is to be excluded from public church meetings (vs. 3-6)
3. Gifts of the spirit provide protection against deception for saints who properly seek them (vs. 7-10)
4. Various gifts of the spirit (vs. 11-33)

Historical Setting

Joseph Smith, Jun.

The next day after the above was received, [Section 45] I also received the following revelation, relative to the gifts of the Holy Ghost: . . . (HC, Vol. 1, p. 163)

B.H. Roberts

. . .With reference to the matters mentioned in verses 1-7 in this revelation, John Whitmer writes: "In the beginning of the

Church, while yet in her infancy, the disciples used to exclude unbelievers, which caused some to marvel and converse of this matter because of the things written in the Book of Mormon. [3 Nephi 18:22-34] Therefore the Lord deigned to speak on this subject, that His people might come to understanding, and said that He had always given to His Elders to conduct all meetings as they were led by the Spirit." —John Whitmer's *History of the Church*, Ch. 4. (HC, Vol. 1, pp. 163-164, Footnote)

Sacred Truths

Introduction

Though this revelation was given as a result of the problem described in the historical setting in this chapter, the Lord's answer contained a principle that is much broader and more far-reaching than the original problem might have suggested. The Lord gave the church the answer to the question pertaining to non-member attendance at public church meetings. (See D&C 46:3-6) However, this problem, like every other problem, should be resolved by applying the teachings revealed in this revelation. We will discuss three of these teachings in this chapter:

1. Guidance by the Holy Spirit
2. Protection against deception
3. Gifts of the Holy Spirit

Guidance By The Holy Spirit

The Lord said:

> But not withstanding those things which are written, it always has been given to the elders of my church from the beginning, and ever shall be, to conduct all meetings as they are directed and guided by the Holy Spirit. (D&C 46:2)

In the above quoted verse, the Lord reminds us of the importance of modern-day revelation. Though instruction had been given and recorded in an ancient scriptural text (Book of Mormon), the way it was to be applied in a modern-problem setting was not clear. The Lord instructed the brethren, that the guidance of the spirit was the way by which the program of His Church should be conducted and problems should be solved. In other words, handbooks of instruction (important though they may be) will never contain answers to all problems. We must always rely upon spiritual guidance, coupled with that which has been previously given, to do that which is right in the sight of the Lord.

Protection Against Deception

One of the purposes of having the Holy Spirit for our guidance is that we might make decisions in harmony with the Lord's will. Failure to respond to such guidance may very easily result in making unwise decisions and yielding to temptation. We would then be vulnerable to the influence of the adversary and be much more subject to deception.

Protection against deception is assured when we follow the counsel of the Lord, who said:

> But ye are commanded in all things to ask of God, who giveth liberally; and that which the Spirit testifies unto you even so I would that ye should do in all holiness of heart, walking uprightly before me, considering the end of your salvation, doing all things with prayer and thanksgiving, that ye may not be seduced by evil spirits, or doctrines of devils, or the commandments of men; for some are of men, and others of devils. (D&C 46:7)

The Lord commanded us to pray and seek divine guidance in all things that we might avoid deception. We are also directed to seek for the specific ways by which the Holy Spirit can provide spiritual help and insight and thus avoid deception. Those specific helps are referred to as the gifts of the spirit. As pertaining to the gifts and our opportunity to receive the benefits thereof, the Lord directed:

> Wherefore, beware lest ye are deceived; and that ye may not be deceived seek ye earnestly the best gifts, always remembering for what they are given:
> For verily I say unto you, they are given for the benefit of those who love me and keep all my commandments, and him that seeketh so to do; that all may be benefited that seek or that ask of me, that ask and not for a sign that they may consume it upon their lusts.
> And again, verily I say unto you, I would that ye should always remember, and always retain in your minds what those gifts are, that are given unto the church.
> For all have not every gift given unto them; for there are many gifts, and to every man is given a gift by the Spirit of God. (D&C 46:8-11)

Gifts of the Holy Spirit

There are several important principles revealed in the verses quoted above. For instance, the Lord declared that we must earnestly "seek" these gifts. He will not force them upon us nor will they be accessible to us until we make a personal effort to obtain them.

These gifts are available and will be given to those " . . .who love me and keep all my commandments, and him that seeketh so to do, . . ." (D&C 46:9) There are two categories of people mentioned here. There are those among us who are so conducting their lives that they are in harmony with the Savior by keeping His commandments. Though they are not perfect they have acquired the ability to keep the commandments. There are also many among us whose hearts and desires are right and are earnestly striving to develop the capacity to keep His commandments. Both of these groups of people are promised by the Lord that they will not seek these gifts in vain.

From these verses we also learn that we have a responsibility to " . . .always remember, and always retain in [our] minds what those gifts are, . . ." (D&C 46:10) There are many gifts of the spirit. They are not all mentioned in any one place but reference is made of them throughout the scriptures. one would find several of these gifts spoken of by reading the following:

1. Bible, 1 Corinthians Chapters 12 through 14
2. B. of M., Moroni Chapter 10
3. D&C Section 46

The Lord told us to seek the "best gifts." (D&C 46:8) What makes a gift "best"? Simply stated, it is that gift which best satisfies the need and provides the desired spiritual assistance at a given time and according to the circumstances at that time. It is comforting to know that the earnest seeker can receive one or more of these gifts whenever need arises. Elder Joseph Fielding Smith has said:

> That the saints might not be deceived the Lord pointed out to them the proper gifts of the Spirit (Section 46) which are distributed among the members as the Lord sees good to bestow. Yet more than one gift may be received by any person [Saints] who diligently seeks for these things . . .(CHMR, Vol. 1, p. 184)

These gifts have benefited and blessed the lives of many members of the church. We will comment on three specific gifts mentioned in this revelation:

1. Gift of Prophecy

To help with our understanding of the usefulness of this gift, Elder Joseph Fielding Smith has taught:

> All members of the church should seek for the gift of

prophecy, for their own guidance, which is the spirit by which the word of the Lord is understood and his purposes made known. (See 1 Cor. 14:1) (CHMR, Vol. 1, p. 184)

The word of the Lord is declared to the world through living prophets who are endowed with the gift of prophecy. Therefore, if we are to recognize and understand their messages and teachings we must also seek that same gift. It is vital that we recall the value of these gifts. This gift along with all of the others, is truly a protection against deception. (See D&C 46:8)

2.   *Gift of Tongues*

This gift is blessing the lives of people all over the earth. Because of it's power, men and women are able to communicate the teachings of the gospel to one another in the various languages of the world. The Prophet Joseph Smith declared that "[the gift of] tongues were [was] given for the purpose of preaching among those whose language is not understood; . . ." (TPJS, pp. 148-149) How beautifully this principle is manifested as missionaries of the church seek for and receive the gift of tongues in connection with their learning of languages that they might teach the gospel in countries of foreign language.

3.   *Gift of Knowing Jesus Christ is the Son of God*

One of the greatest gifts of all is to know Jesus Christ. It is only through the power of the Holy Spirit that such knowledge is given. (See Bible, 1 Corinthians 12:3; D&C 46:13) Many people do not have such knowledge. The attainment of such comes sometimes by hearing others testify that they know that Jesus is the Christ. Their testimony carries the witness of the spirit and the hearer can know that the testimony is true. It is given to him to "believe on their words, . . ." (D&C 46:14) Speaking of this spiritual gift, President Harold B. Lee taught a group of Latter-day Saint college students as follows:

You young Latter-day Saints here tonight, some of you may not have that testimony as firmly rooted as you would like to. May I ask you then, if you don't have, to cling to my testimony tonight, until you can develop one for yourselves. Say that you believe in one who holds the holy apostleship, that you believe what I said and then you start now to so search in the way that the scriptures have told us, as I have explained to you here tonight, until you too can say, as I say tonight, yes I know, by a witness that is more powerful than sight, I know that Jesus is the Savior of the world. (LDSSA Fireside, Utah State University, October 1971)

Summary and Conclusion

As we conclude this chapter, we hearken back to the major principle emphasized in this revelation. As covenant people in the Lord's church we need to be governed and directed by the influence of the Holy Spirit. To aid us in this endeavor, the Lord has extended help to us through the many gifts of the Holy Spirit. We must, however, seek them for righteous purposes. The Prophet Joseph Smith cautioned:

> The gifts of God are all useful in their place, but when they are applied to that which God does not intend, they prove an injury, a snare and a curse instead of a blessing. (HC, Vol. 5, pp. 31-32)

Emphasizing the blessing these gifts can be in our lives, President George Q. Cannon has said:

> How many of you . . .are seeking for these gifts that God has promised to bestow? How many of you, when you bow before your Heavenly Father in your family circle or in your secret places, contend for these gifts to be bestowed upon you? How many of you ask the Father, in the name of Jesus, to manifest Himself to you through these powers and these gifts? . . .
>
> If any of us are imperfect, it is our duty to pray for the gift that will make us perfect. Have I imperfections? I am full of them. What is my duty? To pray to God to give me the gifts that will correct these imperfections. If I am an angry man, it is my duty to pray for charity, which suffereth long and is kind. Am I an envious man? It is my duty to seek for charity, which envieth not. So with all the gifts of the Gospel. They are intended for this purpose. No man ought to say, "Oh, I cannot help this; it is my nature." He is not justified in it, for the reason that God has promised to give strength to correct these things, and to give gifts that will eradicate them. If a man lacks wisdom, it is his duty to ask God for wisdom. The same with everything else. That is the design of God concerning His Church. He wants His Saints to be perfected in the truth. For this purpose He gives these gifts, and bestows them upon those who seek after them, in order that they may be a perfect people upon the face of the earth, notwithstanding their many weaknesses, because God has promised to give the gifts that are necessary for their perfection. (MS, Vol. 56, pp. 260-261, Apr, 23, 1894)

Chapter 37

Doctrine and Covenants Section 47

Suggested Title

John Whitmer—Church Historian

Overview of Section Content

The Lord calls John Whitmer to write and keep the history of the Church. (vs. 1-4)

Historical Setting

Joseph Smith, Jun.

The same day that I received the foregoing revelation, [Section 46] I also received the following, setting apart John Whitmer as a historian, inasmuch as he is faithful: . . . (HC, Vol. 1, p. 166)

B.H. Roberts

Previous to this, Oliver Cowdery had acted as historian and recorder. John Whitmer, according to his own representations, said he would rather not keep the Church history, but observed—"The will of the Lord be done, and if He desires it, I wish that He would manifest it through Joseph the Seer."—John Whitmer's *History of the Church*, ch. vi.—accordingly the revelation was given. (HC, Vol. 1, p. 166, Footnote)

Sacred Truths

Introduction

The importance of record keeping has been emphasized by the Lord. On the day His Church was organized (April 6, 1830), the Lord commanded that a record be kept. (See D&C 21:1) From that day to the present, various people have been called to direct and assist in this endeavor. In 1831, John Whitmer was called by revelation to be the Church Historian. (See D&C Section 47)

Because of the faithfulness of the Lord's servants since the beginning of man's history, we now reap the benefits of their endeavors. We have at our disposal volumes of records which give evidence of the Lord's dealings with mankind. It is from ancient as well as modern records that we are able to read the revelations of the Lord to His people. We learn of people who have struggled, who have feared, who have loved, who have succeeded, who have failed, and who have lived lives with and without covenants. But the most important message that we read is that there have been people who had hope in Jesus Christ since the beginning of mankind. These teachings are given to us through the medium of records written by faithful historians over the centuries.

In this chapter we will discuss the sacred nature of records as well as John Whitmer's contribution to the recorded history of the church.

Sacred Records

There is a related lesson that can be drawn from this revelation. Record keeping is not restricted to those who keep the history of the church. All members of the Church have been counseled to keep personal histories. Though we may not be appointed Church Historian's, we are all responsible to be historians in the Church. Each of us is charged with the responsibility of recording our own history and providing a written record that can serve and benefit others who may read therefrom.

Members of the church have been counseled as to the value of this important endeavor as follows:

> The family books of remembrance in Latter-day Saint homes today should rate in importance second only to the standard works. These family records are supplements to the scriptures, aiding in teaching the gospel of Jesus Christ to the posterity of faithful members of the Church. A knowledge of the written testimonies and spiritual experiences of family members and of the proved genealogies of the fathers serves to bind the hearts of the children to their fathers and helps them to understand the doctrines that pertain to the exaltation of the family.

Every faithful family should be diligently compiling a book of remembrance. In it should be found the story of the family, especially the story of its spiritual life, written by inspiration. It should also contain a genealogy of the family so that the children may have an opportunity to acquire knowledge of their fathers. (I.E., April 1966, pp. 294-295)

John Whitmer's History of the Church

After his excommunication in 1838, John Whitmer refused to deliver to the Church the history written by himself. Because of his refusal to yield the historical documents, the Prophet Joseph Smith wrote him a letter in which he indicated that Church authorities would proceed to write a history of the Church in lieu therof. (See HC 3:5-16) At that point in time (1838), Joseph Smith proceeded to dictate and caused to be written accounts of the Church history from its beginning. This recording of history continued by various clerks appointed to assist Joseph in this work. From these records, the Church has published the "History of the Church" from its inception to the death of the Prophet Joseph Smith and a short time period thereafter. It should be noted that many years after Joseph's death, the Church acquired a copy of the brief history written by John Whitmer during the period from 1831 to 1838. Commenting on the nature of that history, Roy W. Doxey has written:

The history of the Church written by John Whitmer was only 'a mere sketch of the things that transpired.' His total work consisted of eighty-five pages which included many of the revelations given while he was in office. During the period when many brethren became disaffected, he was in the Presidency of the Church in Missouri. The members of the Church in that area did not sustain him and his associates in the Presidency. Although the presiding brethren demanded that he deliver the history of the Church to them he refused. Years after his death, a copy of the history was obtained by the Church. (D&C Speaks, Vol. 1, p. 327)

Summary and Conclusion

The purpose and value of records has been eloquently expressed by Pres. Wilford Woodruff who wrote as follows:

The devil has sought to take away my life from the day I was born until now, more so even than the lives of other men. I seem to be a marked victim of the adversary. I can find but one reason for this: the devil knew if I got into the Church of Jesus Christ of Latter-day Saints, I would write the history of that Church and leave on record the works and teachings of the prophets, of the apostles and elders. I have recorded nearly all the sermons and teachings that I ever heard from the Prophet Joseph, I have in my journal many of the sermons of President Brigham Young, and such men as Orson Hyde, Parley P. Pratt and others. Another reason I was moved upon to write in the early days was that nearly all the historians appointed in those times apostatized and took the journals away with them.

(Wilford Woodruff, History of
His Life and Labors, p. 477)

Chapter 38

Doctrine and Covenants Section 48

Suggested Title

Land For the Gathering in Ohio—Preparation for Missouri

Overview of Section Content

1. The Lord directs Ohio saints to remain in Ohio and share their land with brethren from the East (vs. 1-3)
2. The Lord counsels the Ohio saints to save money for eventual purchase of lands for an inheritance (vs. 4-6)

Historical Setting

Joseph Smith, Jun.

Upon inquiry how the brethren should act in regard to purchasing lands to settle upon, and where they should finally make a permanent location, I received the following . . . (HC, Vol. 1, p. 166)

B.H. Roberts

This question was agitating the minds of the brethren in consequence of the expected arrival in the near future, of the Saints from New York, who had been commanded to gather to Ohio, and for whose reception it was necessary to make preparations. (HC, Vol. 1, p. 166, Footnote)

Hyrum M. Smith and Janne M. Sjodahl

In former Revelations (Secs. 37:3; 38:32; 39:15) our Lord had commanded the Saints in the East to gather in Ohio, where they would be "endowed with power from on high." The spirit of gathering was poured out upon them, and in the spring of 1831, shortly after the arrival of the Prophet Joseph in Kirtland, many Saints began the westward move from the State of New York. The Saints in Kirtland then began to make inquiries as to how the newcomers could obtain land to settle upon, and where they should make a permanent location. This Revelation was given in answer to their inquiries. (DCC, p. 280)

Sacred Truths

Introduction

There were two questions that prompted the Prophet Joseph Smith to ask the Lord for direction:

1. The Saints living in Ohio were anticipating the arrival of the saints from the East and wondered what their obligations were as to how to assist in providing places for them to settle.

2. The Eastern saints who had been commanded to move to Ohio, (See D&C Sections 37 & 38) were wondering where they could settle their families and how permanent such locations would be.

In answer to the above questions, the Lord counseled the saints in Ohio:

> It is necessary that ye should remain for the present time in your places of abode, as it shall be suitable to your circumstances.
>
> And inasmuch as ye have lands, ye shall impart to the eastern brethren;
>
> And inasmuch as ye have not lands, let them buy for the present time in those regions round about, as seemeth them good, for it must needs be necessary that they have places to live for the present time. (D&C 48:1-3)

In substance, the Lord told both groups that the settlements in Ohio were temporary (for the present time). Historically, we now know such was the case. Ohio was a place of gathering for strength while the Lord prepared the Saints to establish Zion in the land of Missouri. (See D&C 64:21-22)

Preparation For Missouri

After the Lord answered the questions of the Saints, He revealed to them that there would be a future gathering at still another location. They were counseled to prepare for the time when they would gather elsewhere under the Lord's direction. He did not reveal the location of the gathering place. However, He did tell them they would need to purchase lands and would be responsible for the beginning of building a city there. (See D&C 48:4-6)

Again, historically, we know that the place of gathering referred to in this revelation was subsequently revealed to be the land of Missouri. (See D&C 57:1-4)

Summary and Conclusion

There is a lesson for us that can be learned from this revelation. The Lord knows the future, the needs of His people, and how to provide for those needs. Knowing that the Saints would eventually need to purchase lands, He counseled them to save their money that they might be prepared when the time came to purchase. (See D&C 48:4) Unfortunately, many did not follow His counsel and consequently, were not prepared when the time came.

As it was then, so it is now. The Lord knows all things from the beginning to the end. When He counsels us to obtain a year's supply of food, participate in welfare projects, stay out of debt, etc. it is in our best interest to heed His counsel.

Chapter 39

Doctrine and Covenants Section 49

Suggested Title

The Shaking Quakers

Overview of Section Content

1. Elders called to preach the gospel to the Shakers (vs. 1-4, 26-28)
2. The Savior will continue to reign in Heaven until His second coming (vs. 5-7, 22-23)
3. Salvation in the Lord's kingdom available through faith, repentance, baptism and the Gift of the Holy Ghost (vs. 8-14)
4. Marriage is ordained of God (vs. 15-17)
5. Man can obtain food and raiment from beasts, fowls, and the earth (vs. 18-21)
6. Lamanites shall blossom and Zion will flourish upon the mountains before the Savior's second coming (vs. 24-25)

Historical Setting

Joseph Smith, Jun.

At about this time came Leman Copley, one of the sect called Shaking Quakers, and embraced the fulness of the everlasting Gospel, apparently honest-hearted, but still retaining the idea that the Shakers were right in some particulars of their faith. In order to have more perfect understanding on the subject, I inquired of the Lord, and received the following . . . (HC, Vol. 1, p. 167)

B.H. Roberts

"This sect of Christians arose in England, and Ann Lee has the credit of being its founder. They derive their name from their manner of worship, which is performed by singing and dancing, and clapping their hands in regular time, to a novel but rather pleasant kind of music. This sect was persecuted in England, and came to America in 1774. They first settled in Watervliet, near Albany, New York. They have, or think they have, revelations from heaven, or gifts from the Holy Spirit which direct them in the choice of their leaders, and in other important concerns. Their dress and manners are similar to those of the society of friends (Quakers); hence they are often called Shaking Quakers."—Hayward's *Book of All Religions*, pp. 84-85. "They assert, with the Quakers, that all external ordinances, especially baptism and the Lord's supper, ceased in the apostolic age; and that God had sent no one to preach since that time till they were raised up, to call in the elect in a new dispensation. They deny the doctrine of the Trinity and a vicarious atonement, as also the resurrection of the body."—Burder's *History of All Religions*, p. 502. (HC, Vol. 1, p. 167, Footnote)

Roy W. Doxey

To appreciate fully the teachings received in Section 49 of the Doctrine and Covenants, some knowledge of the origin and beliefs of the "Shakers," whose correct name was "The United Society of Believers in Christ's Second Appearing," is necessary.

At the beginning of the 18th century (1706), a group of religionists from France went to England and were known there as the French Prophets. James Wardley, a tailor, and his wife Jane, who were seceders from Quakerism came under their influence. In 1747 the Wardleys founded a society in Manchester and began to preach. They declared that Christ was soon to return to reign on the earth, and that he would come in the form of a woman. The society increased in numbers although suffering much from persecution. One of their converts was Ann Lee. She was born February 29, 1736, the daughter of a blacksmith, and was married to a blacksmith at an early age. She gave birth to four children who died in infancy. In 1758 she was converted by Jane Wardley and also began to preach. Among her claimed revelations was one regarding the nature of God described in this manner: "The duality of Diety, God both Father and Mother; one in essence—one God, not two; but God who possesses two natures, the masculine and the feminine, each distinct in function yet one in being, co-equal in Diety." This belief is the basis for the later claim that Ann Lee became the incarnation of the Christ Spirit.

Because of persecution and lack of progress in making converts, Ann Lee and eight of her followers decided to go to America. Arriving there in 1774, they established themselves at Watervliet near Albany, New York. Ann Lee saw two other Shaker communities founded before her death in 1784. The period of greatest growth of this sect was between 1792 and 1835. At one time they numbered nearly 5,000. The sect no longer exists. (Anne White and Leila S. Taylor. "Shakerism, Its Meaning and Message"; *Encyclopedia Americana* [1949] Vol. 24, p. 642) (*The Doctrine and Covenants Speaks*, Vol. 1, pp. 336-337)

Sacred Truths

Introduction

To better appreciate the purpose for which the doctrines in this section are discussed, it is necessary to understand some of the teachings of the Shaking Quakers. In substance, they included the following:

1. Jesus Christ has come the second time and He came in the form of a woman for God is both male and female in nature.
2. Celibacy
3. Eating of meat forbidden
4. External ordinances not necessary
5. Doctrines of the Trinity, the vicarious atonement, and the resurrection of the body are untrue.

In this revelation, several of the brethren were called by the Lord to serve missions among the Shaking Quakers. They were to teach them the correct doctrines as revealed in this revelation which would serve to eliminate false notions that were so prevalent among them. (See D&C 49:1-4, 11)

In this chapter, we will discuss the Lord's teachings concerning the first three subject areas listed above.

The Lord's Second Coming

We learn several things from this revelation that pertain to this subject. The Lord Jesus Christ reigns now in the heavens and His second coming is still future. As to the hour and the day when this event will occur, no one knows, not even the angels in Heaven. When he comes, He will not come in the form of a woman, nor as an ordinary mortal man. He will come in His glory and there will be no mistake as to his identity. (See D&C 49:5-7, 22)

Three great events will transpire prior to His second coming: (See D&C 49:24-25)

1. Jacob will flourish in the wilderness.
2. The Lamanites will blossom.
3. Zion shall be assembled and rejoice upon the mountains.

The Savior's doctrine is clear and renders a great service to the seeker of truth. No one needs to be deceived by those who claim that the Savior's second coming is a past event or that there is an announced date set aside for His second coming. Furthermore, He will not appear as an ordinary mortal man or woman but rather as the glorified Savior and Redeemer of the world.

In anticipation of that great event, we are strengthened in our faith as we watch the fulfillment of the events predicted by the Savior that would precede His coming. As to one of the events referred to in this revelation; President Joseph F. Smith has clearly taught the following:

> Again, in the revelation given in March, 1831, to Parley P. Pratt and Leman Copley, the following remarkable prediction is found:
> 'But before the great day of the Lord shall come, Jacob shall flourish in the wilderness, and the Lamanites shall blossom as the rose. Zion shall flourish upon the hills and rejoice upon the mountains, and shall be assembled together unto the place which I have appointed.' (Doctrine and Covenants, 49:24, 25)
> Who, let me ask, unless he was inspired of the Lord, speaking by the gift and power of God, at that remote period of the Church's history, when our numbers were few, when we had no influence, name or standing in the world—who, I would ask, under the circumstances in which we were placed when this prediction was made, could have uttered such words unless God inspired him? Zion is, indeed, flourishing on the hills, and it is rejoicing on the mountains, and we who compose it are gathering and assembling together unto the place appointed. I now ask this congregation if they cannot see that this prediction (which was made many years before the idea prevailed at all among this people that we should ever migrate and gather out to these mountain valleys) has been and is being literally fulfilled? If there were no other prophecy uttered by Joseph Smith, fulfillment of which could be pointed to, this alone would be sufficient to entitle him to the claim of being a true prophet. (GD, pp. 486-487)

Marriage Ordained of God

This earth was organized for one primary purpose. The earth was to serve as a dwelling place for Father's children. In order for those children to come to this dwelling place, the Lord designed in the beginning the means whereby His spirit children could receive physical bodies and come here to dwell in mortality. The plan provided that a man and a woman would come together in a marriage covenant and participate, with God, in multiplying and replenishing the earth. The institution of marriage and one's loyal faithfulness to the marriage partner is ordained of God. (See D&C 49:15-17)

It is comforting to know that the earth did not just happen to be and that we are not a by-product of chance. We have the word of the Lord to the effect that God is the creator and designer of this planet earth. Furthermore, it was created that it might be filled with all of Father's spirit children who were designated to come here. The number of those so designated was determined before the world was organized. (See D&C 49:16-17) Therefore, we know the earth can and will sustain the number of people who come to dwell thereon.

The following statements by two latter-day prophets aid us in our understanding of these principles:

Joseph F. Smith

...spirits have been coming to this earth to take upon them tabernacles, that they might become like unto Jesus Christ, being "formed in his likeness and image," from the morn of creation until now, and will continue until the winding up scene, until the spirits who were destined to come to this world shall have come and accomplished their mission in the flesh. (G.D., p. 94)

Joseph Fielding Smith

The people who inhabit this earth were all living in the spirit life before they came to this earth. The Lord informs us that this earth was designed, before its foundations were formed, for the abode of the spirits who kept their first estate and all such must come here and receive their tabernacles of flesh and bones, and this is according to the number, or measure, of man according to his creation before the world was made. It is the duty of mankind, in lawful and holy wedlock, to multiply according to the commandments given to Adam and Eve and later to Noah, until every spirit appointed to receive a body in this world has had that privilege. Those who teach celibacy and look upon marriage as sinful are in opposition to the word and commandment of the Lord. (CHMR, Vol. 1, p. 192)

Animals For The Use of Man

The Lord declared in this revelation that the eating of meat is ordained of God.

He further taught that the lower forms of life are useful to man for raiment. However, man is obligated to share with his fellow man and refrain from shedding blood or wasting flesh unnecessarily. (See D&C 49:18-21)

As one reflects upon what the Lord has said he comes to the realization that man's motive for using animals either justifies or condemns him before the Lord.

A fitting summary of the above principles is provided by Pres. Joseph F. Smith as follows:

> I do not believe any man should kill animals or birds unless he needs them for food, and then he should not kill innocent little birds that are not intended for food for man. I think it is wicked for men to thirst in their souls to kill almost everything which possesses animal life. It is wrong, and I have been surprised at prominent men whom I have seen whose very souls seemed to be athirst for the shedding of animal blood. They go off hunting deer, antelope, elk, anything they can find, and what for? "Just for the fun of it!" Not that they are hungry and need the flesh of their prey, but just because they love to shoot and to destroy life. I am a firm believer, with reference to these things, in the simple words of one of the poets:
>
> > 'Take not away the life you cannot give,
> > For all things have an equal right to live.'
>
> (G.D., p. 266)

Summary and Conclusion

Through the missionary work of the church, the Lord makes gospel truths available to all of His children. Such truths serve to correct mistaken ideas. These truths are also the means by which people can attain unto salvation.

Chapter 40

Doctrine and Covenants Section 50

Suggested Title

False Spirits—Be Not Deceived

Overview of Section Content

1. False spirits abroad in the earth (vs. 1-3)
2. A warning against hypocrisy in the Church (vs. 4-9)
3. The Lord counsels how to determine that which is of God (vs. 10-23)
4. Those who are purified from sin have power over evil spirits (vs. 24-36)
5. Personal instructions to several of the elders (vs. 37-39)
6. Covenant children who build on the rock of Christ shall never fall (vs. 40-46)

Historical Setting

Joseph Smith, Jun.

During the month of April, I continued to translate the Scriptures as time would allow. In May, a number of Elders being present, and not understanding the different spirits abroad in the earth, I inquired and received from the Lord the following ... (HC, Vol. 1, p. 170)

Soon after the Gospel was established in Kirtland, and during the absence of the authorities of the Church, many false spirits were introduced, many strange visions were seen, and wild, enthusiasic notions were entertained: men ran out of doors under the influence of this spirit, and some of them got upon the stumps of trees and shouted, and all kinds of extravagances were entered into by them; one man pursued a ball that he said he saw flying in the air, until he came to a precipice, when he jumped into the top of a tree, which saved his life; and many ridiculous things were entered into, calculated to bring disgrace upon the Church of God, to cause the Spirit of God to be withdrawn, and to uproot and destroy those glorious principles which had been developed for the salvation of the human family. (HC, Vol. 4, p. 580)

Joseph Fielding Smith

...This influence of the devil entered into the Church in an early day and had to be rebuked by the Prophet, for such unseemly conduct was prevalent in that day among many religious groups and some of the Saints were deceived in thinking this disorderly conduct was a manifestation of the Spirit of the Lord. It was to correct this evil and to warn the Saints against all false spirits, whether of men or of devils, that this revelation (Sec. 50) was given. Members of the Church had already come in contact with the "Shakers," or "Shaking Quakers," who believed in and were subject to these evil gifts.

Speaking of these manifestations as they crept into the Church, Parley P. Pratt has written:

"As I went forth among the different branches, some very strange spiritual operations were manifested, which were disgusting, rather than edifying. Some persons would seem to swoon away, and make unseemly gestures, and be drawn or disfigured in their countenances. Others would fall into ecstasies and be drawn into contortions, cramps, fits, etc. Others would seem to have visions and revelations which were not edifying, and which were not congenial to the doctrine and spirit of the gospel. In short, a false and lying spirit seemed to be creeping into the Church.

"All these things were new and strange to me, and had originated in the Church during the absence, and previous to the arrival of President Joseph Smith from New York.

"Feeling our weakness and inexperience, and lest we should err in judgment concerning the spiritual phenomena, myself, John Murdock, and several other Elders, went to Joseph Smith, and asked him to inquire of the Lord concerning these spirits or manifestations.

"After we had joined in prayer in his translating room, he dictated in our presence the following revelation: each sentence was uttered slowly and very distinctly, and with a pause between each, sufficiently long for it to be recorded by an ordinary writer in long hand." (*Autobiography of P.P. Pratt,* pp. 61-62)

In this way and under these circumstances Section Fifty was received for the Church.

If the members of the Church will carefully consider the word of the Lord and follow the precepts here given they will not be deceived by the evil spirits of man or devils. The promise is made in a positive manner that all "who buildeth upon this rock shall never fall." Yes, sad to say, there are members of the Church who are ready to follow any theory, philosophy, or strange doctrine especially if with it there is something mysterious.

Even in that day there were hypocrites and deceivers drawn into the Church and with them they brought their abominations which had to be speedily eliminated by the Lord making known their evil practices. (CHMR, Vol. 1, pp. 183-184)

Sacred Truths

Introduction

As can be seen from the Historical Setting, there was a need for the Lord to assist the Church leaders and members to detect false spirits. In this revelation, the Lord provided guidelines pertaining to at least three subject areas that may be used as a protection against deception:

1. Hypocrisy within the Church
2. Edification
3. Lack of knowledge and understanding

Hypocrisy Within The Church

Sometimes a member of the Church has difficulty staying active and faithful in the Church. Such difficulty sometimes arises from acts of hypocrisy and the resulting negative influence seen in the lives of some members of the Church. When such an individual allows hypocrisy in the lives of others to justify his own failure to perform according to his covenants, he is doing so because he has not come to an understanding of the Lord's counsel. He has been deceived. As early as 1831, the Lord revealed that there were deceivers and hypocrites in the Church and warned of the possible destructive influence such people might have in the lives of the members. (See D&C 50:4-7) As members of the Church, we ought to be wise enough to understand the problem and heed the counsel of the Lord. There are hypocrites in the Church and the Lord said so. The Lord also said that when such conditions exist, He will deal with the hypocrite in this life or in the next. Church action may need to be taken in mortality or the hypocrite may find himself shut out of the Lord's presence in eternity. Either way, it is the Lord's prerogative to take action. No one else is justified in concerning themselves about the Lord's business. Furthermore, Church members are counseled to do what is right before the Lord and not justify their own inappropriate action because of the unrighteousness of others. (See D&C 50:8-9) No one needs to be deceived by the hypocritical actions of some who have membership standing in the Church whose motives are not pure when they fail to live by the standards of the church.

Edification

This revelation was given to people who had received the gospel message from authorized servants of the Lord. And when that message was delivered, it was done by the power and influence of the Lord's spirit. Thus, they were acquainted with the correct method of teaching in the Lord's Church. So the Lord reminded them of that method by asking the question:

> Wherefore, I the Lord ask you this question—unto what were ye ordained?
> To preach my gospel by the Spirit, even the Comforter which was sent forth to teach the truth. (D&C 50:13-14)

Then He inquired of them why, when they were exposed to a method other than the Lord's, they were confused and failed to detect the source and the falsity of such behavior. (See D&C 50:15-16)

So that there would be no misunderstanding, the Lord proceeded to emphasize the principle through repetitive declarations. Several times, He stated that whatsoever comes from the Lord by the Spirit of truth edifieth and is of God. In other words, it uplifts one both morally and spiritually. (See D&C 50:17:23)

Though these principles in this revelation were called forth to deal with particular problems facing the Church in 1831, the principles still have broad application in many phases of our lives today. That which doth not edify is still not of God and is still darkness. For instance, the Lord is not the author or the source of inspiration behind the creation of movies that portray degrading behavior that is not uplifting spiritually and morally. The source of such is evil and is darkness. Such criteria can be used to judge teachings and writings of men, language, works of art, courtship relationships and every other experience that confronts mankind in mortality. No one needs to be deceived in thinking otherwise.

Lack of Knowledge and Understanding

We have been taught that there is a right and a wrong to every question. But man's knowledge and understanding is not sufficient to always accurately identify truth from error. In this revelation, the Lord described man's inadequacies when He said "But no man is possessor of all things . . ." (D&C 50:28) There are many situations when man's knowledge, intellect, and experience is insufficient to make wise and proper decisions. When such situations arise, divine help is available. The Lord said:

> And if ye are purified and cleansed from all sin, ye shall ask whatsoever you will in the name of Jesus and it shall be done . . .
>
> Wherefore, it shall come to pass, that if you behold a spirit manifested that you cannot understand, and you receive not that spirit, ye shall ask of the Father in the name of Jesus; and if he give not unto you that spirit, then you may know that it is not of God.
>
> And it shall be given unto you, power over that spirit; and you shall proclaim against that spirit with a loud voice that it is not of God. (D&C 50:29, 31-32)

The pre-requisite for obtaining divine guidance is cleanliness of soul, obtained by repentance and obedience to the commandments of the Lord. When a person is free from sin, he is invited to ask for information that will enable him to separate truth from error. The Lord promised to provide such insights from on High. No one needs to be deceived through lack of knowledge and understanding. Keeping one's self clean before the Lord opens the windows of heaven (which is revelation). By gaining divine knowledge one walks in the Spirit of truth.

Summary and Conclusion

Satan's motives are to deceive and destroy. The Savior's work provides detection and deliverance from the evil one for the Lord's children. Through living prophets, the Lord reveals to the saints sufficient knowledge that they might avoid being deceived.

Chapter 41

Doctrine and Covenants Sections 51 and 54

Suggested Titles

Section 51—Law of Consecration and Stewardship
Section 54—Obeying and Disobeying the Law of Consecration

Overview of Section Content

Section 51

1. The Lord instructs Bishop Edward Partridge how to organize the Saints gathered in Thompson, Ohio (vs. 1-2)
2. The Lord describes the process of establishing stewardships under the law of consecration (vs. 3-6)
3. Rules respecting the common property of the people and the establishment of a storehouse (vs. 7-13)
4. The Bishop and his family to be provided for by the Church while he is employed in Church business (vs. 14)
5. The Saints in Thompson, Ohio to be an example of living the law of consecration (vs. 15-20)

Section 54

1. Some of the Saints at Thompson, Ohio to receive the Lord's mercy for keeping consecration covenants, while others in Thompson, Ohio must suffer for breaking them (vs. 1-6)

2. Thompson, Ohio Saints who had kept their covenants directed to go to Missouri (vs. 7-10)

Historical Setting

Both these sections deal with the Colesville, New York Branch of the Church (also known as the Thompson, Ohio Branch) in their attempt to live the Law of Consecration as revealed through the Prophet. This group of Saints was given the special privilege of gaining the experience of living the principles of this law. (See D&C 51:15-18) Later, the entire Church would be required to live this law. Because of the common nature of these revelations we will discuss them together in this chapter.

Section 51

Joseph Smith, Jun.

Not long after the foregoing was received, [Section 50] the Saints from the State of New York began to come on, and it seemed necessary to settle them; therefore at the solicitation of Bishop Partridge, I inquired, and received the following . . . (HC, Vol. 1, p. 173)

Hyrum M. Smith and Janne M. Sjodahl

Shortly after the Revelation recorded in Section 50 had been received, the Saints from Colesville, N.Y., began to arrive in Ohio. They had been directed to gather in that locality (Sec. 37:3) and they had been promised that there they would receive The Law (Sec. 38:32). The Saints in Ohio had been instructed to divide their land with their Eastern brethren (Sec. 48:2), and it was the duty of Edward Partridge, who had been appointed Bishop (Sec. 41) to take care of the newcomers, as far as possible. Under the circumstances, Bishop Partridge asked for divine guidance. The Prophet inquired of the Lord for him, and received this answer to his prayers. (DCC, p. 296)

Joseph Fielding Smith

. . .the Lord endeavored to teach these members in part, at least, and train them in the great principle of consecration as a preparatory step before they should be permitted to journey to Zion, for it was in keeping with this law upon which the City of Zion was to be built. Thus these saints from the East were to be organized according to the law of God. (Sec. 51:4-6) This land in

Ohio was in this manner to be consecrated unto them "for a little season," until the Lord should provide for them otherwise, and command them to go hence. (Sec. 51:15-16) (CHMR, Vol. 1, p. 187)

Section 54

Joseph Smith, Jun.

The branch of the Church in Thompson, on account of breaking the covenant, and not knowing what to do, they sent in Newel Knight and other Elders, to ask me to inquire of the Lord for them; which I did, and received the following. (HC, Vol. 1, p. 180)

B.H. Roberts

It is difficult to determine with exactness in what the transgressions of the Saints at Thompson consisted, but it is evident that selfishness and rebellion were at the bottom of their trouble, and that Leman Copley and Ezra Thayre were immediately concerned in it. The Saints comprising the Colesville branch, when they arrived at the gathering place in Ohio, were advised to remain together and were settled at Thompson, a place in the vicinity of Kirtland. On their arrival Bishop Edward Partridge urged the Prophet Joseph to inquire of the Lord concerning the manner of settling them, and providing for them. Wereupon the Prophet inquired of the Lord and received the revelation [D&C Section 51] found on page 173. [HC, Vol. 1] It will be seen from that revelation that the Saints of the Colesville branch were to be organized under the law of consecration and stewardship. That is, in brief, the Saints were to make a consecration of whatsoever things they possessed unto the Bishop, and then each man receive from the Bishop a stewardship. Every man was to be equal in his stewardship, according to his family, his circumstances, and his needs. For details in the matter the reader is referred to the revelation itself. It is evident that some of the brethren already living at Thompson, had agreed to enter into the law of consecration and stewardship with the Saints from Colesville; and that afterwards they broke this covenant. Among these were Leman Copley and Ezra Thayre. "A man by the name of Copley," says Newel Knight in his journal, "had a considerable tract of land there [in Thompson] which he offered to let the Saints occupy. Consequently a contract was agreed upon, and we commenced work in good faith. But in a short time Copley broke the engagement, and I went to Kirtland to see Brother Joseph," etc . . . (HC, Vol. 1, p. 180, Footnote)

Joseph Fielding Smith

...it appears that Copley, who had not been fully converted, and some others in Thompson, violated their covenants which caused confusion among the Colesville Saints and placed them at the mercy of their enemies. In their distress they sent Newel Knight, who was in charge of this branch, to the Prophet to learn what they should do. The Lord spoke to them by revelation (Sec. 54) saying since their covenant was broken and of no effect, they would have to flee to Missouri or their enemies would be upon them... (CHMR, Vol. 1, pp. 187-188)

Sacred Truths

Introduction

As noted in the Historical Setting, Bishop Partridge was concerned how he was to help the Colesville Saints settle in Ohio. Section 51 is the Lord's response to this inquiry through the Prophet Joseph Smith. The revelation begins as follows:

Hearken unto me, saith the Lord your God, and I will speak unto my servant Edward Partridge, and give unto him directions; for it must needs be that he receive directions how to organize this people.

For it must needs be that they be organized according to my laws; if otherwise, they will be cut off. (D&C 51:1-2)

When the Lord refers to "my laws" in the above quotation, He has reference to His Law of Consecration as first recorded in Doctrine and Covenants 42:30-42. In Section 51, the Lord gave additional insights pertaining to that law and gave a commandment for the Colesville Saints. They were to organize themselves under the provisions of the law and thus become the first people of this dispensation to live under the Law of Consecration. This experience served somewhat as a pilot program and provided Bishop Partridge the opportunity to learn and gain experience with the law. (See D&C 51:15, 18)

Although the rudiments of this law were revealed in Section 42, no discussion of that law was provided in Chapter 32 of this text. Therefore, our discussion in this chapter includes references to verses in both Sections 42 and 51.

Furthermore, inasmuch as difficulties arose in the living of this law, the Colesville Saints were commanded to cease practicing the principles of the law until further directed by the Lord. In this chapter, we will also discuss Section 54.

The Law of Consecration

Before we discuss this law, we should be reminded of a certain basic truth upon which this law rests:

The earth and all things contained therein belong to the Lord. (See D&C 104:14-17, 54-57)

The Law of Consecration is a celestial law and is a means by which the Lord provides for His saints. There are two aspects to this law:

1. The consecration (See D&C 42:30-31)
2. The stewardship (See D&C 42:32; 51:3-5)

An explanation of the law and some of its functions was given in General Conference by Pres. J. Reuben Clark, Jr. as follows:

The basic principle of all the revelations on the United Order is that everything we have belongs to the Lord; therefore, the Lord may call upon us for any and all of the property which we have, because it belongs to Him. This, I repeat, is the basic principle. (D&C 104:14-17, 54-57)

One of the places in which some of the brethren are going astray is this: There is continuous reference in the revelations to equality among the brethren, but I think you will find only one place where that equality is really described, though it is referred to in other revelations. That revelation (D&C 51:3) affirms that every man is to be "equal according to his family, according to his circumstances and his wants and needs." (See also D&C 82:17; 78:5-6) Obviously, this is not a case of "dead level" equality. It is "equality" that will vary as much as the man's circumstances, his family, his wants and needs, may vary.

In the next place, under the United Order every man was called to consecrate to the Church all of the property which he had; the real estate was to be conveyed to the Church, as I understand the revelations, by what we would call a deed in fee simple. Thus the man's property became absolutely the property of the Church. (D&C 42:30; 72:15) Then the bishop deeded back to the donor by the same kind of deed, that is, in fee simple, and also transferred to him by an equivalent instrument, so far as personal property was concerned, that amount of real and personal property, which, the two being taken together, would be required by the individual for the support of himself and his family "according to his family, according to his circumstances and his wants and needs." This the man held as his own property. (D&C 42:32; 51:4-6; 83:3)

In other words, basic to the United Order was the private ownership of property, every man had his own property from which he might secure that which was necessary for the support of himself and his family. There is nothing in the revelations that would indicate that this property was not freely alienable at the will of the owner. It was not contemplated that the Church should own everything or that we should become in the Church, with reference to our property and otherwise, the same kind of automaton, manikin, that communism makes out of the individual, with the State standing at the head in place of the Church.

Now, that part of a man's property which was not turned back to him, if he had more than was needed under this rule of "equality" already stated, became the common property of the Church, and that common property was used for the support of the poor of the Church. It is spoken of in the revelations as the "residue" of property. (D&C 42:34-36)

The land which you received from the bishop by deed, whether it was part of the land which you, yourself, had deeded to the Church, or whether it came as an out-right gift from the Church as just indicated, and the personal property which you received, were all together sometimes called a "portion" (D&C 51:4-6) sometimes a "stewardship" (D&C 104:11-12), and sometimes an "inheritance." (D&C 83:3)

The fundamental principle of this sytem was the private ownership of property. Each man owned his portion, or inheritance, or stewardship, with an absolute title, which he could alienate, or hypothecate, or otherwise treat as his own. The Church did not own all of the property, and the life under the United Order was not a communal life, as the Prophet Joseph, himself, said, (*History of the Church*, Volume III, p. 28). The United Order is an individualistic system, not a communal system.

We have all said that the Welfare Plan is not the United Order and was not intended to be. However, I should like to suggest to you that perhaps, after all, when the Welfare Plan gets thoroughly into operation—it is not so yet—we shall not be so very far from carrying out the great fundamentals of the United Order.

In the first place I repeat again, the United Order recognized and was built upon the principle of private ownership of property; all that a man had and lived upon under the United Order, was his own. Quite obviously, the fundamental principle of our system today is the ownership of private property. (CR, October 1942, pp. 55-57)

The foregoing discussion presents not only the basic mechanics of the law, but also teaches us about the spirit of the law. The spirit of the law is of at least equal importance and sometimes is not emphasized when one discusses the law. What is a Latter-day Saint really doing when he consecrates his property or makes any other form of consecration? He is acknowledging unto God, that he is aware that all things belong to the Lord. He has reached a level of spiritual maturity where things of the world are not the only source of his security. He is at peace because he has placed his trust in the living God. He has put himself and all that he possesses at the disposal of the Lord by rendering obedience to the law as administered by the authorized servants of the Lord. At that point, he is worthy to receive an inheritance from the Lord both in time and in eternity.

Obeying and Disobeying the Law of Consecration

As mentioned earlier in this chapter, the Colesville Saints settled in Thompson, Ohio and were instructed to implement the provisions of the Law of Consecration. Other members of the Church, already living in the vicinity, also made covenants to live under this law and some of them failed to keep their covenants. It is to them the Lord made reference when he said:

> And as the covenant which they made unto me has been broken, even so it has become void and of none effect.
> And wo to him by whom this offense cometh, for it had been better for him that he had been drowned in the depth of the sea. (D&C 54:4-5)

Though some of the Thompson Saints broke their covenants, the Colesville group, by and large, observed to keep their commitments and covenants with the Lord. To them the Lord said:

> But blessed are they who have kept the covenant and observed the commandment, for they shall obtain mercy. (D&C 54:6)

They were then instructed to leave Ohio and settle in the land of Missouri. (See D&C 54:7-8)

There is a lesson for us today in this revelation. Making covenants with the Lord is a serious and sacred matter. To those who keep their covenants with Him, the Lord has made clear that His mercy is extended to them. The Lord's mercy includes forgiveness of sin, compassion for the sinner, and promises of redemption and exaltation. Those who earnestly desire these great blessings realize and understand that making and keeping covenants with the Lord is a sacred and personal matter.

On the other hand, those who break their sacred covenants and fail to repent of such sin, will find they have no access to the Lord's mercy. They will face, instead, the consequences of a broken law.

Summary and Conclusion

The spirit of the law of consecration is available to us today. We have opportunity to give of our selves and our resources through contributions of time, talent and material means to the building of the kingdom of God. Such opportunities come through the welfare program, living the law of tithing, contributing to building programs, etc. The principles are still the same. The Lord's mercy will be extended to those who make and keep covenants with Him. The decisions to be made are still the same. Will we choose to have the Lord's mercy or choose, instead, the consequences of violating covenants made with the Lord?

Chapter 42

Doctrine and Covenants Section 52

Suggested Title

A Pattern in all Things—Teach What the Apostles and Prophets Have Written

Overview of Section Content

1. The Lord appoints a conference to be held in Missouri (vs. 1-2)
2. The Lord calls Joseph Smith and others to journey to Missouri and instructs them concerning their duties while enroute (vs. 3-13, 22-34)
3. The Lord provides a pattern in all things as a protection against deception (vs. 14-21)
4. Two elders are called on a mission to the East (vs. 35-36)
5. Instructions of the Lord to various brethren (vs. 37-44)

Historical Setting

Joseph Smith, Jun.

On the 3rd of June, the Elders from the various parts of the country where they were laboring, came in; and the conference before appointed [See D&C Section 44] convened in Kirtland; and the Lord displayed His power to the most perfect satisfaction of the Saints. The man of sin was revealed, and the authority of the

Melchizedek Priesthood was manifested and conferred for the first time upon several of the Elders. [. . .The Prophet does not mean that the Melchizedek Priesthood was given for the first time in the Church. It was at this conference, however, that the special office of High Priest was for the first time conferred upon men in this dispensation, except in so far as Apostles are also High Priests (Doctrine and Covenants, sec. lxxxiv: 63); and of course as there were men who had been ordained to the apostleship before this conference of June, 1831, in that manner there had been High Priests in the Church, but not otherwise.] (HC, Vol. 1, p. 176, Footnote.) It was clearly evident that the Lord gave us power in proportion to the work to be done, and strength according to the race set before us, and grace and help as our needs required. Great harmony prevailed; several were ordained; faith was strengthened; and humility, so necessary for the blessing of God to follow prayer, characterized the Saints.

The next day, as a kind continuation of this great work of the last days, I received the following . . . (HC, Vol. 1, pp. 175-177)

B.H. Roberts

The manner in which the man of sin was revealed and the authority of the Melchizedek Priesthood manifested, is related by John Whitmer, in his *History of the Church* (ch. vii). After giving the names of those who were ordained High Priests the day on which the two powers were manifested, he says: "Joseph Smith, Jun., prophesied the day previous that the man of sin would be revealed. While the Lord poured out His Spirit upon His servants, the devil took a notion to make known his power. He bound Harvey Whitlock and John Murdock so that they could not speak, and others were affected but the Lord showed to Joseph, the seer, the design of the thing; he commanded the devil in the name of Christ, and he departed, to our joy and comfort." (HC, Vol. 1, p. 175, Footnote)

Joseph F. Smith

". . .The man of sin was revealed, and the authority of the Melchizedek Priesthood was manifested, and conferred for the first time upon several of the elders." Now, if this does not mean that on this occasion several elders received their first ordination, then it must mean that these several elders who had previously been ordained, then, for the first time, received the power or authority of their ordinations. The words "conferred for the first time upon several of the elders," would seem at first glance to mean that several were then ordained elders, but taking the complete sentence together, namely, "The man of sin was revealed, and the authority of the Melchizedek Priesthood was manifested, and conferred for the first time upon several of the elders," we naturally conclude that several who had previously been ordained elders, had not yet received the spirit, or power, or authority of their ordinations, but that now for the first time, the authority of the priesthood having been manifested, it fell upon them. It is evident from the context that the word authority as used in this quotation means power . . . (GD, pp. 195-196)

Sacred Truths

Introduction

In Section 44 of the Doctrine and Covenants, the Lord commanded that the elders should come together from various parts of the country and assemble in conference. This revelation (Section 52) was given during that conference. The Lord announced that the next conference of the Church would be held in Missouri. (See D&C 52:1-2) He also appointed some of the elders to journey together to Missouri that they might be in attendance at the appointed conference. (See D&C 52:22-32) The Lord had designed that while they were in Missouri, He would reveal the location for the city of Zion and the land of their inheritance. (See D&C 52:3-5)

It should be remembered that in Section 48 of the Doctrine and Covenants, the Saints were directed to save their money in order that they might purchase lands for an inheritance at the place the Lord would later reveal. After the brethren arrived in Missouri, as they had been appointed so to do, the Lord revealed to them the location of Zion, the city of the New Jerusalem with its temple, and the land of their inheritance. (See D&C Section 57)

Inasmuch as many of the brethren had been called to represent the Lord and His Church throughout various parts of the country, He counseled them that they might not be deceived. As part of that counsel He said:

> And again, I will give unto you a pattern in all things, that ye may not be deceived; for Satan is abroad in the land, and he goeth forth deceiving the nations—
>
> Wherefore, by this pattern ye shall know the spirits in all cases under the whole heavens. (D&C 52:14, 19)

A Pattern in All Things

In the Lord's pattern, He provided a description of a person whose actions and attributes are acceptable to Him. This pattern includes the following: (See D&C 52:15-21)

1. He is one who prays
2. He is one whose spirit is contrite, or humble
3. He is one who receives the Lord's ordinances and obeys the requirements thereof
4. He is one whose language is meek and uplifting
5. He is one who receives and recognizes the Lord's power
6. He is one whose works and teachings will reflect truths given by revelation from the Lord

In an effort to better understand how this pattern is applicable to us in order that we might be "accepted" of the Lord, we call attention to the following personal questions:

1. Am I one who has sufficient faith in the God of Heaven that I seek divine guidance through the channels of prayer?

2. Am I one who recognizes my sins and failings and whose spirit is contrite enough to plead before the Lord for forgiveness?

3. Am I one who desires to maintain a covenant relationship with the Lord which is only available through the ordinances authorized by Him through His priesthood?

4. Am I one whose language uplifts my associates and reflects honor upon the Lord?

5. Am I one who recognizes the power of the Lord not only in the manifestations and outpouring of temporal blessings, but also, as it is given to us through those servants who are authorized to represent Him?

6. Am I one who not only accepts but also teaches truth as it has been and will yet be given by the Lord through His apostles and prophets? (See D&C 52:9, 36)

Summary and Conclusion

There are two major concepts that need to be emphasized:

1. If we will learn and remember this pattern, we need never be deceived by anyone who is not in harmony with the Lord. We can recognize such disharmony if such a person is not endeavoring to meet the standards established in the Lord's pattern.

2. We will never deceive ourselves nor will we become a source of deception to others if we will so order our lives as to be in harmony with the Lord's pattern in all things.

Chapter 43

Doctrine and Covenants
Section 53

Suggested Title

Sidney Gilbert—Forsake the World—Endure to the End

Overview of Section Content

1. Sidney Gilbert comanded to forsake the world and perform the duties
   of an elder (vs. 1-3, 5-7)
2. Sidney Gilbert appointed to be a business agent for the Church (vs. 4)

Historical Setting

Joseph Smith, Jun.

Shortly after the foregoing was received, [Section 52] at the
request of Algernon Sidney Gilbert I inquired, and obtained the
following . . . (HC, Vol. 1, p. 179)

Sacred Truths

Introduction

In verse one of Section 53, the Lord indicates He is giving this
revelation as a result of Sidney Gilbert's desire to know of his spiritual
standing in the Church. In response to his inquiry, the Lord directed him,
through the prophet, in the following ways:

1. Forsake the world (See D&C 53:2)
2. Act in the office of an elder and preach the gospel (See D&C 53:3)
3. Be an agent unto the Church (See D&C 53:4)
4. Endure unto the end (See D&C 53:7)

Forsake the World

Elder David O. Mckay has defined the term "world" as it relates to the Church and its members. He said:

> Now, what do we mean by the world? It is sometimes used as an indefinite term. I take it that the world refers to the inhabitants who are alienated from the Saints of God. They are aliens to the Church, and it is the spirit of this alienation that we should keep ourselves free from. We are told by Paul not to conform to the fashions of the world. Titus was warned not to partake of those things, the evils of the world, and to "Flee also youthful lusts: but follow righteousness, faith, charity, peace, with them that call on the Lord out of a pure heart." (II Tim. 2:22) Purity of heart—Zion is the pure in heart, we have been told, and the strength of this Church lies in the purity of the thoughts and lives of its members, then the testimony of Jesus abides in the soul, and strength comes to each individual to withstand the evils of the world. (CR, October 1911, p. 58)

A person forsakes the world when he becomes a member of the Lord's Church by entering into and keeping a covenant relationship with the Savior. He is still in the world but not of the world. In this Section the Lord reminded Sidney Gilbert that he needed to remain free from the ways of the world and be true to the covenants he had made with the Lord.

Act in the Office of an Elder
And Preach the Gospel

What is the office of an elder? Pres. Harold B. Lee taught the following:

> The term "elder," which is applied to all holders of the Melchizedek Priesthood, means a defender of the faith. That is our prime responsibility and calling. Every holder of the Melchizedek Priesthood is to be a defender of the faith. (CR, April 1970, p. 54)

In this section, the Lord taught Brother Gilbert of the responsibility of an elder in the Lord's Church. He has an obligation to Jesus Christ to declare His gospel. As he fulfills that obligation he becomes a defender of the faith.

Be An Agent Unto The Church

The Lord called Sidney Gilbert to be an agent unto the Church. For insights as to the nature of that calling, we refer to the following:

> Sidney Gilbert was an able business man. The crucified Redeemer asks him to give his business talents to the Church. The Lord was about to gather His Saints in a new locality, even in Missouri, and they needed men like Sidney Gilbert to transact business for them. Business talents, when consecrated to the service of mankind, are just as good and necessary as so-called spiritual gifts. It is only when they are used to serve the purposes of selfishness and greed that they become a snare and a curse. In the service of the Lord they are a blessing. As an agent he could help in building up the Church. (DCC, p. 313)

Endure Unto The End

As was noted previously in this chapter, one forsakes the world by leaving the spirit of worldly things and coming into the spiritual environment of covenant relationships with the Savior. But such a step is not sufficient unto itself. One must continue to remain free of worldly interests that are in conflict with the growth of the spiritual life. By so doing he overcomes the world and is thus obedient to the scriptural injunction given by the Savior to Sidney Gilbert:

> And again, I would that ye should learn that he only is saved who endureth unto the end. Even so. Amen. (D&C 53:7)

What we are at the end of our probation is what determines our eternal destiny. Our past, whatever mistakes it contained, becomes insignificant if we have come to the truth, repented of our sins, and are living in harmony with Jesus Christ.

Summary and Conclusion

As it was with Sidney Gilbert, so it is for all Latter-day Saints. Those who desire to be acceptable before the Lord would do well to follow the instructions contained in the simple pattern revealed to Sidney Gilbert:

1. Forsake the world.
2. Be faithful in the office of appointed church callings.
3. Endure to the end.

Chapter 44

Doctrine and Covenants Section 55

Suggested Title

William W. Phelps—Remission of Sins

Overview of Section Content

1. William W. Phelps is conditionally promised remission of sins and an opportunity to perform the duties of an elder (vs. 1-3)
2. William W. Phelps is called to Missouri and is to assist Oliver Cowdery in printing and writing for the Church (vs. 4-5)
3. Joseph Coe is instructed to travel to Missouri (vs. 6)

Historical Setting

Joseph Smith, Jun.

About the middle of June, while we were preparing for our journey to Missouri, William W. Phelps and his family arrived among us—"to do the will of the Lord," he said: so I inquired of the Lord concerning him and received the following ... (HC, Vol. 1, pp. 184-185)

Hyrum M. Smith and Janne M. Sjodahl

About the middle of June, 1831, William W. Phelps with his family, arrived in Kirtland. He was born at Hanover, Morris

County, N.J., February 17th, 1792. In the State of New York he had edited a newspaper and taken an active part in politics. In Missouri, whither he went in company with the Prophet Joseph, he founded The Evening and Morning Star, a monthly magazine devoted to the interests of the Church, and published by the Church. Its first number appeared at Independence, June, 1832. The printing office was destroyed by a mob in July, 1833, but in the following December another printing office was established at Kirtland, and the publication of the *Star* was resumed there. Phelps, in 1837, was appointed to act, with David and John Whitmer, as a President of the Church in Zion. In 1848 he came to Utah, where he attained some prominence. He assisted in the drafting of the Constitution of Deseret, and became preceptor in the University. He died in Salt Lake City, March 7th, 1872, eighty years of age. Many inspiring hymns, popular among the Latter-day Saints, were composed by him. (DCC, p. 317)

Andrew Jenson

...At a meeting held in Far West, Missouri, Feb. 6, 1838, Wm. W. Phelps and his co-laborers in the presidency were rejected by the saints in the Carter settlement, Missouri. Other branches of the Church subsequently voted the same way. During the sessions of the court of inquiry held at Richmond, Mo., in November, 1838, Wm. W. Phelps, who had become bitter in his feelings, was among those who testified against the Church leaders. He was finally excommunicated from the Church at a conference held at Quincy, Illinois, March 17, 1839, but early in 1841 he was received back into fellowship in the Church . . . (LDSBE, Vol. 3, p. 695)

Sacred Truths

Introduction

The Lord instructed and counseled W.W. Phelps as noted in the Overview of Section Content. A discussion of the process of seeking and obtaining a remission of sins will be presented in this chapter.

Seeking and Obtaining a Remission of Sins

William W. Phelps was taught how he or anyone else could seek for and obtain a remission of his sins. He was told that such remission can only be obtained by having an eye single to the glory of God. (See D&C 55:1) Or in other words, he must do things the Lord's way. The Lord's way includes faith on His name, repentance, and entering into a covenant relationship with the Lord. That covenant is consummated through the rebirth process which includes baptism by immersion and the reception of the Holy Ghost by the laying on of hands by one who has authority in the church. Such a person is then eligible for a remission of his sins through the power of the atonement of Jesus Christ.

When a person yields to temptation and fails to keep his covenants, how does he again obtain a remission of his sins? Does he need to be re-baptized? No, baptism does not provide a remission of sins. The atonement of the Savior is the only power that remits sin. The sinner must repent and renew his baptismal covenant by partaking of the sacrament of the Lord's supper. Thus, he again becomes eligible for a remission of his sins.

An incident in the life of William W. Phelps provides an illustration of his breaking of covenants and his seeking to renew and re-establish his covenants with the Lord. As a result of his improper actions, he was excommunicated from the Church. So in his case, there needed to be a re-baptism.

Seeking to rectify his errors, he wrote a letter to the Prophet Joseph Smith, confessing his sins and pleading for forgiveness of the Saints. We call attention to three important portions of that letter:

1. Reference is made to a prophetic blessing given by Joseph Smith to William W. Phelps.

2. William W. Phelps referred to his dream that related to the prophetic blessing.

3. The repentant spirit of William W. Phelps is apparent in the way he pled for forgiveness.

The following is a copy of the letter dated June 29, 1840, written at Dayton, Ohio:

BROTHER JOSEPH:—I am alive, and with the help of God I mean to live still. I am as the prodigal son, though I never doubt or disbelieve the fulness of the Gospel. I have been greatly abused and humbled, and I blessed the God of Israel when I lately read your prophetic blessing on my head, as follows:

"The Lord will chasten him because he taketh honor to himself, and when his soul is greatly humbled he will forsake the evil. Then shall the light of the Lord break upon him as at noonday and in him shall be no darkness."

I have seen the folly of my way, and I tremble at the gulf I have passed. So it is, and why I know not. I prayed and God answered, but what could I do? Says I, "I will repent and live, and ask my old brethren to forgive me, and though they chasten me to death, yet I will die with them, for their God is my God. The least place with them is enough for me, yea, it is bigger and better than all Babylon." Then I dreamed that I was in a large house with many mansions, with you and Hyrum and Sidney, and when it was said, "Supper must be made ready," by one of the cooks, I saw no meat, but you said there was plenty, and you showed me much, and as good as I ever saw; and while cutting to cook, your heart and mine beat within us, and we took each other's hand and cried for joy, and I awoke and took courage.

I know my situation, you know it, and God knows it, and I want to be saved if my friend will help me. Like the captain that was cast away on a desert island; when he got off he went to sea again, and made his fortune the next time, so let my lot be. I have done wrong and I am sorry. The beam is in my own eye. I have not walked along with my friends according to my holy anointing. I ask forgiveness in the name of Jesus Christ of all the Saints, for I will do right, God helping me. I want your fellowship; if you cannot grant that, grant me your peace and friendship, for we are brethren, and our communion used to be sweet, and whenever the Lord brings us together again, I will make all the satisfaction on every point that Saints or God can require. Amen. (HC, Vol. 4, pp. 141-142)

In response to the above letter, Joseph Smith wrote a letter to William W. Phelps. In his letter, the Prophet expressed his personal feelings regarding the petition he had received. We call attention to the manner in which the prophet of the living God represented the Savior in handling this case. The following is a copy of the letter of Joseph Smith dated July 22, 1840, written at Nauvoo, Illinois:

Dear Brother Phelps:—I must say that it is with no ordinary feelings I endeavor to write a few lines to you in answer to yours of the 29th ultimo; at the same time I am rejoiced at the privilege granted me.

You may in some measure realize what my feelings as well as Elder Rigdon's and Brother Hyrum's were, when we read your letter—truly our hearts were melted into tenderness and compassion when we ascertained your resolves, etc. I can assure you I feel a disposition to act on your case in a manner that will meet the approbation of Jehovah, (whose servant I am), and agreeable to the principles of truth and righteousness which have been revealed; and inasmuch as long-suffering, patience, and mercy have ever characterized the dealing of our Heavenly Father towards the humble and penitent, I feel disposed to copy the example, cherish the same principles, and by so doing be a savior of my fellow men.

It is true, that we have suffered much in consequence of your behavior—the cup of gall, already full enough for mortals to drink, was indeed filled to overflowing when you turned against us. One with whom we had oft taken sweet counsel together, and enjoyed many refreshing seasons from the Lord—"had it been an enemy, we could have borne it." "In the day that thou stoodest on the other side, in the day when strangers carried away captive his forces, and foreigners entered into his gates, and cast lots upon [Far West], even thou wast as one of them; but thou shouldest not have looked on the day of thy brother, in the day that he became a stranger, neither shouldst thou have spoken proudly in the day of distress."

However, the cup has been drunk, the will of our Father has been done, and we are yet alive, for which we thank the Lord. And having been delivered from the hands of wicked men by the mercy of our God, we say it is your privilege to be delivered from the powers of the adversary, be brought into the liberty of God's dear children, and again take your stand among the Saints of the Most High, and by diligence, humility, and love unfeigned, commend yourself to our God, and your God, and to the Church of Jesus Christ.

Believing your confession to be real, and your repentance genuine, I shall be happy once again to give you the right hand of fellowship, and rejoice over the returning prodigal.

Your letter was read to the Saints last Sunday and an expression of their feeling was taken, when it was unanimously Resolved, that W.W. Phelps should be received into fellowship.

"Come on, dear brother, since the war is past,
For friends at first, are friends again at last."
Yours as ever,
Joseph Smith, Jun.
(HC, Vol. 4, pp. 162-164)

Summary and Conclusion

We have learned from this section that the most important thing in our life is to properly seek for and obtain a remission of sins through the atonement of Jesus Christ. Thus, we can be sanctified and stand approved of Him.

Chapter 45

Doctrine and Covenants Section 56

Suggested Title

The Lord Commands and Revokes

Overview of Section Content

1. The Lord's anger is kindled against the rebellious—He commands and revokes as seemeth Him good (vs. 1-4)
2. The Lord gives commandments and changes assignments for some of the brethren (vs. 5-13)
3. The Lord warns the rich and the poor concerning greediness (vs. 14-20)

Historical Setting

Joseph Smith, Jun.

Soon after I received the foregoing, [Section 55] Elder Thomas B. Marsh came to inquire what he should do; as Elder Ezra Thayre, his yokefellow in the ministry, could not get ready to start on his mission as soon as he (Marsh) would: and I inquired of the Lord, and received the following . . . (HC, Vol. 1, p. 186)

Sacred Truths

Introduction

The Lord had previously commanded Thomas B. Marsh and Ezra Thayre to go to Missouri as missionary companions. (See D&C 52:22) However, in the Historical Setting for Section 56, we are alerted to a problem. Ezra Thayre was not prepared to fulfill his appointment. Without a companion Thomas B. Marsh wondered what he should do and sought advice from the Lord through the Prophet Joseph Smith.

As a result of Ezra Thayre's failure to be obedient the Lord revoked the former commandment. (See D&C 56:5)

The Lord Commands and Revokes

It is important that we realize that this is the Lord's Church. The commandments are of Him. It is His prerogative to give commandments to His church as well as to revoke commandments when He sees fit. The principle is stated plainly by the Lord:

> Wherefore I, the Lord, command and revoke, as it seemeth me good; and all this to be answered upon the heads of the rebellious, saith the Lord. (D&C 56:4)

It is also important that we remember what the Lord has revealed in earlier sections of the Doctrine and Covenants. Any commandment, or revocation thereof, will be channelled through the Lord's mouthpiece, the living prophet. (See D&C Sections 21, 28, 43)

Again, it is important to know that there may be many reasons why the Lord revokes a commandment. But the one He mentions in Section 56 is rebellion. (See D&C 56:1-4) This same reason is echoed again as discussed by the Lord in a later revelation:

> Who am I that made man, saith the Lord, that will hold him guiltless that obeys not my commandments?
>
> Who am I, saith the Lord, that have promised and have not fulfilled?
>
> I command and men obey not; I revoke and they receive not the blessing.
>
> Then they say in their hearts: This is not the work of the Lord, for his promises are not fulfilled. But wo unto such, for their reward lurketh beneath, and not from above. (D&C 58:30-33)

What should we learn? The Lord directs His church and all policies and practices will come from Him through His living prophets. Let us not be guilty of resisting changes and rebelling against revelations coming from the Lord, whether they be new commandments or the revocation of previous ones.

One of the great evidences of a Latter-day Saint's faith in Jesus Christ is his willingness to accept and render obedience to policies, directions, practices, and commandments that have been given and will yet be given by the Lord as announced by His authorized servants.

The Savior set the example of such obedience for every Latter-day Saint and also the world if they would hearken. His commitment to obedience was verbalized in the Garden of Gethsemane when He said to His Father, "...not as I will, but as thou wilt." (Bible, Matthew 26:39) That mortal commitment was culminated as He took up His cross by voluntarily giving His life, that His Father's will might be done.

In this revelation, the Lord said:

> And he that will not take up his cross and follow me, and keep my commandments, the same shall not be saved. (D&C 56:2)

What is meant by our cross? It is a voluntary act of submitting our will to the Lord. When a Latter-day Saint is obedient to the Lord, whether it be to a new commandment or the revocation of a former one, he is demonstrating his desire to follow the Savior by taking up his own cross of obedience. Thus, he subjugates his own will, interests, and desires to be in harmony with the will of the Master. But by so doing, he has the priceless promise of salvation in the Lord's kingdom.

Summary and Conclusion

This is the Lord's church, His priesthood, and His gospel. All principles and practices within the church are subject to the will and direction of the Lord and will be made known by Him through His living prophet. The Lord commands and revokes as seemeth Him good.

Chapter 46

Doctrine and Covenants Section 57

Suggested Title

The Center Place of Zion

Overview of Section Content

1. Missouri is a land of promise (vs. 1-2)
2. The center place of Zion and the Temple (vs. 3)
3. Counsel to purchase land in Missouri (vs. 4-5)
4. Specific instructions to certain elders and other members (vs 6-16)

Historical Setting

Joseph Smith, Jun.

The meeting of our brethren, [in Missouri] who had long awaited our arrival, was a glorious one, and moistened with many tears. It seemed good and pleasant for brethren to meet together in unity. But our reflections were many, coming as we had from a highly cultivated state of society in the east, and standing now upon the confines or western limits of the United States, and looking into the vast wilderness of those that sat in darkness; how natural it was to observe the degradation, leanness of intellect, ferocity, and jealousy of a people that were nearly a century behind the times, and to feel for those who roamed about without the benefit of civilization, refinement, or religion; yea, and exclaim in the language of the Prophets: "When will the wilderness blossom as the rose? When will Zion be built up in her glory, and where will Thy temple stand, unto which all nations shall come in the last days?" Our anxiety was soon relieved by receiving the following . . . (HC, Vol. 1, p. 189)

Joseph Fielding Smith

. . .When the Prophet Joseph and his brethren arrived in Jackson County they were all anxious for the Lord to make known to them the location for the city of Zion—New Jerusalem. In answer to their pleading they received the revelation (Sec. 57) . . . (CHMR, Vol. 1, p. 188)

Hyrum M. Smith and Janne M. Sjodahl

In the Book of Mormon the Saints were told (Ether 13:1-12), that the new Jerusalem and Holy Sanctuary of the Lord should be located in America (Comp. III Nephi 20:22; 21:23), and they were anxious to know where the site for the City was. In September, 1830, the Lord gave them to understand that the City should be erected "on the borders by the Lamanites" (Sec. 28:9). In February, 1831, they were promised that a Revelation should be given on that subject, if they would pray for it (Sec. 42:62). On the 7th of March, the same year, they were given to understand that the gathering from the eastern States and the sending out of Elders on the mission to the West were preparatory steps to the establishment of that City, wherefore the Saints should gather up their riches and purchase an inheritance in the place to be indicated, which should be a place of refuge for the Saints of the most High God (Sec. 45:64-66). The time had now come for the fulfilment of the promise referred to (Sec. 42:62), and this Revelation was received . . . (DCC, pp. 327-328)

Sacred Truths

Introduction

We remember that in a previous revelation the Lord counseled the Ohio Saints to be prepared to purchase lands for the establishment of a city, the location of which was yet to be revealed. (See D&C 48:4-6) A few months later, the Lord directed Joseph Smith to travel to the land of Missouri where the Lord would then reveal the specific location of the city to be built. (See D&C 52:3-5) As noted in the Historical Setting of this chapter, Joseph was obedient to the Lord's directive. (See accompanying map) He was anxious to receive revelation as the Lord had promised that the Saints might know the location of the city of Zion. The prophet was aware of the significance of the establishment of Zion in the latter days. On one occasion he later said:

> The building up of Zion is a cause that has interested the people of God in every age; it is a theme upon which prophets, priests and kings have dwelt with peculiar delight; they have looked forward with joyful anticipation to the day in which we live; and fired with heavenly and joyful anticipations they have sung and written and prophesied of this our day. (HC, Vol. 4, pp. 609-610)

We can partially realize and understand the excitement felt in the prophet's bosom. He stood on the threshold of reality as it was about to be made known to him by the Lord concerning a tangible fulfillment of the long-looked-for establishment of the place for the city of Zion.

The Center Place of Zion

The Lord identified the specific location for the city of Zion when He said to Joseph who was then in the land of Missouri:

> Wherefore, this is the land of promise, and the place for the city of Zion. (D&C 57:2)

This revelation not only contains the revealing of the place for the city of Zion, but we are also told that there is more to the establishment of Zion than just building a city. The Lord alerts us to a vital aspect of the Zion concept. We learn that a temple is to be an essential part of such an endeavor. Speaking of the inclusion of a temple, the Lord said:

> And thus saith the Lord your God, if you will receive wisdom here is wisdom. Behold, the place which is now called Independence is the center place; and a spot for the temple is lying westward, upon a lot which is not far from the court-house. (D&C 57:3)

We are aware that much more will be revealed by the Lord in later sections that pertains to the establishing and building of Zion. It is in this section, however, that we first learn that Zion cannot be established without a temple. The two are inseparably connected.

It should be remembered that before the church was ever established in this dispensation the Lord referred to the need for the establishment of Zion. (See D&C 6:6; 11:6; 12:6; 14:6) On the day the church was organized the Lord revealed that one of the inspired functions of the prophet was that he would "...move the cause of Zion..." (D&C 21:7) It is interesting to note that the first recorded instance in the Doctrine and Covenants of false revelation in this dispensation dealt with the upbuilding of Zion. (See Historical Setting, Chap. 20, this volume) Satan attempted to mislead the saints in their understanding of this important work of the Lord. (See D&C 28:9-11)

As far as a temple is concerned, an intimation that temples would be built in this dispensation came in the revelation given to Edward Partridge. (see D&C 36:8; see also DCC, p. 192)

As has been noted, the bringing together of these two concepts (Zion and temples) first appears in the Doctrine and Covenants in Section 57. Subsequent revelations in the Doctrine and Covenants will continue to stress the association and relationship of temples to Zion.

Summary and Conclusion

When the Lord gave this revelation, He revealed two important facts pertaining to the establishment of Zion:

1. The location of the center place
2. The inclusion of a temple in the establishing of Zion

In addition to these two facts, the Lord counseled us to receive wisdom. (See D&C 57:3) What wisdom should we receive? Whether we are building the center place of Zion, or building up any of the stakes of Zion, or strengthening the family units in Zion, an essential truth prevails: There will only be a Zion place, organization, and people when there is a temple constructed and the Saints are endowed with the power of God therein. May we be wise enough to understand and receive the values of having access to the blessings of the temples in Zion.

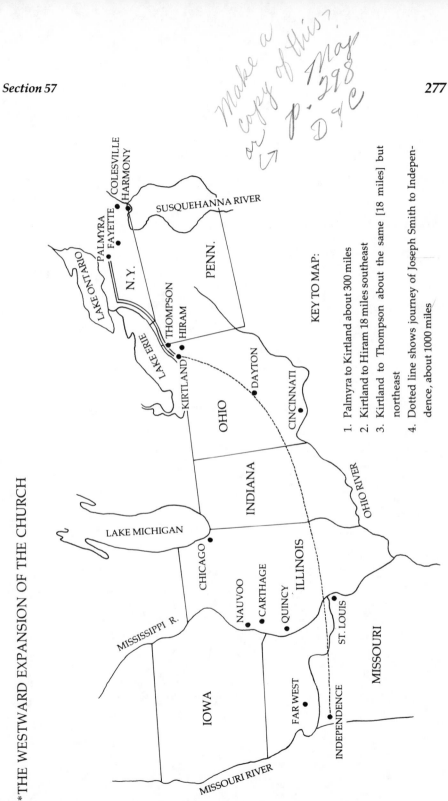

THE WESTWARD EXPANSION OF THE CHURCH

KEY TO MAP:

1. Palmyra to Kirtland about 300 miles

2. Kirtland to Hiram 18 miles southeast

3. Kirtland to Thompson about the same [18 miles] but northeast

4. Dotted line shows journey of Joseph Smith to Independence, about 1000 miles

Chapter 47

Doctrine and Covenants Section 58

Suggested Title

The Lord's Will Concerning the Land of Zion and His People

Overview of Section Content

1. Blessings promised to the faithful in Zion (vs. 1-5)
2. Some purposes for the saints being in Missouri in 1831 (vs. 6-14)
3. Some duties of Edward Partridge and others as Bishops in Zion (vs. 15-20)
4. Saints to obey the laws of the land and the laws of the church (vs. 21-23)
5. Instructions to Edward Partridge and those who assist him (vs. 24-25)
6. The Lord's commandments and man's own free will (vs. 26-33)
7. The Lord's counsel to Martin Harris (vs. 34-39)
8. The Lord's counsel to William W. Phelps (vs. 40-41)
9. The repentant to receive the Lord's forgiveness (vs. 42-43, 60)
10. The Lord's counsel to the saints pertaining to their gathering in Zion (vs. 44-49, 52-57)
11. The Lord's commandment to Sidney Rigdon (vs. 50-51)
12. The Lord's counsel to the saints traveling to and from Zion (vs. 58-59, 61-65)

Historical Setting

Joseph Smith, Jun.

The first Sabbath after our arrival in Jackson county, Brother W.W. Phelps preached to a western audience over the boundary of the United States, wherein were present specimens of all the families of the earth; Shem, Ham and Japheth; several of the Lamanites or Indians—representative of Shem; quite a respectable number of negroes—descendants of Ham; and the balance was made up of citizens of the surrounding country, and fully represented themselves—pioneers of the West. At this meeting two were baptized, who had previously believed in the fulness of the Gospel.

During this week the Colesville branch, referred to in the latter part of the last revelation, and Sidney Rigdon, Sidney Gilbert and wife and Elders Morley and Booth, arrived. I received the following . . . (HC, Vol. 1, pp. 190-191)

Sacred Truths

Introduction

Chapter 46 of this volume contains a discussion of Joseph Smith's first journey to Missouri. While there, he received a revelation (D&C Section 57) identifying the place for the New Jerusalem (City of Zion). In addition to that revelation, the Lord also gave instructions in subsequent revelations pertaining to the laws and standards that must be observed in Zion. Some of these requirements, blessings promised to the obedient, as well as various instructions of the Lord are contained in Section 58 of the Doctrine and Covenants.

The Lord addressed the saints in Missouri as follows:

Hearken, O ye elders of my church, and give ear to my word, and learn of me what I will concerning you, and also concerning this land unto which I have sent you. (D&C 58:1)

In the above verse, the Lord reveals that His will pertains not only to the land of Zion, but also to the people who are to live there.

In this chapter we will discuss some of the counsel given by the Lord in this revelation.

Saints in Missouri in 1831

On occasion, people have mistakenly concluded that the Lord directed the saints to go to Missouri with the understanding that they would complete the building of Zion at that time. Even some of the early saints labored under such an impression. However, the Lord made it plain in this revelation, that the establishment of Zion and her people would not take place at that time but would only come after much tribulation. (See D&C 58:2-5) Elder B.H. Roberts discussed this portion of the Lord's revelation as follows:

> These promises to the Saints respecting Zion; these descriptions given to them of her future sanctified and glorified state; their connection with a work so exalted and far-reaching, was apt to fire their minds with a zeal not always tempered with wisdom. It was in vain that limitations of time and conditions were placed upon these general descriptions of the future greatness and glory of the city of God; nor could they understand that their own relationship to these great things was merely to lay the foundation of them, to locate the site of the future city and temple, and then bear witness of it to the world. Yet that their work in connection with the founding of Zion was chiefly this, is clearly to be seen in the revelations of God to them.
>
> The immediate and triumphant establishment of Zion, though expected by many of the Saints, was nowhere contemplated in the revelations of God to the Church. That hope of immediate establishment and glorification of Zion was the result of faulty deductions from the revelations of God; but the Lord was not blind respecting the events about to take place on the land of Zion, nor did He hold out any false hope to His people had they but read His revelations aright. A few days before the first conference held by the Elders on the land of Zion, the Lord said to them through His Prophet: [Quotes D&C 58:1-7, 13, 44-45]
>
> These statements, when rightly considered, dispel all notion of the immediate establishment of Zion. The Lord distinctly warns His servants against any such supposition. He predicts "tribulation" before the glory shall come. It is only after "much tribulation" that the blessings are promised. (HC, Vol. 3, Introduction, pp. xxxiv-xxxvi)

What were some of the purposes for the saints to be in Missouri in 1831?

1. Learn obedience

It is interesting that the saints were to learn obedience in the midst of tribulation. (See D&C 58:4, 6) The apostle Paul said the Savior Himself learned obedience " . . . by the things which He suffered." (Bible, Hebrews 5:8) It is one thing to be obedient. It is quite another to learn obedience.

Unless we face and overcome opposition through the use of our agency, we don't really learn obedience.

2. Prepare to bear testimony

The saints were to have their hearts prepared that they might bear testimony of things to come. (See D&C 58:6) How is a person's heart prepared to bear testimony? By exercising faith and being obedient to the teachings and commandments of the Lord. Afterwards, comes the witness of the Spirit and a testimony is born. (See B. of M., Ether 12:6) Thus he is prepared to bear testimony. What are some of the things to come in Missouri of which testimony was to be borne?

A. The house of the Lord is to be built.
B. The building of the New Jerusalem (City of Zion) is to take place.
C. The Savior will appear to His saints.
D. The law will go forth from Zion.

The above list is not exhaustive. But we know of these things because of the testimony borne by those whose hearts were prepared by the Lord and who testified to others of these things to come.

3. Lay the foundation of Zion

Though they would not complete the building of Zion, the saints would be honored with the privilege of laying the foundation thereof. (See D&C 58:7) It was while they were there that the land was dedicated for the establishment of Zion and the building of temples unto the Lord. The Prophet Joseph Smith provided the following account of the formal proceedings of dedication:

> On the second day of August, I assisted the Colesville branch of the Church to lay the first log, for a house, as a foundation of Zion in Kaw township, twelve miles west of Independence. The log was carried and placed by twelve men, in honor of the twelve tribes of Israel. At the same time, through prayer, the land of Zion was consecrated and dedicated by Elder Sidney Rigdon for the gathering of the Saints. It was a season of joy to those present, and afforded a glimpse of the future, which time will yet unfold to the satisfaction of the faithful.
>
> On the third day of August, I proceeded to dedicate the spot for the Temple, a little west of Independence, and there were also present Sidney Rigdon, Edward Partridge, W.W. Phelps, Oliver Cowdery, Martin Harris and Joseph Coe.
>
> The 87th Psalm was read . . .
>
> The scene was solemn and impressive. (HC, Vol. 1, pp. 196, 199)

4. *Prepare a feast*

The saints were to prepare to offer a feast to the world. (See D&C 58:8-11) By way of explanation of this responsibility, the following commentary is provided:

> One great purpose of God in establishing Zion is to save the world, through its laws and institutions, from the curse of poverty and destitution. The object is to give to the world an entirely new social order, to establish a community in which even the poor would share the "fat things" with "the rich and the learned, the wise and the noble" (v. 10) Zion is to be a place for the "supper of the house of the Lord"—a banquet hall—"unto which all nations shall be invited." There "the marriage feast of the Lamb" will be held when the time has come for God Omnipotent to reign upon this Earth (Rev. 19:7-9). It is the New Jerusalem, consisting of the City of Zion and the "Jerusalem which is above," that is, "the Bride of the Lamb" (Rev. 21:2; Gal. 4:26; Eph. 5:27). The two will be united when our Savior comes in His glory. "Blessed are they who are called unto the marriage supper of the Lamb." Yea, blessed are they who will be called to become citizens in the City of Zion. (DCC, pp. 336-337)

The Lord's Bishops

By divine decree, the Lord has assigned bishops to be judges in Israel in the dispensation of the fulness of times as well as in ancient days. (See D&C 58:17-18)

Any man who is called to be a Bishop (judge in Israel) should always keep in mind what the Lord has said to them.

> Let no man think he is ruler; but let God rule him that judgeth, according to the counsel of his own will, or, in other words, him that counseleth or sitteth upon the judgement seat. (D&C 58:20)

In other words, a Bishop is here reminded that he ought not to rely on his own wisdom but should always be sure that his judgment is compatible with the will of the Lord who is truly the ruler.

Knowing that the Lord rules through His Bishops, Latter-day Saints can and should have confidence in the counsel and judgment given by one who occupies that sacred position by appointment of the Lord. The Saints should be humbly grateful to have such an intimate relationship with the Lord through His equally-humble servant, the Bishop. In Zion, such is the relationship among the Saints, the Bishops, and the Lord.

Laws of the Land

Pertaining to the responsibility of the saints towards the laws of the land, the Lord said:

Let no man break the laws of the land, for he that keepeth the laws of God hath no need to break the laws of the land.

Wherefore, be subject to the powers that be, until he reigns whose right it is to reign, and subdues all enemies under his feet. (D&C 58:21-22)

An analysis of these verses reveals a relationship between the laws of the land, the laws of the Lord and the Lord's people. To stand approved of the Lord, as people of Zion, the saints cannot be disobedient to the laws of the land and at the same time expect the Lord's blessings. Our responsibilities in this regard have been explained by Pres. N. Eldon Tanner:

It is a fact that the laws of the land are made by the governing body in the interest of the safety and well-being of the citizens. Consider, for example, the laws pertaining to drunken driving and other regulations pertaining to highway traffic control, health, zoning restrictions, building codes, etc. Even taxes make it possible for us to have better roads, better schools, and other public services, all of which are for our comfort and convenience and self-improvement.

If all people were to recognize law as a benefit to man and then honor and obey it, it would contribute greatly to our health, well-being, and happiness. Laws are essential. Imagine a city, community, state, or country without law and regulations. To the extent we disregard, disobey, and flaunt the law, we are losing our freedom, depriving others of theirs, and leading to anarchy. If a bad law exists, then the people should take proper legal measures through their governing bodies to improve or change the law, but while it is law, it should be obeyed. (CR, April 1970, pp. 62-63)

Commandments—Good Causes—Free Will

The Lord expects His Saints to be people of initiative in doing good things. (See D&C 58:26-29) What is meant by "good"? The Lord has informed us through His prophet Mormon's teachings that " . . .everything which inviteth to do good, and to persuade to believe in Christ, is sent forth by the power and gift of Christ; wherefore ye may know with a perfect knowledge it is of God." (B. of M., Moroni 7:16)

Being engaged in a good cause means that efforts expended in that cause are intended to result in bringing people to a closer relationship with the Lord and strengthening them in their personal capacities of goodness.

A modern-day prophet, Spencer W. Kimball, has illustrated how people in Zion might apply this principle:

> Seemingly small efforts in the life of each member could do so much to move the Church forward as never before. Think, brothers and sisters, what would happen if each active family were to bring another family or individual into the Church before next April conference: We would be joined by several hundred thousand new members of the Church. Imagine, if only one additional mature couple were to be called on a full-time mission from each ward—our missionary force would go from 27,500 to over 40,000! Contemplate the results if each family were to assist—between now and next April conference—an inactive family or individual into full activity. How we would revel in the association of those tens of thousands!
>
> Think of the blessings here and on the other side of the veil if each holder of a temple recommend were to do just one more endowment this next year! And how would our nonmember neighbors and friends feel if we were each to do just one more quiet act of Christian service for them before October conference—regardless of whether or not they are interested in the Church!
>
> Imagine how much richer our family life would be if our spouses and children were to receive a few more minutes of individual attention each month! (CR, April 1979, p. 114)

The Lord's Forgiveness

The greatest message of peace ever declared to mortal man is that he can gain peace in his soul only as he is freed from the effects of sin through the atonement of Jesus Christ. In order to obtain such peace, mankind must repent in accordance with the instructions of the Savior as follows:

> Behold, he who has repented of his sins, the same is forgiven, and I, the Lord, remember them no more.
>
> By this ye may know if a man repenteth of his sins—behold, he will confess them and forsake them. (D&C 58:42-43)

The greatest blessing for compliance with these divine instructions is the assurance one has that the Lord will remember his sins no more. Sins repented of, will not be used in judgment against a repentant soul. The Lord revealed to Ezekiel:

> But if the wicked will turn from all his sins that he hath committed, and keep all my statutes, and do that which is lawful and

right, he shall surely live, he shall not die.

All his transgressions that he hath committed, they shall not be mentioned unto him: in his righteousness that he hath done he shall live. (Bible, Ezekiel 18:21-22)

There is another vital point that must not be overlooked. The Savior has told us to do that which we have seen Him do. (See B. of M., III Nephi 27:21) Therefore, when the Savior assures us He will never accuse a repentant soul, then we ought to do likewise for ourselves and others. If one has truly repented, he will not harbor feelings of guilt over sins repented of. Instead, his faith in Jesus Christ will cause him to look forward with peace in His heart and a determination to be obedient to the will of the Lord. Truly, people in Zion are pure in heart.

Summary and Conclusion

This revelation has provided insights as to the will of the Lord concerning the land of Zion and His people. Those who adhere to the teachings contained in this revelation will be assisted in preparing to live in a society of Zion. Such people will always be approved of the Lord.

Chapter 48

Doctrine and Covenants Section 59

Suggested Title

Blessings and Commandments—Sabbath Day

Overview of Section Content

1. Blessings promised by the Lord to the obedient in Zion (vs. 1-4, 15-19, 23-24)
2. Commandments of the Lord to the inhabitants of Zion (vs. 5-14)
3. It pleases the Lord to bless man (vs. 20)
4. The way man offends God (vs. 21-22)

Historical Setting

Joseph Smith, Jun.

On the 7th, I attended the funeral of Sister Polly Knight, the wife of Joseph Knight, Sen. This was the first death in the Church in this land, and I can say, a worthy member sleeps in Jesus till the resurrection.

I also received the following . . . (HC, Vol. 1, p. 199)

B.H. Roberts

Polly Knight's health had been failing for some time, according to a statement made by her son, Newel. She was very ill during her journey from Kirtland to Missouri, "Yet," says her son, "She would not consent to stop traveling; her only, or her greatest desire was to set her feet upon the land of Zion, and to have her body interred in that land. I went on shore and bought lumber to make a coffin in case she should die before we arrived at our place of destination— so fast did she fail. But the Lord gave her the desire of her heart, and she lived to stand upon that land."—*Scraps of Biography*, p. 70. (HC, Vol. 1, p. 199, Footnote)

Sacred Truths

Introduction

As with Section 58, so also Section 59 of the Doctrine and Covenants contains the instructions of the Lord pertaining to Zion and her people. There are standards of conduct that the Lord expects His people to observe in a Zion society. In this revelation, He has given several commandments for this purpose. We will discuss some of these in this chapter.

Standards of Conduct in a Zion Society

In this revelation, the Lord reaffirmed the two great commandments upon which all other commandments are founded: (See D&C 59:5-6)

1. Love and serve God in the name of Jesus Christ, with all thy heart, might, mind, and strength.
2. Love thy neighbor as thyself.

In the verses that follow, the Lord revealed several commandments, the observing of which, would bring us into compliance with the two great commandments mentioned above.

1. Stealing, Adultery, Killing

The Lord's people are commanded not to steal, commit adultery or kill. (See D&C 59:6) In that same verse the Lord also said " . . .nor do anything like unto it."

Stealing has always been wrong. But stealing is only one form of dishonesty. Dishonesty in any form might be seen as "like unto it". The Lord places the requirement for people of Zion to be totally honest and not engage in any form of violation of the standards of integrity.

Adultery is one of the most serious sins committed in mortality. Any act or thought that leads to or that might culminate in an adulterous act is "like unto it" and is condemned by the Lord. With such a divine injunction, no one can expect to live in Zion who justifies or fails to repent of acts of petting, masturbation, homosexuality, etc.

Killing is a sin for which there is no forgiveness (See D&C 42:18, 79) Not only has the Lord warned us against this horrible sin, but He has also warned us against doing anything "like unto it." One act of sin that is identified as being like unto killing is abortion. Speaking of such a degrading act, the First Presidency has said:

> In view of a recent decision of the United States Supreme Court, we feel it necessary to restate the position of the church on abortion in order that there be no misunderstanding of our attitude.
>
> The church opposes abortion and counsels its members not to submit to or perform an abortion except in the rare cases where, in the opinion of competent medical counsel, the life or good health of the mother is seriously endangered or where the pregnancy was caused by rape and produces serious emotional trauma in the mother. Even then it should be done only after counseling with the local presiding priesthood authority and after receiving divine confirmation through prayer.
>
> Abortion must be considered one of the most revolting and sinful practices in this day, when we are witnessing the frightening evidence of permissiveness leading to sexual immorality.
>
> Members of the church guilty of being parties to the sin of abortion must be subjected to the disciplinary action of the councils of the church as circumstances warrant. In dealing with this serious matter, it would be well to keep in mind the word of the Lord stated in the 59th section of the Doctrine and Covenants, verse 6, "Thou shalt not steal; neither commit adultry, nor kill, nor do anything like unto it."
>
> As to the amenability of the sin of abortion to the laws of repentence and forgiveness, we quote the following statement made by President David O. McKay and his counselors, Stephen L. Richards and J. Reuben Clark Jr., which continues to represent the attitude and position of the church:
>
> "As the matter stands today, no definite statement has been made by the Lord one way or another regarding the crime of abortion. So far as is known, He has not listed it alongside the crime of the unpardonable sin and shedding of innocent human blood. That He has not done so would suggest that it is not in that class of crime and therefore that it will be amenable to the laws of repentance and forgiveness."
>
> This quoted statement, however, should not, in any sense, be construed to minimize the seriousness of this revolting sin. (Church News, Jan. 27, 1973, p. 7)

2. Giving Thanks

One of the characteristics of people in Zion is that they will " . . .thank the Lord . . .in all things." (D&C 59:7) Pres. Joseph F. Smith has described how the spirit of gratitude in individuals can permeate and influence a whole society for good. He said:

> The spirit of gratitude is always pleasant and satisfying because it carries with it a sense of helpfulness to others; it begets love and friendship, and engenders divine influence. Gratitude is said to be the memory of the heart.
>
> And where there is an absence of gratitude, either to God or man, there is the presence of vanity and the spirit of self-sufficiency. (GD, p. 262)

The absence of this divine attribute is looked upon by the Lord as an offense unto God. (See D&C 59:21) Pres. Joseph F. Smith described such a condition as sin:

> And I believe that one of the greatest sins of which the inhabitants of the earth are guilty today is the sin of ingratitude, the want of acknowledgement, on their part, of God and his right to govern and control. We see a man raised up with extraordinary gifts, or with great intelligence, and he is instrumental in developing some great principle. He and the world ascribe his great genius and wisdom to himself. He attributes his success to his own energies, labor and mental capacity. He does not acknowledge the hand of God in anything connected with his success, but ignores him altogether and takes the honor to himself; this will apply to almost all the world. In all the great modern discoveries in science, in the arts, in mechanics, and in all material advancement of the age, the world says, "We have done it". The individual says, "I have done it", and he gives no honor or credit to God. Now, I read in revelations through Joseph Smith, the prophet, that because of this, God is not pleased with the inhabitants of the earth but is angry with them because they will not acknowledge his hand in all things. (GD, pp. 270-271)

3. Sacrifice

Since the days of Adam the Lord has required His people to offer sacrifice. Anciently, the law required the shedding of the blood of animals in similitude of the great atoning sacrifice of the Savior. Following the Savior's own sacrifice, He addressed the Nephites and commanded them as follows:

And ye shall offer up unto me no more the shedding of blood;
yea, your sacrifices and your burnt offerings shall be done away, for
I will accept none of your sacrifices and your burnt offerings.

And ye shall offer for a sacrifice unto me a broken heart and a
contrite spirit. And whoso cometh unto me with a broken heart and
a contrite spirit, him will I baptize with fire and with the Holy
Ghost, even as the Lamanites, because of their faith in me at the
time of their conversion, were baptized with fire and with the Holy
Ghost, and they knew it not. (B. of M., III Nephi 9:19-20)

In the dispensation of the fulness of times, the Lord reaffirmed the new
law of sacrifice. (See D&C 59:8) In a later revelation, the Lord spoke of
conditions in Zion and declared that not only should the saints have a
broken heart and a contrite spirit, but they should also be *willing* to observe
their covenants by sacrifice. (See D&C 97:8)

How does a Latter-day Saint comply with the law of sacrifice? Pres. J.
Reuben Clark, Jr. discussed this law and compliance therewith as follows:

...Under the new covenant that came in with Christ, the
sinner must offer the sacrifice out of his own life, not by offering the
blood of some other creature; he must give up his sins, he must
repent, he himself must make the sacrifice, and that sacrifice was
calculated to reach out into the life of the sinner in the future so that
he would become a better and changed man. (Behold the Lamb of
God, pp. 107-108)

Zion's people not only sacrifice unrighteousness out of their lives, but
willingly offer to be obedient and make whatever sacrifice the Lord may
require of them. The condition of willingness is far more important than the
sacrifice itself.

4. Sabbath Day

This revelation was given at the site of the future city of Zion in
Missouri on Sunday, Aug. 7, 1831, "the Lord's day." (See D&C 59:12)

Along with keeping the previously mentioned commandments, the
Lord said that keeping the Sabbath day holy would also serve to help keep
His people unspotted from the world. (See D&C 59:9)

The Lord directed His people to participate in several activities
appropriate to a proper Sabbath-day observance: (See D&C 59:9-15)

a. Go to the house of prayer (house of worship)
b. Offer up sacraments to the Lord (pledges, oblations, covenants,
   consecrations, etc.)
c. Rest from man's temporal labors

d. Pay devotions to the Lord (prayer, worship, etc.)
e. Confess sins
f. Prepare food without detracting from the spirit of the Sabbath

The First Presidency has given guidelines as to what constitutes appropriate observance of the Sabbath day:

> The Sabbath is not just another day on which we merely rest from work, free to spend it as our lightmindedness may suggest. It is a holy day, the Lord's Day, to be spent as a day of worship and reverence. All matters extraneous thereto should be shunned. (Deseret News, June 20, 1959)

A simple way for each person to judge as to whether his Sabbath-day activities are in harmony with the spirit of the Lord's day is to evaluate them in light of the above criteria. We might ask ourselves the following question:

Do my thoughts and actions contribute to the spirit of worship and reverence of the Lord?

Summary and Conclusion

As the Lord declared in the beginning of this revelation, commandments are given as blessings for His people. One of these blessings is the receiving of additional commandments in their time. (See D&C 59:4) The commandments of the Lord provide the formula by which one masters the flesh and remains unspotted from the world. This is the doorway to obtaining " . . .peace in this world, and eternal life in the world to come." (D&C 59:23)

Pres. George Q. Cannon emphasized the value of keeping the Lord's commandments when he said:

> Jesus, the Son of God, has attained to His exalted station by obeying the very principles that constitute our religion. The angels that surround the throne of our Almighty Father have received their exaltation and glory by obeying these principles, observing one law after another until the whole character is transformed and becomes Godlike. (Gospel Truth, Vol. 2, p. 12)

This is the spirit of this revelation and the purpose of Zion.

Chapter 49

Doctrine and Covenants Section 60

Suggested Title

Talent

Overview of Section Content

1. The Lord counsels the elders concerning their return journey from Zion to Kirtland (vs. 1, 5-11)
2. The Lord's counsel on the importance of sharing the gospel with others (vs. 2-4)
3. The Lord counsels those who will yet come up to the land of Zion to preach the gospel (vs. 12-17)

Historical Setting

Joseph Smith, Jun.

On the 8th, as there had been some inquiry among the Elders what they were to do, I received the following... (HC, Vol. 1, p. 201)

Joseph Fielding Smith

...On the 8th day of August, 1831, at the close of the first conference held in Missouri, the elders inquired what they were to do. The Prophet inquired of the Lord and received a revelation

giving them direction in relation to their return journey...
(CHMR, Vol. 1, p. 203)

Sacred Truths

Introduction

The Prophet Joseph Smith was still in Missouri. He had been commanded to travel from Ohio that the Lord might reveal unto him the location for the future city of Zion (New Jerusalem). (See D&C Section 57) This had all been accomplished. In addition, the Lord had also given counsel and commandments that defined acceptable behavior and standards for those who would live in Zion. (See D&C Sections 58 & 59)

The time had now come to consider matters pertaining to the return journey to Ohio. Some of the brethren had inquired of Joseph concerning this matter, and he in turn sought direction from the Lord.

The Lord's Counsel Concerning the Return Journey to Ohio

In this revelation there are at least three items of counsel pertaining to this journey.

1.   A Proper Time and Way

Now that the particular assignment given to Joseph was completed, it was time to move on and be about other phases of the Lord's work. There was no need to stay longer in Missouri, but instead, they were to " . . .return speedily to the land from whence they came." (D&C 60:1)

As to the means of transportation, they were instructed to make their own decision. (See D&C 60:5) There are occasions when the Lord does not initiate divine direction on certain matters. This was one of those times. He expects people to use their intelligence to make wise decisions. He will confirm correct judgment. But he may leave the decision-making process to the individual. (See also D&C 61:22)

The Lord cautioned, that while on their journey home, the elders were not to go in haste. They were to preach the gospel enroute and not be in such a hurry that they failed to teach the people along the way. (See D&C 60:8)

2.   Talent

Some of the brethren had failed in their responsibility to teach others of the gospel message. A knowledge and testimony of the gospel comes from the Lord and He expects this God-given talent to be shared with others. The Savior said:

> But with some I am not well pleased, for they will not open their mouths, but they hide the talent which I have given unto

them, because of the fear of man. Wo unto such, for mine anger is kindled against them . . .

Behold, they have been sent to preach my gospel among the congregations of the wicked; wherefore, I give unto them a commandment, thus: Thou shalt not idle away thy time, neither shalt thou bury thy talent that it may not be known. (D&C 60:2, 13)

One of the benefits that comes from sharing our testimony talent has been explained by Pres. Brigham Young as follows:

A man who wishes to receive light and knowledge, to increase in the faith of the Holy Gospel, and to grow in the knowledge of the truth as it is in Jesus Christ, will find that when he imparts knowledge to others he will also grow and increase. Be not miserly in your feelings, but get knowledge and understanding by freely imparting it to others, and be not like a man who selfishly hoards his gold; for that man will not thus increase upon the amount, but will become contracted in his views and feelings. So the man who will not impart freely of the knowledge he has received, will become so contracted in his mind that he cannot receive truth when it is presented to him. Wherever you see an opportunity to do good, do it, for that is the way to increase and grow in the knowledge of the truth. (JD, Vol. 2, p. 267)

3. Rejection of the Lord's Servants

The sharing of the gospel must always be accompanied by the bearing of testimony as a witness that the message is true. Those who are recipients of the message may choose to receive it or reject it according to their use of their agency. There may be occasions when someone rejects it in such a way as to be offensive to the Lord. Under such circumstances, the Lord may desire that the testimony of the elders be sealed by the shaking off of the dust of the feet as a testimony against those who so rejected the message. (See D&C 60:15) The bearing of this type of testimony has been discussed and counsel has been given as follows:

Our Lord instructed His first Apostles to shake the dust off their feet, when they departed from a house or a city in which their message had been rejected. Paul and Barnabas did so, when they were forced to leave Antioch in Pisidia (Acts 13:50-1). Paul, at Corinth, when the Jews opposed him and blasphemed, shook his raiment and said, "Your blood be upon your own heads; I am clean" (Acts 18:6). The significance of this solemn act is made clear in Nehemiah 5:13. This prophet, after having taken a promise of the priests, shook his lap and said, "God shake out every man from his house, and from his labor, that performeth not this promise, even thus be he shaken out and empty." To shake the dust of the feet signified the same thing. The Elders of the Church were to perform this act in secret, as a testimony against scoffers and persecutors on the day of judgment, and only when prompted by the Spirit, lest they should make a serious mistake. (DCC p. 360, underlining added)

Summary and Conclusion

Church service rendered is a means of providing an opportunity for the gospel to become a blessing in the lives of the Lord's children. Sharing the gospel is of primary importance in the work of the kingdom. Such talent must not be hidden.

Chapter 50

Doctrine and Covenants Section 61

Suggested Title

The Waters and the Land—Satan

Overview of Section Content

1. The Lord forgives sins of those who confess with humble hearts (vs. 1-2)
2. Dangers upon the waters (vs. 3-5)
3. The Lord affords protection upon the waters (vs. 6)
4. The Lord's counsel to Sidney Gilbert and William W. Phelps (vs. 7-12)
5. The Lord's judgments upon the land and waters (vs. 13-19)
6. The Lord counsels His saints in their travels by land and water (vs. 20-29)
7. Specific assignments to this company of elders as they traveled (vs. 30-35)
8. The Lord's counsel and encouragement to the saints (vs. 36-39)

Historical Setting

Joseph Smith, Jun.

On the 9th, in company with ten Elders, I left Independence landing for Kirtland. We started down the river in canoes, and went the first day as far as Fort Osage, where we had an excellent wild turkey for supper. Nothing very important occurred till the third day, when many of the dangers so common upon the western waters, manifested themselves; and after we had encamped upon the bank of the river, at McIlwaine's Bend, Brother Phelps, in open vision by daylight, saw the destroyer in his most horrible power, ride upon the face of the waters; others heard the noise, but saw not the vision.

The next morning after prayer, I received the following. (HC, Vol. 1, pp. 202-203)

Sacred Truths

Introduction

From the Historical Setting of this chapter, we learn that this revelation was received by the Prophet Joseph Smith as he journeyed with some of the elders from Missouri to his home in Ohio. While enroute, they encountered dangerous conditions on the river. At this time the Lord revealed information pertaining to the waters and the land.

In this chapter we will discuss two doctrinal principles that are contained in Section 61 of the Doctrine and Covenants.

Power of the Lord

In this revelation, the Lord declared that Satan has some power and control over the elements of the earth. (See D&C 61:19) Speaking of this power, Elder Joseph Fielding Smith has said:

> . . .These brethren while encamped at McIlwaine's Bend on the Missouri, beheld the power of the destroyer as he rode upon the storm. One of that number saw him in all his fearful majesty, and the Lord revealed to the entire group something of the power of this evil personage. It may seem strange to us, but it is the fact that Satan exercises dominion and has some control over the elements . . . Paul speaks of Satan as the "prince of the power of the air." (Eph.2:2) The Lord revealed to these brethren some of the power of the adversary of mankind and how he rides upon the storm, as a means of affording them protection. They were commanded to use judgment as they traveled upon these waters, and the saints coming to Zion were instructed to travel by land on their way up to Zion. Moreover, notwithstanding the great power of Satan upon the waters, the Lord still held command and he could protect his people whether on land or by water as they journeyed. (CHMR, Vol. 1, p. 207)

Though it is true that Satan has certain powers, the Lord has even greater powers over Satan. (See D&C 61:6) The Lord can protect the faithful and will do so according to His judgment.

The Waters and the Land

In this revelation, the Lord provided information pertaining to the waters and the land. He indicated that the land was originally cursed, but has been blessed in the latter days. Whereas the water was originally blessed, but the blessing has been withdrawn in the latter days. (See D&C 61:14-17)

Elder Joseph Fielding Smith has provided some very helpful insights and understanding pertaining to the meaning of the verses mentioned above:

> In the beginning the Lord blessed the waters and cursed the land, but in these last days this was reversed, the land was to be blessed and the waters to be cursed. A little reflection will bear witness to the truth of this declaration. In the early millenniums of this earth's history, men did not understand the composition of the soils, and how they needed building up when crops were taken from them. The facilities at the command of the people were primitive and limited, acreage under cultivation was limited, famines were prevalent and the luxuries which we have today were not obtainable. Some one may rise up and say that the soil in those days was just as productive as now, and this may be the case. It is not a matter of dispute, but the manner of cultivation did not lend itself to the abundant production which we are receiving today. It matters not what the causes were, in those early days of world history, there could not be the production, nor the varieties of fruits coming from the earth, and the Lord can very properly speak of this as a curse, or the lack of blessing, upon the land. In those early periods we have every reason to believe that the torrents, floods, and the dangers upon the waters were not as great as they are today, and by no means as great as what the Lord has promised us. The early mariners among the ancients traversed the seas as they knew them in that day in comparative safety. In Norway may be seen the boats which the early vikings used to traverse the Atlantic ocean. Today this manner of travel in such boats would be of the most dangerous and risky nature. Moreover, we have seen the dangers upon the waters increase until the hearts of men failed them and only the brave, and those who were compelled to travel the seas, ventured out upon them. In regard to the Missouri-Mississippi

waters, we have seen year by year great destruction upon them, and coming from them. Millions upon millions of dollars, almost annually are lost by this great stream overflowing its banks. Many have lost their lives in these floods as they sweep over the land and even upon this apparently tranquil, or sluggish stream there can arise storms that bring destruction. Verily the word of the Lord has been, and is being, fulfilled in relation to those waters. While the Lord has spoken of the sea heaving itself beyond its bounds, and the waves roaring, yet we must include the great destruction upon the waters by means of war, and especially by submarine warfare as we have learned of it in recent years. (CHMR, Vol. 1, pp. 206-207)

Summary and Conclusion

Satan has certain powers over the elements. It is not wise to deliberately place one's self in a position where Lucifer's power can prevail over the individual. The faithful saints are assured of the Lord's prevailing power and of his protection.

The Lord reigns. He will protect and provide for His faithful saints.

Chapter 51

Doctrine and Covenants
Section 62

Suggested Title

Needs of Man—Testimonies

Overview of Section Content

1. Jesus Christ is our advocate and our strength (vs. 1)
2. The Lord's blessings and counsel to those who are gathering to Missouri (vs. 2-9)

Historical Setting

Joseph Smith, Jun.

On the 13th [August] I met several of the Elders on their way to the land of Zion, and after the joyful salutations with which brethren meet each other, who are actually "contending for the faith once delivered to the Saints," I received the following . . . (HC, Vol. 1, p. 205)

Joseph Fielding Smith

. . .Section Sixty-two is a revelation of instructions to those who were on their way to Zion. They were instructed to assemble themselves upon the land of Zion, and the faithful were promised that they would be preserved and rejoice together in the land of

Missouri. There was a great desire on the part of many to go to Missouri because that was indeed to be the land of Zion, the holy city which had been spoken of by ancient prophets. (CHMR, Vol. 1, p. 208)

Sacred Truths

Introduction

Joseph Smith and company continued journeying to their homes in Ohio. While enroute, they met a group of Elders who were journeying to Missouri. This revelation was given through the Prophet Joseph Smith to this group of Elders. From these instructions of the Lord, we will focus on the following two principles:

The Knowledge of God and the Needs of Man

All people have needs. But mortal man does not always know what those needs are. He cannot always accurately identify the needs of another individual and sometimes not even his own. Secondly, mortals do not always know how to fill those needs. The Lord knows our limitations and yet desires that man's righteous needs be filled. He said:

> Behold, and hearken, O ye elders of my church, saith the Lord your God, even Jesus Christ, your advocate, who knoweth the weakness of man and how to succor them who are tempted. (D&C 62:1)

How does it help us to know that the Lord knows our weaknesses and how to help us? Think what it could mean to parents, missionaries, home teachers, priesthood leaders, etc. to go to the source and get the knowledge that would enable them to labor in the best interests of others.

Such help and assistance is not only available for the helping of others, but is useful to us individually in conquering our own weaknesses. Think of the value of learning from the Lord that our spiritual growth is being impeded by our impatience, selfishness, dishonest tendencies, etc. Our recognition and awareness of the problem becomes the first step to overcoming it. As we then go to our Heavenly Father through our advocate, Jesus Christ, we find that weakness being changed into a personal strength. (See B. of M., Ether 12:27)

The Blessing of Bearing Testimony

Whereas, the Lord had rebuked certain elders in Missouri for failing to express their knowledge and convictions of the gospel, (See D&C 60:2) He blessed another group of elders for their willingness to bear their testimony. He said:

> Nevertheless, ye are blessed, for the testimony which ye have borne is recorded in heaven for the angels to look upon; and they rejoice over you, and your sins are forgiven you. (D&C 62:3)

We don't know the extent to which the Lord blesses saints who bear testimony. But it is evident that blessings are bestowed by the Lord that effect people in many ways. First of all, the individual who bears testimony by the Spirit of the Lord is strengthened spiritually. Those who hear the expression of testimony can likewise receive spiritual strength when they receive it by the Spirit. Furthermore, a non-member of the Church may be blessed to have his first spiritual witness of the gospel of Jesus Christ as he hears a testimony borne.

The Savior said that a testimony is recorded in heaven. The extent of the use or disposition that is made of these recorded testimonies we do not know. One thing is certain, they serve as blessings to the angels who look upon them, in that they have cause to rejoice.

Summary and Conclusion

The Lord is the source of all blessings. He knows all the needs of His children. To those who heed the Lord's counsel will come a fulfillment of their needs. Testimonies of the obedient are a source of blessing in helping to fulfill the needs of others.

Chapter 52

Doctrine and Covenants Section 63

Suggested Title

Zion and Her People

Overview of Section Content

1. The Lord's warning to the wicked and rebellious (vs. 1-19, 32-35)
2. The righteous to receive an inheritance upon the glorified earth (vs. 20-21)
3. The saints to purchase land in Zion, assist in the establishing of Zion and assemble in the land of Zion (vs. 22-31, 36-48)
4. The resurrection, Zion, and the millennial reign (vs. 49-54)
5. The Lord's chastisement of Sidney Rigdon (vs. 55-56)
6. A day of warning (vs. 57-58)
7. That which is of the Lord is sacred (vs. 59-64)
8. Counsel to Joseph Smith and Sidney Rigdon (vs. 65)
9. Rewards for those who overcome (vs. 66)

Historical Setting

Joseph Smith, Jun.

In these infant days of the Church, there was a great anxiety to obtain the word of the Lord upon every subject that in any way concerned our salvation; and as the land of Zion was now the most important temporal object in view, I enquired of the Lord for further information upon the gathering of the Saints, and the purchase of the land, and other matters, and received the following . . . (HC, Vol. 1, p. 207)

Joseph Fielding Smith
. . .When the report spread among the members of the Church that the Lord had revealed definitely where the city New Jerusalem was to be built, naturally there was rejoicing and many expressed the desire to know what they were to do in order to obtain inheritances . . .(CHMR, Vol. 2, p. 3)

Sacred Truths

Introduction
As can be seen from the Historical Setting, this revelation pertains to Zion and her people. The message of this revelation is summarized by Elder Joseph Fielding Smith as follows:

The Lord has given instruction repeatedly that all who go to Zion shall obey His law—the celestial law on which Zion was to be built. Those who were weak in the faith, or indifferent to the commandments, were warned that they would not be made welcome in that land unless they repented. "Hearken, O Ye People, and open your hearts, and give ear from afar: and listen, you that call yourselves the people of the Lord, and hear the word of the Lord and His will concerning you." These are the words by which this revelation is introduced . . . (CHMR, Vol. 2, p. 3)

It should be remembered that Joseph Smith had just returned from Missouri. While there he had received revelations pertaining to the location of Zion and some instructions to the saints who desired to be a part of the building of Zion. (See D&C Sections 57, 58, 59)

Now that the Prophet had returned home, the Lord gave this revelation containing further instructions and information pertaining to Zion and her people.

Zion and Her People
We will discuss four subjects from this revelation as they pertain to Zion.

1. *Faith of the Saints in Zion* (See D&C 63:1-21)
The Ohio saints were anxious to be a part of the establishment of Zion.

In this revelation, the Lord gave a warning to those who had not sufficient faith and were unbelieving. He spoke of them as the wicked and rebellious. (See D&C 63:2, 6)

One cannot live in Zion without faith in the Lord Jesus Christ. Without such faith, one cannot live the celestial laws on which Zion will be built.

What is faith? First, it is not a perfect knowledge. Secondly, one who has faith trusts in the Lord, even though the individual may not understand or see the purpose or end result of exercising faith. Third, one who has faith has a hope in things to come that are not yet seen, but are true. (See B. of M., Alma 32:21)

The Lord warned that some of these saints were seeking evidence or signs as proof that things pertaining to the Lord's work of Zion were really true. They wanted to know before they were willing to exercise faith. (See D&C 63:1, 7-11) The Lord expressed His displeasure at such behavior when He said:

> Wherefore, I, the Lord, am not pleased with those among you who have sought after signs and wonders for faith, and not for the good of men unto my glory. (D&C 63:12)

There were others among these saints who were not capable of having the Spirit in their lives because they lacked faith in the Lord's standards of morality. They were also warned that they must repent and exercise faith in Him and His teachings. Otherwise, they would live in a state of fear of the judgments that would come upon them. Such conditions were not compatible with the requirements for people to live in Zion. Thus, their actions evidenced a lack of faith in the Lord Jesus Christ. (See D&C 63:13-19)

To those who had sufficient faith in the Savior, the Lord promised the following:

> Nevertheless, he that endureth in faith and doeth my will, the same shall overcome, and shall receive an inheritance upon the earth when the day of transfiguration shall come. (D&C 63:20)

2. The land of Zion (See D&C 63:24-31, 36-48)

As early as March 1831, the Lord counseled the saints to save their money that they might be able to purchase lands. (See D&C 48:4) Then, at the time when the Lord revealed the location of these lands, He directed the saints to buy land in Missouri. (See D&C 58:49) Now, in this revelation, the Lord reaffirmed the need for the saints to purchase lands in Missouri for the purpose of building Zion. It was not to be assumed that the Lord would justify the obtaining of land in any other way than the legal process. (See D&C 63:25-27, 29-31)

Once the land was purchased, then the saints could respond to the will of the Lord and assemble in Missouri. He counseled them, however, that they should not gather in haste. (See D&C 63:24) There is a great principle taught in this verse. The fruits of doing things in haste are:

a. Confusion
b. Pestilence

Note the sequence. Haste produces confusion and confusion results in pestilence, or in other words misery and suffering. The Lord does not direct His church to act in haste. All things therein are done only after there has been thorough thinking and evaluation of proper courses of action. Inspired decisions are made based on proper preparation. Well might we apply this principle as we anticipate marriage, buying a home, choosing careers, etc. We might wonder how much misery might have been and could be avoided if the saints of God would hearken to this principle, collectively and individually.

The fruits of patience and of heeding the Lord's counsel to avoid haste are beautifully illustrated by President Joseph F. Smith as follows:

> God's way of educating our desires are, of course, always the most perfect, and if those who have it in their power to educate and direct the desires of children would imitate his prudence, the children would be much more fortunate in combating the difficulties that beset men everywhere in the struggle for existence. And what is God's way? Everywhere in nature we are taught the lessons of patience and waiting. We want things a long time before we get them, and the fact that we wanted them a long time makes them all the more precious when they come. In nature we have our seedtime and harvest; and if children were taught that the desires that they sow may be reaped by and by through patience and labor, they will learn to appreciate whenever a long-looked-for goal has been reached. Nature resists us and keeps admonishing us to wait; indeed, we are compelled to wait.
>
> A man has a much greater capacity to enjoy that for which he has labored for a number of years than one who has a similar object given to him. It is, therefore, most unfortunate for children when their parents greatly weaken or almost wholly destroy the children's capacity for the enjoyment of some of the most wholesome pleasures of life. The child who has everything he wants and when he wants it is really to be pitied, for he has no ability to enjoy it. There may be a hundred times more pleasure in a dollar piece for one child than for another. (GD, pp. 297-298)

3. The future of the people of Zion (See D&C 63:49-54)

The Savior revealed some future blessings promised to His people. Some of these promises include the following:

a. An inheritance in Zion
b. Participation in the millennial era
c. Coming forth in the first resurrection
d. Separation from the wicked

A true disciple of Jesus Christ is aware of these promised blessings and is looking forward to the fulfillment of these promises. The Savior counseled him as follows:

> These things are the things that ye must look for; and, speaking after the manner of the Lord, they are now nigh at hand, and in a time to come, even in the day of the coming of the Son of Man. (D&C 63:53)

4. Sacred things in Zion (See D&C 63:59-64)

People who desire to receive an inheritance in Zion will realize the sacredness of all things that come from God. They will heed the counsel given of the Lord:

> Remember that that which cometh from above is sacred, and must be spoken with care, and by constraint of the Spirit; and in this there is no condemnation, and ye receive the Spirit through prayer; wherefore, without this there remaineth condemnation. (D&C 63:64)

What things are sacred? The Lord said "that which cometh from above." What, then, comes from above?

Life comes from above. It is sacred. No one has the right to wantonly destroy life. Creating life by participating with God through the use of procreation powers is a sacred responsibility and should be exercised in harmony with the Lord's teachings on this subject.

Some titles and names are sacred. The word "Father" identifies not only our Heavenly Father, but also our earthly parent. This name ought to be used only under conditions that reflect honor and dignity. The same principle applies to titles such as apostle, elder, or bishop. Such come from the Lord and accordingly ought to receive due respect.

The above illustrations serve only as a sample of sacred things that come from above. Many more illustrations could be given. But the important principle to remember is, that there are sacred things. It is our responsibility to identify and be sensitive to that which should be "...spoken of with care, and by constraint of the Spirit." (D&C 63:64)

Summary and Conclusion

The saints were anxious to know how they might prepare themselves to receive an inheritance in Zion. The worthy saint today is also desirous of obtaining such a blessing.

In this revelation, the Lord instructs the saints in such a way that dispels all doubt as to the importance of applying the principles revealed herein.

Chapter 53

Doctrine and Covenants Section 64

Suggested Title

Forgiving Others—More About Zion and Her People

Overview of Section Content

1. The saints overcome the world by forgiving others and obtaining forgiveness from the Lord (vs. 1-11)
2. Unrepentant church members to be dealt with by the church (vs. 12-14)
3. The Lord rebukes and counsels several brethren (vs. 15-22, 26)
4. Today is the time to prepare for the Lord's second coming (vs. 23-25)
5. The Lord's counsel on debt (vs. 27-28)
6. Requirements for those who are on the Lord's errand and the destiny of Zion (vs. 29-43)

Historical Setting

Joseph Smith, Jun.

The early part of September was spent in making preparations to remove to the town of Hiram, and renew our work on the translation of the Bible. The brethren who were commanded to go up to Zion were earnestly engaged in getting ready to start in the coming October. On the 11th of September I received the following . . . (HC, Vol. 1, p. 211)

Joseph Fielding Smith

. . .Because of interference and because he needed a quiet place in which to work, the Prophet on September 12, 1831, moved to the home of John Johnson in the township of Hiram. This was in Portage County, Ohio, about thirty miles southeast of Kirtland. From the time he moved until early in October, the Prophet spent most of his spare time preparing for the continuation of the translation of the Bible. By translation is meant a revision of the Bible by inspiration or revelation as the Lord had commanded him, and which was commenced as early as June 1830. (D.H.C. 1:215) Sidney Rigdon continued to write for the Prophet in the work of revision. The day before the Prophet moved from Kirtland he received an important revelation, section 64, as it now appears in the Doctrine and Covenants. This revelation contained a wealth of information, counsel and warning, for the guidance of the members of the Church . . . (CHMR, Vol. 2, pp. 7-8)

Sacred Truths

Introduction

As noted in the historical setting, Joseph Smith mentioned that some of the brethren had been commanded to go to Zion. Before they left on their journey, the Lord gave this revelation containing instructions and teachings that would assist them to better understand and live for the glorious promises associated with Zion.

The discussion of the contents of this revelation will be presented in three categories:

1. Forgiveness of sins
2. The Lord's errand
3. Destiny of Zion and her people

Forgiveness of Sins

Some of these brethren were not pure in heart. Their feelings towards the Lord's prophet were not appropriate. (See D&C 64:1-6) The Lord acknowledged that His prophet was not perfect. (See D&C 64:7) However, these same brethren who were critical of Joseph had also sinned and were in need of forgiveness from the Savior. Yet, they were unwilling to extend similar compassion and mercy towards their brother, the prophet Joseph Smith.

One of the great truths taught in this revelation is that the Lord forgives sins. (See D&C 64:7) Furthermore, the revelation teaches that forgiveness is dependent upon several principles:

1. *Confession of sins* (See D&C 64:7)

This essential part of the process of repentance has been discussed by Elder Marion G. Romney as follows:

> My brothers and sisters, there are many among us whose distress and suffering are unnecessarily prolonged because they do not complete their repentance by confessing their sins . . .
>
> I would assume that we are to confess all our sins unto the Lord. For transgressions which are wholly personal, affecting none but ourselves and the Lord, such confession would seem to be sufficient.
>
> For misconduct which offends another, confession should also be made to the offended one, and his forgiveness sought.
>
> Finally, where one's trangressions are of such a nature as would, unrepented of, put in jeopardy his right to membership or fellowship in the Church of Jesus Christ, full and effective confession would, in my judgment, require confession by the repentant sinner to his bishop or other proper presiding Church officer—not that the Church officer could forgive the sin (this power rests in the Lord himself and those only to whom he specifically delegates it) but rather that the Church, acting through its duly appointed officers, might with full knowledge of the facts take such action with respect to Church discipline as the circumstances merit.
>
> One having forsaken his sins and, by proper confession, cleared his conduct with the Lord, with the people he has offended, and with the Church of Jesus Christ, where necessary, may with full confidence seek the Lord's forgiveness and go forth in newness of life, relying upon the merits of Christ. (CR, October 1955, pp. 124-125)

2. *Asking for forgiveness* (See D&C 64:7)

The Lord does not violate the eternal principle of agency. The Lord is willing to extend forgiveness but He does not impose it. If man desires to obtain forgiveness, he must exercise his agency and initiate a request for it.

3. *Forgiving others* (See D&C 64:8-11)

If we fail to forgive others, our own salvation is in jeopardy. The Lord referred to such an act as being evil and for such action, we stand condemned before the Lord. Under these conditions, there remains in us the greater sin.

Why is our salvation at stake when we fail to forgive others? Because such an act is " . . .the greater sin." (D&C 64:9) Why is it "the greater sin"? When we take the position of withholding forgiveness from our fellow men, we are attempting to block his progress towards salvation. This position is satanical and our motive is not Christlike. We are endeavoring to impede the progress of a living soul and deny him the forgiving blessings of the atonement. This philosophy is saturated with impure motives that are designed to destroy the soul. What greater sin is there than this? Perhaps many Latter-day Saints have failed to realize the seriousness of refusing to forgive others. But the Lord called it evil and for such we do stand condemned before Him and the greater sin remaineth.

An example from the life of Elder Heber J. Grant would help to illustrate this principle:

> Some years ago a prominent man was excommunicated from the Church. He, years later, pleaded for baptism. President John Taylor referred the question of his baptism to the apostles, stating that if they unanimously consented to his baptism, he could be baptized, but that if there was one dissenting vote, he should not be admitted into the Church. As I remember the vote, it was five for baptism and seven against.
>
> A year or so later the question came up again and it was eight for baptism and four against. Finally all of the council of the apostles, with the exception of your humble servant, consented that this man be baptized, and I was then next to the junior member of the quorum. Later I was in the office of the president, and he said:
>
> "Heber, I understand that eleven of the apostles have consented to the baptism of Brother So and So," naming the man, "and that you alone are standing out. How will you feel when you get on the other side and you find that this man has pleaded for baptism and you find that you have perhaps kept him from entering in with those who have repented of their sins and received some reward?"
>
> I said, "President Taylor, I can look the Lord squarely in the eye, if he asks me that question, and tell Him that I did that which I thought was for the best good of the kingdom . . .I can tell the Lord that he had disgraced this Church enough, and that I did not propose to let any such man come back into the Church."

"Well," said President Taylor, "my boy, that is all right. Stay with your convictions; stay right with them."

I said, "President Taylor, your letter said you wanted each one of the apostles to vote the convictions of his heart. If you desire me to surrender the convictions of my heart, I will gladly do it. I will gladly vote for this man to come back. But while I live I never expect to consent if it is left to my judgement. That man was accused before the apostles several years ago and he stood up and lied and claimed that he was innocent, and the Lord gave to me a testimony that he lied, but I could not condemn him because of that. I got down on my knees that night and prayed God to give me the strength not to expose that man, seeing that he had lied but that we had no evidence except only the testimony of the girl that he had seduced. And I prayed the Lord that some day additional testimony might come, and it did come, and we then excommunicated him. And when a man can lie to the apostles, and when he can be guilty while proclaiming repentance of sin, I think this Church has been disgraced enough without ever letting him come back into the Church."

"Well," repeated President Taylor, "my boy, don't you vote for him as long as you live, while you hold those ideas; stay right with them."

I left the president's office. I went home. My lunch was not ready. I was reading the Doctrine and Covenants through for the third or fourth time systematically, and I had my bookmark in it. But as I picked it up, instead of opening where the bookmark was, it opened to—

Wherefore, I say unto you, that ye ought to forgive one another; for he that forgiveth not his brother his trespasses standeth condemned before the Lord . . .

I, the Lord, will forgive whom I will forgive, but of you it is required to forgive all men.—(D&C 64:9, 10)

And I closed the book and said: "If the devil applies for baptism and claims that he has repented, I will baptize him."

After lunch I returned to the office of President Taylor and I said, "President Taylor, I have had a change of heart. One hour ago I said, never while I live, did I expect to ever consent that Brother So and So should be baptized, but I have come to tell you he can be baptized, so far as I am concerned."

President Taylor had a habit, when he was particularly pleased, of sitting up and laughing and shaking his whole body.

He laughed and said, "My boy, the change is very sudden, very sudden. I want to ask you a question. How did you feel when you left here an hour ago? Did you feel like you wanted to hit that man right squarely between the eyes and knock him down?"

I said, "That is just the way I felt."

He said, "How do you feel now?"

"Well, to tell you the truth, President Taylor, I hope the Lord will forgive the sinner."

He said, "You feel very happy, don't you, in comparison. You had the spirit of anger, you had the spirit of bitterness in your heart toward that man, because of his sin and because of the disgrace he had brought upon the Church. And now you have the spirit of forgiveness and you really feel happy, don't you?"

And I said, "Yes, I do. I felt mean and hateful and now I feel happy."

And he said: "Do you know why I wrote that letter?"

I said: "No, sir."

"Well, I wrote it, just so you and some of the younger members of the apostles would learn the lesson that forgiveness is in advance of justice where there is repentance; and that to have in your heart the spirit of forgiveness and to eliminate from your hearts the spirit of hatred and bitterness, brings peace and joy; that the gospel of Jesus Christ brings joy, peace and happiness to every soul that lives it and follows its teachings." (CR, October 1920, pp. 5-7)

The Lord's Errand

Whether the assignment and calling was to go to Missouri in 1831 or to serve a mission, give a talk in sacrament meeting or teach a class in the Church today, we all should realize the importance of the principle revealed by the Lord when He said:

> Wherefore, as ye are agents, ye are on the Lord's errand; and whatever ye do according to the will of the Lord is the Lord's business. (D&C 64:29)

Each person who serves in the Lord's kingdom needs to know that he is on the Lord's errand and is about the Lord's business. Such an awareness serves two purposes:

1. The servant goes forth with courage, confidence, and authority knowing that, as the Lord's representative, he is supported by the Lord.

2. The servant realizes that he is accountable in his service not only to the Lord's authorized representatives, but also to the Lord Himself.

The importance of being aware of the source of one's calling has been explained by Elder Loren C. Dunn as follows:

> There are many in the Church who may not be as attentive to their duties as they might be, not because they haven't been called of God by revelation but because they did not fully realize that fact when they were called. Again, let me refer to the fifth Article of Faith: "We believe that a man must be called of God, by prophecy, and by the laying on of hands, by those who are in authority to preach the Gospel and administer in the ordinances thereof."
>
> A calling in the Church is both a personal and a sacred matter, and everyone is entitled to know he or she has been called to act in the name of God in that particular position. Every person in this church has the right to know that he has been called of God. If he does not have that assurance, then I would suggest he give his calling serious, prayerful consideration so that he can receive what he has a right to receive.
>
> Also, if a priesthood leader realizes that there are those under him who may not have this clear understanding, there is something he can do. He cannot call them again, but he can bring them in and reassure them of the divine nature of their callings.
>
> I am most grateful for the great leaders of the Church who have helped me to feel and understand the divine nature of the callings to which I have been called over the years.
>
> I can't ever remember coming away from a personal audience with a priesthood leader who was delivering a call to me but what I felt in my heart the realization and assurance that I had been called of God and that that priesthood leader was a servant of the Lord and acting in his own office and calling. (CR, April 1972, p. 20)

Destiny of Zion and Her People

Even though this revelation pertained to matters of the church in Missouri at that time, we should be aware that the ultimate dimensions of Zion are greater than any one geographical location. Stakes of Zion presently serve as gathering places for the saints throughout the earth, and the cause of Zion will eventually fill the entire earth. (See D&C 101:17-21; 115:6: Bible, Daniel Chap. 2)

In this revelation we get a glimpse of the destiny of Zion as it is presently being unfolded and as it will ultimately come to pass. The following list contains some of the grand and glorious events and conditions surrounding the development of the Zion of God:

1. The saints will have an inheritance in Zion (See D&C 64:30-32)
2. Zion is destined to become great (See D&C 64:33)

3. The willing and the obedient shall enjoy the fruits of the land (See D&C 64:34)
4. There will be no rebelliousness in Zion (See D&C 64:35-36)
5. Descendants of Ephraim will be among the host of Zion (See D&C 64:36)
6. The Lord's Church is the standard by which the inhabitants of the world will be judged (See D&C 64:37-40)
7. Zion shall flourish (See D&C 64:41)
8. The glory of the Lord shall be upon Zion (See D&C 64:41)
9. All nations shall flow unto Zion (See D&C 64:42)
10. Zion shall be an ensign to all nations (See D&C 64:42)
11. Nations of the earth shall acknowledge the greatness of Zion (See D&C 64:43)

Summary and Conclusion

It is important for us to remember that anyone who desires an inheritance in Zion must seek for and obtain a remission of his sins.

It is of equal importance that one who is called to assist in the building of the Lord's kingdom should understand and remember the divine nature of his call.

Thus, those who are clean before the Lord and help build the cause of Zion shall be participants in and heirs of the blessings promised in connection with the ultimate destiny of Zion.

Chapter 54

Doctrine and Covenants Section 65

Suggested Title

Destiny and Purpose of the Kingdom of God

Overview of Section Content

1. Destiny and purpose of the Kingdom of God (vs. 1-3)
2. Saints to pray for the fulfillment of God's purposes (vs. 4-6)

Historical Setting

Joseph Smith, Jun.

In the fore part of October, I received the following prayer through revelation: . . . (HC, Vol. 1, p. 218)

Hyrum M. Smith and Janne M. Sjodahl

The prophet Joseph was now living at Hiram, about thirty miles south-east of Kirtland. He had gone there, on invitation of Father Johnson, in order to devote himself to his work on the Bible revision. From September 12, 1831, until the first of October, he did little more than prepare to re-commence the translation of the Bible. (*HC*, Vol. I., p. 215) What the preparations consisted in is not stated, but this revelation, which is an inspired prayer, indicates that an important part of such preparation was communion with God in prayer.

At Hiram, several important conferences were held. There thirteen Revelations were received, including the memorable vision recorded in Section 76. There a mob, excited by the agitation of Ezra Booth, who had denied the faith and become an enemy, tried to take the life of the prophet and Sidney Rigdon. No doubt, this Revelation came to strengthen them for the work and experiences before them . . . (DCC, p. 397)

Sacred Truths

Introduction

This revelation is a prayer revealed to the prophet Joseph Smith. It affords the Latter-day Saint a great opportunity to visualize the magnitude and destiny of the kingdom of God. Likewise we are able to see, in part, the great purpose of having membership in that kingdom.

In this chapter, we will discuss the following topics:

1. Destiny of the kingdom of God
2. Purpose of the kingdom of God

Destiny of the Kingdom of God

The terms "kingdom of God" and "kingdom of heaven" are sometimes used interchangeably. However, in modern revelation, there is often a distinctive meaning given to each. (See D&C 65:5-6) Elder James E. Talmage discussed these distinctions as follows:

> In modern revelation, the expressions "kingdom of God" and "kingdom of heaven" are sometimes used with distinctive meanings—the former phrase signifying the Church, and the latter the literal kingdom which is to supersede and comprise all national or racial divisions. In this sense, the kingdom of God has been set up already in these the last days; its beginning in and for the present dispensation was the establishment of the Church on its latter-day and permanent foundation. This is consistent with our conception of the Church as the vital organ of the kingdom in general. The powers and authority committed to the Church are, then, the keys of the kingdom. (Articles of Faith, p. 366)

The keys of the kingdom of God provide the authority and power given to the Lord's church in this dispensation. Through the use of such authority the church is able and responsible to take the message and ordinances of the gospel to the ends of the earth. (See D&C 65:2) We learn from this revelation that the Lord's kingdom is destined to fill the whole earth. It is not the work of man, as evidenced by the statement that " . . .the gospel [shall] roll forth unto the ends of the earth, as the stone which is cut out of the mountain without hands . . ." (D&C 65:2) This kingdom is not in the hands of man. It is directed by the Savior.

No one understood the destiny of this church and kingdom better than the prophet Joseph Smith. On one occasion, he said:

> The ancient prophets declared that in the last days the God of heaven should set up a kingdom which should never be destroyed, nor left to other people; and the very time that was calculated on, this people were struggling to bring it out . . .
>
> I calculate to be one of the instruments of setting up the kingdom of Daniel by the word of the Lord, and I intend to lay a foundation that will revolutionize the whole world. I once offered my life to the Missouri mob as a sacrifice for my people, and here I am. It will not be by sword or gun that this kingdom will roll on: the power of truth is such that all nations will be under the necessity of obeying the Gospel. (HC, Vol. 6, pp. 364-365)

Purpose of the Kingdom of God

The Church of Jesus Christ has many functions. It provides opportunity for blessings to come into the lives of people in many ways. But if one were to summarize the purpose of it all, it could be said that the Church is designed to help the Lord's children be prepared to meet the Savior. (See D&C 65:3-5)

The value of knowing this purpose, as revealed in this section, is that such knowledge serves as a guideline in all that we do in the kingdom. By understanding the purpose of church activity, we then do the right thing for the right reason.

So important is this mission of the kingdom, that the Lord revealed a prayer as a guideline for the Saints. They are counseled to "Call upon the Lord, that his kingdom may go forth upon the earth, that the inhabitants thereof may receive it, and be prepared for the days to come, in the which the Son of Man shall come down in heaven, clothed in the brightness of his glory, to meet the kingdom of God which is set up on the earth." (D&C 65:5)

Summary and Conclusion

Latter-day Saints should realize they are a part of the greatest cause that has ever been known to mankind. As members of the kingdom of Christ, they are not only preparing themselves, but are also helping others prepare to meet their king. What a privilege.

Chapter 55

Doctrine and Covenants Section 66

Suggested Title

William E. M'Lellin—A Covenant Relationship with the Savior

Overview of Section Content

1. William E. M'Lellin is blessed by the Lord for receiving the fulness of the gospel (vs. 1-2)
2. William E. M'Lellin is counseled by the Lord to repent, proclaim the gospel, and forsake all unrighteousness (vs. 3-13)

Historical Setting

Joseph Smith, Jun.

At the request of William E. M'Lellin, I inquired of the Lord, and received the following: . . . (HC, Vol. 1, p. 220)

Joseph Fielding Smith

. . .October 11th and 25th [1831] an important conference of the Church was held. It commenced on the 11th and was adjourned until the 25th, after much business had been transacted . . .

. . .William E. M'Lellin on the first day of the conference held October 25, 1831, sought for a blessing by revelation from the Lord. He accepted the Gospel in the spirit of faith but he had many weaknesses. In seeking this blessing he did so with full desire to know the will of the Lord concerning himself . . . (CHMR, Vol. 2, pp. 16-17)

Sacred Truths

Introduction

This revelation was given at the request of William E. M'Lellin and contains the will of the Lord for him at that time. The Lord revealed the way by which a proper covenant relationship is established with Him. The Lord identified the following two aspects of that relationship:

Receiving the fulness of the Gospel

In this revelation the Lord refers to the fulness of the gospel as His " . . .everlasting covenant . . ." (D&C 66:2) How does one receive the fulness of the gospel? When one is properly baptized by proper authority, he enters into a covenant with the Savior. As he progresses in understanding and obedience to his covenant, he is given opportunity to receive additional ordinances and covenants until he has received the " . . .fulness of my gospel . . ." (D&C 66:2) By coming to the Savior through this process, one knows, from this revelation, that his actions are a blessing to him. (See D&C 66:1-2)

Worthiness

On occasion, some people have entered into a covenant with the Savior without being worthy of that relationship with him. They may not have understood certain aspects or requirements of the gospel. Or they may not have been taught the required standards. Or some may not have been willing to comply with gospel principles. It is also conceivable that some may simply have been dishonest, though they were aware and knew the Lord's expectations.

We do not know which, if any, of the above were reasons for William E. M'Lellin's failure to be completely worthy of his covenant relationship with the Lord. But in this revelation, the Lord called his attention to the fact that he was not totally clean. (See D&C 66:3)

If one's heart is right, the Lord will show him those things that are not pleasing in His sight. (See D&C 66:4) The Lord may reveal to us our sins that might include unrepented sins that have been forgotten. He may also reveal to us our sins that we may not have previously understood or realized were actions that were not pleasing unto Him. In this revelation, the Lord showed unto William E. M'Lellin his sins. (See D&C 66:10) Without repentance, his covenant relationship with the Savior was in jeopardy.

Summary and Conclusion

As with William E. M'Lellin, so it is with every Latter-day Saint. A covenant relationship with Jesus Christ is dependent upon our receiving proper ordinances from His authorized representives and being worthy of those covenants so established.

Chapter 56

Doctrine and Covenants Section 67

Suggested Title

Language of the Revelations—Test of Scripture

Overview of Section Content

1. The Lord knows the hearts of all men (vs. 1-3)
2. The Lord gives a testimony of the truth of His scriptures (vs. 4-9)
3. The faithful are given a promise of the privilege of seeing the Savior (vs. 10-14)

Historical Setting

Joseph Smith, Jun.

After this revelation was received, [Section 1] some conversation was had concerning revelations and language. I received the following . . . (HC, Vol. 1, p. 224)

Joseph Fielding Smith

. . .For some months before the Prophet moved to Hiram he was inspired by the Lord to prepare the important revelations from the beginning for publication. This selection was well under way at the close of the conference of October 25th. As Oliver Cowdery and

John Whitmer were making preparations to go to Missouri to attend to the duties assigned them at an earlier date, a conference was called to assemble November 1, 1831, to consider matters as might need attention before their departure. The most important matter to be considered was the publishing of "The Book of Commandments," as it had been decided that the compilation of revelations should be called. On the first day of the conference (November 1st) the Lord gave his endorsement to the publication by giving one of the greatest revelations ever received by man as his Preface to the Book of his Commandments.

　. . .On the second day of the conference, the Prophet said that "inasmuch as the Lord had bestowed a great blessing upon us in giving commandments and revelations," he asked the conference what testimony they were willing to attach to these commandments which would shortly be sent to the world. A number of the brethren arose and said that they were willing to testify to the world that they knew that they (the commandments) "were of the Lord . . ."

　However there were a few of the brethren present who felt because of their superior education that there should be some improvement in the language of the revelations. Considerable time was spent in discussion concerning the language as it had been given, whereupon the Prophet through prayer received a revelation in which the Lord submitted a challenge to these learned brethren. It appears that this revelation silenced the critics, all except one. William E. M'Lellin who was given to some boasting in his own strength, and evidently who had forgotten the word of the Lord given to him at his request at the conference of October 25th, accepted the challenge.

　In this revelation (Sec. 67) the Lord acknowledged the prayers that had been offered, and he declared that he knew the hearts of those who were assembled . . .(CHMR, Vol. 2, pp. 18-19)

Sacred Truths

Introduction

　In the Historical Setting, we note that a problem had risen in connection with the first publication containing the revelations of the Lord to the Prophet Joseph Smith. Some of the brethren felt they could improve upon the language of the revelations. Because of this attitude, the Lord challenged and instructed these brethren in this revelation.

　In this chapter we will discuss three principles the Lord revealed pertaining to His scriptures.

Language of Scripture

The words used by prophets in the writing of scripture are generally those of the prophets themselves. For instance, Isaiah wrote the book of Isaiah. There are rare occasions when the revelation contains the dictated words of the Savior (Sacramental prayers, etc.). But for the most part, the Lord reveals principles, concepts, ideas, etc. It is the responsibility of the prophet to verbalize them in his own language.

In a revelation given at this conference (D&C Section 1) the Lord said:

> Behold, I am God and have spoken it; these commandments are of me, and were given unto my servants in their weakness, after the manner of their language, that they might come to understanding. (D&C 1:24)

When some of these brethren failed to understand this process of revelation, the Lord clarified the role of His prophet as pertaining to the language of the scripture. The Lord said to them:

> Your eyes have been upon my servant Joseph Smith, Jun., and his language you have known, and his imperfections you have known; and you have sought in your hearts knowledge that you might express beyond his language; this you also know. (D&C 67:5)

In summary, might we refer to the words of Elder John A. Widtsoe. Speaking of the language used in the Doctrine and Covenants, he said:

> The language, with the exception of the words actually spoken by heavenly beings, is the language of the Prophet. The ideas were given to Joseph Smith. He wrote them in the best language at his command. (MDC, p. 9)

Test of Scripture

Some of the brethren felt they were capable of writing the revelations in language that would be superior to that of the Prophet Joseph Smith. Because of this attitude, the Lord revealed criteria by which they could test the scripture and determine the divine origin thereof. There are two principles by which the Lord's scripture can be tested:

1. Cannot be duplicated

The Lord challenged these men to search through the revelations and select one which they thought was most poorly written. Then, they were to select a man to represent them and he was challenged to " . . .make one like

unto it, . . ." (D&C 67:7) One of the brethren, who was in attendance at the
conference was William E. M'Lellin. He represented some of the brethren
and attempted to duplicate one of the Lord's revelations. Commenting on
this attempt, Joseph Smith said:

> After the foregoing was received, William E. M'Lellin, as the
> wisest man, in his own estimation, having more learning than
> sense, endeavored to write a commandment like unto one of the
> least of the Lord's, but failed; it was an awful responsiblity to write
> in the name of the Lord. The Elders and all present that witnessed
> this vain attempt of a man to imitate the language of Jesus Christ,
> renewed their faith in the fulness of the Gospel, and in the truth of
> the commandments and revelations which the Lord had given to
> the Church through my instrumentality. (HC, Vol. 1, p. 226)

Even if a man wrote sentences and paragraphs equal to the language of
the revelations, he still could not duplicate the revelations of the Lord. And
why not? The Lord gave the answer as follows:

> These words are not of men nor of man, but of me; wherefore,
> you shall testify they are of me and not of man;
> For it is my voice which speaketh them unto you; for they are
> given by my Spirit unto you, and by my power you can read them
> one to another; and save it were by my power you could not have
> them;
> Wherefore, you can testify that you have heard my voice, and
> know my words. (D&C 18:34-36)

Only the Lord can give revelation by the spirit and thus create scripture
that is to be understood and received by the spirit. Man cannot provide the
spirit which giveth life. Hence, man cannot duplicate the Lord's scripture
given by the spirit in the language of the Lord's prophet.

Speaking of man's inability to create scripture, Elder Orson F. Whitney
illustrated this principle when he spoke about William E. M'Lellin's vain
attempt. Elder Whitney said:

> . . .one of them, who thought himself the wisest, and who
> posessed some learning, took up the challenge and actually at-
> tempted to frame a revelation; but it was a flat failure. He could
> utter, of course, certain words, and roll out a mass of rhetoric; but
> the divine spirit was lacking, and he had to acknowledge himself
> beaten.

It is not so easy to put the spirit of life into things. Man can make the body, but God alone can create the spirit. You have heard, have you not, of the scientist who took a grain of wheat and endeavored to make one just like it? First he separated the grain of wheat into its component parts, and found that it contained so much lime, so much silica, so much of this element and that; and then he took other parts corresponding thereto, brought them together by means of his chemical skill, and produced a grain of wheat so exactly similar to the other that the natural eye could not detect any difference between them. But there was a difference, a vast difference, and it was demonstrated when he planted the two grains. The one that God made sprang up, and the one that man made stayed down. Why? Because the manmade grain of wheat had no spirit—only a body, and the body without the spirit is dead. Man cannot breathe into the body of things the breath of life; that is a function and prerogative of Deity. It is not so easy to frame revelations from God. A vain boaster making ridicule of the proverbs of Solomon, said: "Anybody can make proverbs." His friend answered, "Try a few," and the conversation ended. (CR, April 1917, p. 42)

2. No unrighteousness in them

When the Lord reveals a concept to His prophet which is then written by the prophet as scripture, it is sacred and righteous. The Lord has never revealed or taught principles that were unrighteous. (See D&C 3:2) The Lord made this point very clear to the brethren when He said:

> For ye know that there is no unrighteousness in them, and that which is righteous cometh down from above, from the Father of lights. (D&C 67:9)

The Lord challenged man to search the revelations and declared that he would search in vain for any unrighteousness in them. There is no false doctrine contained therein. There is nothing taught or suggested that degrades mankind. Rather all things coming from God are true and are for the good of man and his edification.

This principle is also seen in the functioning of the Lord's church. Everything that is authorized to be taught in the Church is designed for the uplifting and improvement of man. This is the greatest evidence of the divinity of the Lord's scriptures and likewise holds true of His church, founded once more on the earth in this dispensation. "Wherefore, by their fruits ye shall know them." (B. of M., III Nephi 14:20)

Testimony of Scripture

The brethren in attendance at the conference of November 1831, received additional witness that the scriptures were of the Lord. They were witnesses to a man's vain attempt to duplicate the Lord's scriptures. They also knew there was no unrighteousness in any of the revelations given through the prophet Joseph Smith. Having received such a testimony of the divine origin of the revelations, the Lord told them, "...ye are under condemnation if ye do not bear record that they are true." (D&C 67:8)

Each of these brethren expressed their willingness to bear testimony to the world that the book of commandments, about to be published, contained revelations of the Lord to His prophet, Joseph Smith. (See HC, Vol. 1 p.226) At that time, (November 1831) the Lord revealed to Joseph Smith, a statement containing such a testimony, that was to be published in the Book of Commandments. Elder B.H. Roberts commented on the publishing of that statement as follows:

> This "Testimony" to the truth of the "Book of Commandments" was doubtless drawn up with the intention of having it signed by the Elders present at the conference; but whether that was done or not does not appear in the Ms. [manuscript] of the Prophet's history. The testimony itself, however, is in the manuscript History. This is remarked because it has not been published heretofore in the History of the Prophet. The matter appears to stand thus: Each of the Elders present at the conference testified to the truth of the revelations then about to be published; and, as already seen (p. 222 note), expressed a willingness to testify to the truth of the revelations to all the world. Accordingly this testimony was prepared with the intention of having it signed and published in the "Book of Commandments." It may have been signed, too, and carried to Missouri, but owing to the fact that the printing press was destroyed by a mob before the "Book of Commandments" was all printed. the "Testimony" does not appear in the part of it that was printed. The names of the Elders present at this special conference, according to the minutes of it in the *Far West Record* (p. 15), are as follows: Joseph Smith, Jun., Oliver Cowdery, David Whitmer, John Whitmer, Peter Whitmer, Jun., Sidney Rigdon, William E. M'Lellin, Orson Hyde, Luke Johnson, Lyman E. Johnson. (HC, Vol. 1, p. 226, Footnote)

The statement containing the revealed testimony is found in HC, Vol. 1, p. 226 and is also published in the Explanatory Introduction pages of the Doctrine and Covenants. It is published as a "Testimony of the twelve apostles to the truth of the book of Doctrine and Covenants". The Quorum of Twelve Apostles was organized in February 1835. Since that time, there have been these special witnesses of the Lord who are responsible to bear witness of the revealed word of the Lord to the ends of the earth. It is appropriate that their names are attached to this published testimony.

Summary and Conclusion

When one reads the scriptures, phrased by a prophet of the Lord, he is assured that the message given is of the Lord. The spirit will bear witness to the honest seeker and give him a testimony of the truthfulness and righteousness of the content. He is then under obligation to bear testimony that these revelations are of God.

Such is the opportunity and responsibility offered to all mankind who would test the scriptures of the Lord.

Chapter 57

Doctrine and Covenants Section 68

Suggested Title

Scripture—The Presiding Bishop—Parents

Overview of Section Content

1. Directions to Orson Hyde and others with the same calling (vs. 1-12)
2. Additional bishops to be called in the future (vs. 14-15)
3. The presiding bishopric and literal descendants of Aaron (vs. 16-21)
4. The Church court for the presiding bishop (vs. 22-24)
5. Laws and instructions to parents and other inhabitants of Zion and her stakes (vs. 25-35)

Historical Setting

Joseph Smith, Jun.

As the following Elders—Orson Hyde, Luke Johnson, Lyman E. Johnson, and William E. M'Lellin—were desirous to know the mind of the Lord concerning themselves, I inquired, and received the following . . . (HC, Vol. 1, p. 227)

Joseph Fielding Smith

. . . At the close of the conference of November 1-2, 1831, Elders Orson Hyde, Luke Johnson, Lyman E. Johnson, and William E.

M'Lellin, came to the Prophet and sought the will of the Lord concerning themselves, and their ministry. The Prophet made inquiry and received the revelation which appears as section sixty-eight. Surely the Lord in his wisdom poured out knowledge, line upon line, precept upon precept as the members of the Church were prepared to receive it. While this revelation was given at the request of these brethren it was not intended for them alone, but for the guidance of all officers and members of the Church. . . . (CHMR, Vol. 2, p. 29)

Sacred Truths

Introduction

In this revelation, the Lord revealed information pertaining to several important areas. We will discuss three of these in this chapter.

Scripture

The four men, to whom this revelation was given, desired to know the Lord's will concerning themselves and their ministry. It is important to note that all four of them were later called into the Quorum of Twelve Apostles when it was organized in February 1835. In this revelation, the Lord gave them to understand some of the dimensions of their future calling as apostles of the Lord. Their ministry would be worldwide. Their calling would include the preaching of the gospel to every creature. (See D&C 68:8-10) In the discharge of their preaching responsibilities, they were to preach by the power of the Holy Ghost. The Lord said:

> And whatsoever they shall speak when moved upon by the Holy Ghost shall be scripture, shall be the will of the Lord, shall be the mind of the Lord, shall be the word of the Lord, shall be the voice of the Lord, and the power of God unto salvation. (D&C 68:4)

Commenting on the blessing it is for us to have inspired leaders in the Lord's Church, Elder Harold B. Lee has said:

> I thank the Lord that we are not dependent alone upon the faith of those who lived centuries ago, or even a hundred years ago, for revelations that were given unto them in that day. In this day He has given us leaders who are possessed of the same spirit of revelation. This is what the Lord said, speaking to those who held Apostleship: [Quoted D&C 68:3-4] (CR, October 1941, p. 114)

It is a blessing to the Church to have a constant flow of scripture for the guidance and benefit of the membership. It is not to be understood that any one or all of the apostles in the Quorum of Twelve ever produce scripture that contains new doctrine. Such a responsibility belongs to the president of the Church only. He is the Lord's prophet, seer, and revelator, and has sole responsibility for the announcing of any new doctrine to the Church.

President J. Reuben Clark gave a masterful discourse on this subject. He said:

> [Quoted D&C 68:2-4] The very words of the revelation recognize that the Brethren may speak when they are not "moved upon by the Holy Ghost," yet only when they do so speak, as so "moved upon" is what they say Scripture. No exceptions are given to this rule or principle. It is universal in its application.
>
> The question is, how shall we know when the things they have spoken were said as they were "moved upon by the Holy Ghost?"
>
> I have given some thought to this question, and the answer thereto so far as I can determine is: We can tell when the speakers are "moved upon by the Holy Ghost" only when we, ourselves, are "moved upon by the Holy Ghost."
>
> In a way, this completely shifts the responsibility from them to us to determine when they so speak.

. . . .

> In considering the problem involved here, it should be in mind that some of the General Authorities have had assigned to them a special calling; they possess a special gift; they are sustained as prophets, seers, and revelators, which gives them a special spiritual endowment in connection with their teaching of the people. They have the right, the power, and authority to declare the mind and will of God to his people, subject to the over-all power and authority of the President of the Church. Others of the General Authorities are not given this special spiritual endowment and authority covering their teachings; they have a resulting limitation, and the resulting limitation upon their power and authority in teaching applies to every other officer and member of the church, for none of them is spiritually endowed as a prophet, seer, and revelator. Furthermore, as just indicated, the President of the Church has a further and special spiritual endowment in this respect, for he is the Prophet, Seer, and Revelator for the whole Church.

. . . .

There are those who insist that unless the Prophet of the Lord declares, "Thus saith the Lord," the message may not be taken as a revelation. This is a false testing standard. For while many of our modern revelations as contained in the Doctrine and Covenants do contain these words, there are many that do not. Nor is it necessary that an actual voice be heard in order that a message from our Heavenly Father shall be a true revelation, as shown by revelations given in former dispensations, as well as in our own. (Address to Seminary and Institute personnel, BYU, July 7, 1954)

The Presiding Bishop

The Lord has also enlightened us on the subject of bishops in the Church. After indicating that additional bishops would be called as needed in the Church (See D&C 68:14-15) He spoke of the presiding bishop in the Church. (See D&C 68:15-21)

Pertaining to these scriptural references to the office of Presiding Bishop of the Church, President Joseph Fielding Smith taught:

> The person spoken of in the revelations as having the right by lineage to the bishopric is the one who is the firstborn. By virtue of his birth he is entitled to hold "the keys or authority of the same." This has reference only to the one who presides over the Aaronic Priesthood. It has no reference whatever to bishops of wards. Further, such a one must be designated by the First Presidency of the Church and receive his anointing and ordination under their hands. The revelation comes from the Presidency, not from the patriarch, to establish a claim to the right to preside in this office. In the absence of knowledge concerning such a descendant, any high priest, chosen by the Presidency, may hold the office of Presiding Bishop and serve with counselors. (DS, Vol. 3, pp. 92-93)

Parents

When a couple accepts the responsibility of parenthood, they also have a spiritual responsibility to their children. The Lord has revealed some of their spiritual obligations. They are to teach their children the saving principles and ordinances of the gospel. (See D&C 68:25-32) Some of these teachings and duties mentioned in this revelation are as follows:

1. Faith in the Lord Jesus Christ
2. Repentance
3. Baptism
4. Gift of the Holy Ghost
5. Having their children baptized

6. Prayer
7. Walk uprightly before the Lord
8. Observe the Sabbath Day to keep it holy
9. Cease to be idle

By being aware and carrying out their specific spiritual duties as parents, fathers and mothers can avoid the consequences of spiritually abusing their children. This spiritual child abuse is referred to by the Lord as sin. (See D&C 68:25)

Think of the positive impact and influence for good that would be made upon the families, the church, and the world, if parents in the stakes of Zion would hearken and give heed to this sacred responsibility. It is the Lord's law to Latter-day Saint parents. (See D&C 68:26)

Summary and Conclusion

The Lord blesses His children in many ways. For instance, He has given the saints access to the message of His prophets as recorded on the pages of scripture. He has also blessed His church and the membership thereof through the functions and services of the Presiding Bishop of the Church. Further, evey family in the church has been designated as a means by which children's lives are blessed through the gospel teachings of parents. When the Lord's children afford themselves of these and other opportunities, blessings flow unto them.

Chapter 58

Doctrine and Covenants Sections 69 and 70

Suggested Titles

Section 69—A Sacred Trust—Book of Commandments
Section 70—Stewardships—Book of Commandments

Overview of Section Content

Section 69

1. John Whitmer is to accompany Oliver Cowdery in transporting the revelations to the land of Zion (vs. 1-2)
2. John Whitmer is to continue writing church history, and preach and expound the gospel (vs. 1-8)

Section 70

1. Several brethren are appointed stewards over the revelations and commandments (vs. 1-8)
2. What the Lord requires of every man in his stewardship (vs. 9-11)
3. Remunerations for temporal and spiritual stewardships (vs. 12-18)

Historical Setting

Both of these revelations pertain to the responsibility of publishing and caring for the Lord's Book of Commandments.

Setting For Section 69

Joseph Smith, Jun.

This Book of Commandments and Revelations was to be dedicated by prayer to the service of Almighty God by me; and after I had done this, I inquired of the Lord concerning these things, and received the following: . . . (HC, Vol. 1, p. 234)

Setting for Section 70

Joseph Smith, Jun.

My time was occupied closely in reviewing the commandments and sitting in conference, for nearly two weeks; for from the first to the twelfth of November we held four special conferences. In the last which was held at Brother Johnson's, in Hiram, after deliberate consideration, in consequence of the book of revelations, now to be printed, being the foundation of the Church in these last days, and a benefit to the world, showing that the keys of the mysteries of the kingdom of our Savior are again entrusted to man; and the riches of eternity within the compass of those who are willing to live by every word that proceedeth out of the mouth of God—therefore the conference voted that they prize the revelations to be worth to the Church the riches of the whole earth, speaking temporally. The great benefits to the world which result from the Book of Mormon and the revelations which the Lord has seen fit in His infinite wisdom to grant unto us for our salvation, and for the salvation of all that will believe, were duly appreciated; and in answer to an inquiry, I received the following: . . . (HC, Vol. 1, pp. 235-236)

Sacred Truths

Introduction

One of the major items of business brought before the conference of November 1831 was the preparing for publication of the Book of Commandments.

After the conference had voted to accept the revelations selected for publication, the prophet Joseph Smith received two revelations. One pertained to the transporting of these revelations to Missouri for printing (see D&C Section 69) and the other concerned custodial responsibility for the revelations in their printed form (see D&C Section 70)

Because of the nature of the subject matter in these two revelations, we will discuss the content of both of them in this chapter under two topics.

A Sacred Trust

By the voice of the conference, Oliver Cowdery was assigned to carry the revelations from Ohio to Missouri for printing. (See HC, Vol. 1, p. 229) The Lord also assigned John Whitmer to accompany Oliver on his journey (See D&C 69:1-2) John Whitmer was reminded by the Lord that his calling as church historian (see D&C Section 47) should not be neglected while on this journey. (See D&C 69:3-8)

Commenting on the need for Oliver Cowdery to have a companion, Elders Joseph Fielding Smith and B.H. Roberts have said:

> In this commandment [Section 69] the Lord declared that it was not wisdom that Oliver Cowdery should make the journey alone. The journey was about one thousand miles and through a sparsely settled country. There were many dangers on the way. The revelations were considered to be priceless and then, besides, Oliver carried with him sums of money to assist in the work in Missouri. John Whitmer was therefore appointed to accompany Oliver . . . (CHMR, Vol. 2, p. 21)

> It must not be understood from the first paragraph of this revelation that Oliver Cowdery was untrustworthy, and therefore it was necessary that a companion be provided for him. The fact was that much of the journey between Kirtland and Independence, or Zion, was through a sparsely settled country, the western portion of it through a frontier country where there is always a gathering, more or less, of lawless people; and it was at considerable risk that a person traveled through such a country, especially when alone and carrying money with him. It was wisdom, then, for the sake of Oliver Cowdery, and to insure the safety of the money and the sacred things he was to carry with him, that one should go with him that would be a true and faithful companion, hence the appointment of John Whitmer. (HC, Vol. 1, p. 234, Footnote)

It is significant that one man's journey from one geographical area to another was important enough to call forth a revelation from the Lord. Why? Because he was being entrusted with the revelations of the Savior given to a latter-day prophet of God. This was a sacred trust. It was not to be taken lightly. This mission was to be accomplished under the direction of the Lord.

As members of the church today, we have the same revelations in our hands. We, too, have been entrusted with the Lord's revelations. They have been given to us that we might obtain understanding, wisdom, knowledge, etc. pertaining to our salvation and exaltation. What a sacred trust.

Stewardships

In anticipation of the publication of the book of commandments, the Lord assigned several brethren to serve as stewards over the publication, distribution, and sale of the book. (See D&C 70:1-8)

As to the nature of this assignment, Elder Joseph Fielding Smith has said:

> At the conference held November, 1831, the Lord issued a proclamation to the inhabitants of Zion, and to all the members of the Church, announcing that he had made Joseph Smith, Jun., Martin Harris, Oliver Cowdery, John Whitmer, Sidney Rigdon, and William W. Phelps, stewards of the revelations and commandments which he had given, and which were yet to be given, and the members of the Church were to hearken to these brethren. An account of the stewardship of these brethren would be required of them in the day of judgment. Not only were these brethren held responsible for the care of the revelations, which the Lord valued so highly, but also for the printing and distribution of the books when they were printed. These books were to be sold, not given away, and all surplus was to be given into the hands of the bishop and placed in the Lord's storehouse where it would be consecrated to the inhabitants of Zion, "inasmuch as they became heirs according to the laws of the kingdom." (CHMR, Vol. 2, p. 39)

The Lord also revealed that other men would be given stewardships by Him from time to time. (See D&C 70:9) The nature of these stewardships may be temporal or they may be spiritual. But two principles are important:

1. Every man will be required to give an account of his stewardship in the day of judgment. This is a law of the Lord. (See D&C 70:4, 9-10)

2. Man's attitude towards his stewardship is vital. If he does not function grudgingly, but has a desire to share equally with his fellowmen, in the temporal things of the earth he is promised " . . .the abundance of the manifestations of the spirit . . ." (D&C 70:14)

Summary and Conclusion

As we come to the end of this chapter, we also conclude this volume of sacred truths from the Doctrine and Covenants, the Lord's book. It is a sacred trust, which the Lord has given, to have in our possession the revelations from the Lord Jesus Christ. We are accountable before Him to not only understand His will, but also to apply His teachings in our individual lives. By so doing, we will be blessed with an abundance of the manifestations of the Spirit of the Lord.

Appendix

Index of Suggested Titles for Doctrine & Covenants Sections

SELECTED BIBLIOGRAPHY

Ballard, Melvin J. *Crusader for Righteousness*. Salt Lake City: Bookcraft, 1968.

Bible, The.

Book of Mormon, The. Salt Lake City: The Church of Jesus Christ of Latter-day Saints.

B.Y.U. Speeches of the Year. Provo: Brigham Young University Press.

B.Y.U. Studies. Provo: Brigham Young University Press.

Cannon, George Q. *Gospel Truth*. 2 vols. Salt Lake City: Deseret Book, 1974.

Church News. Salt Lake City: Deseret News Press.

Clark, J. Reuben, Jr. *Behold the Lamb of God*. Salt Lake City: Deseret Book, 1962.

Conference Reports. Salt Lake City: Deseret News Press.

Cowley, Matthias F. *Wilford Woodruff, History of His Life and Labors* Salt Lake City: Bookcraft, 1964.

Deseret Weekly News. Salt Lake City: Deseret News Press.

Doctrine and Covenants, The. Salt Lake City: The Church of Jesus Christ of Latter-day Saints.

Doxey, Roy W. *The Doctrine and Covenants Speaks*. 2 vols. Salt Lake City: Deseret Book, 1970.

Dunn, Paul H. *The Ten Most Wanted Men*. Salt Lake City: Bookcraft, 1967.

Eighth Annual Priesthood Genealogical Research Seminar. Provo: Brigham Young University Press, 1973.

Ensign. Salt Lake City: The Church of Jesus Christ of Latter-day Saints.

Eusebius. *The History of the Church from Christ to Constantine*. New York: New York University Press, 1966.

Historical Record. The Church of Jesus Christ of Latter-day Saints, Salt Lake City.

Improvement Era. Salt Lake City: Mutual Improvement Association

Jenson, Andrew. *L.D.S. Biographical Encyclopedia*. 4 vols. Salt Lake City: Publishers Press, 1971.

Journal of Discourses. 26 vols. Los Angeles: General Printing and Lithograph Co., 1961.

Kimball, Spencer W. *Faith Precedes the Miracle*. Salt Lake City: Deseret Book, 1972.

Kimball, Spencer W. *Men of Example*. Address to Religious Educators, Assembly Hall, Salt Lake City. 12 September 1975.

Lundwall, N.B., comp. *Lectures on Faith by Joseph Smith*. Salt Lake City.

Mace, Wandle, biography of. Unpublished. Harold B. Lee Library, Brigham Young University, Provo.

Matthews, Robert J. *"A Plainer Translation" Joseph Smith's Translation of the Bible*. Provo: Brigham Young University press, 1975.

McConkie, Bruce R. *Mormon Doctrine*. Salt Lake City: Bookcraft, 1958.

McKay, David O. *Gospel Ideals*. Salt Lake City: Deseret News Press, 1953.

Millennial Star. Manchester, England: The Church of Jesus Christ of Latter-day Saints.

Pearl of Great Price, The. Salt Lake City: The Church of Jesus Christ of Latter-day Saints.

Smith, Hyrum M. and Sjodahl, Janne M. *The Doctrine and Covenants Commentary*. Salt Lake City: Deseret Book, 1950.

Smith, Joseph. *History of the Church of Jesus Christ of Latter-day Saints*. 6 vols. Salt Lake City: Deseret News Press, 1951.

Smith, Joseph F. *Gospel Doctrine*. Salt Lake City: Deseret Book, 1963.

Smith, Joseph Fielding. *Answers to Gospel Questions*. 5 vols. Salt Lake City: Deseret book, 1957.

Smith, Joseph Fielding. *Church History and Modern Day Revelation*. 4 vols. (Pamphlets) Salt Lake City: Deseret News Press, 1946.

Smith, Joseph Fielding. *Doctrines of Salvation*. 3 vols. Salt Lake City: Bookcraft, 1954.

Smith, Joseph Fielding. *Life of Joseph F. Smith*. Salt Lake City: Deseret Book, 1969.

Smith, Joseph Fielding., comp. *Teachings of the Prophet Joseph Smith*. Salt Lake City: Deseret Book, 1963.

Smith, Lucy Mack. *History of Joseph Smith*. Salt Lake City: Bookcraft, 1958.

Sperry, Sidney B. *Doctrine and Covenants Compendium*. Salt Lake City: Bookcraft, 1960.

Talmage, James E. *Articles of Faith*. Salt Lake City: The Church of Jesus Christ of Latter-day Saints, 1952.

Twain, Mark. *Adventures of Huckleberry Finn*. New York and London: Harper and Brothers, 1896.

Tyler, Daniel. *History of the Mormon Battalion*. Chicago: Rio Grande Press, 1964.

Whitney, Orson F. *Life of Heber C. Kimball*. Salt Lake City: Bookcraft, 1967.

Widtsoe, John A. *The Message of the Doctrine and Covenants*. Salt Lake City: Bookcraft, 1969.

Woodruff, Wilford. *The Discourses of Wilford Woodruff*. Salt Lake City: Bookcraft, 1969.